THE BALLAD OF DANNY WOLFE

THE BALLAD OF
DANNY WOLFE

LIFE OF A MODERN OUTLAW

JOE FRIESEN

SIGNAL

McCLELLAND
& STEWART

Cloth edition published 2016

Signal is an imprint of McClelland & Stewart, a division of Penguin Random House
Canada Limited, a Penguin Random House Company

Signal and colophon are registered trademarks of McClelland & Stewart

Library and Archives Canada Cataloguing in Publication
Friesen, Joe, author
The ballad of Danny Wolfe : life of a modern outlaw / Joe Friesen.
Issued in print and electronic formats.
ISBN 978-0-7710-3023-9 (bound).—ISBN 978-0-7710-3031-4 (epub)
1. Wolfe, Danny, 1976-2010. 2. Indian Posse (Gang). 3. Gang members—
Canada—Biography. 4. Indian gangs—Canada—History. I. Title.
HV6248.W64F75 2016   j364.1092   C2014-904602-2
                                               C2014-904603-0

Library of Congress Control Number is available upon request

Typeset in Adobe Caslon by M&S, Toronto
Printed and bound in the USA

Published by Signal,
an imprint of McClelland & Stewart,
a division of Penguin Random House Canada Limited
a Penguin Random House Company

www.penguinrandomhouse.ca

1 2 3 4 5   20 19 18 17 16

To my parents

CONTENTS

AUTHOR'S NOTE

This book would not have been possible without the assistance of Danny Wolfe, Richard Wolfe, and their mother Susan Creeley, as well as their many friends and family members who agreed to help me. I am very grateful to them for being so open and patient. They sat with me for countless interviews over many years and accepted all my phone calls and visits.

Delving into the world of prison and street gangs was made much easier thanks to the many current and former gang members who were willing to share what they knew. In a few cases, names have been changed to protect those who feared for their safety, or were not authorized to speak publicly.

This work is based on dozens of interviews, thousands of pages of Danny's private prison records and psychological reports, extensive court records, government documents obtained through access to information laws, publicly commissioned reports, and several hundred pages of Danny's personal letters.

Here is how it came about.

One night, around midnight, the phone rang and I ran to answer it. I didn't recognize the number.

"Hey, it's Danny," said a voice.

I paused. "Danny . . . ," I said, trying to jog my memory.

"Danny Wolfe," he replied, slightly annoyed that I hadn't twigged. "I'm calling from Regina. I got a letter from you. You said you wanted to talk to me."

Ah, the most wanted man in the country, the one who had just been put back in jail. *That* Danny. I'd written letters to people in jail before, as a journalist chasing a story, but no one had ever responded. This time was different. I had told Danny in my letter that I wanted to write about the history and origins of the Indian Posse, the street gang that he co-founded, and he was enthusiastic.

"I know exactly what you mean. Exactly. I've had the same idea. I wanted to do a documentary like that myself for a long time," he said on the phone that night.

Danny said he would arrange the visiting forms so I could meet with him in prison, and he would also help me get in contact with other members of the gang to hear their stories.

"There's a lot of good bros inside that would talk to you," he said.

Six months later, the visiting forms arrived with a letter. "Sorry it took so damn long to get back to you," Danny wrote. "I'm interested in helping with the history of IP.

"I know there's more members that would like to have an interview as well, old school brothers that are still in the game. There's been dramatic changes in the gang, or gangs in Canada, and that's what I would like to express." We agreed that since he had a major trial coming up, it would be wiser to delay the interview until after. He signed off, saying he hoped to see me soon.

Two years later, I found myself driving through a snowstorm in Saskatchewan with Danny's brother Richard, whom I'd just met.

The snow was so thick that I couldn't see the highway, nor could I see the semi-trucks barreling past in the other lane. I felt certain that if we advanced even a few more feet we would plummet off the road into the Qu'Appelle Valley. Richard, heavily tattooed and fresh out of prison after fifteen years, just laughed. "Keep going," he said. "What else can you do?"

Over the next four years I kept going, always fascinated by what I discovered. Susan Creeley was also extremely helpful, describing her own role in Danny's life in a frank and open way, and always willing to confront difficult topics. She provided me with all of Danny's voluminous court files, his personal effects, and hundreds of letters and photos, which helped me paint what I hope is a detailed portrait of a complex and controversial man.

Any errors or omissions are my own.

Joe Friesen
Toronto, 2016

PROLOGUE

THE BREAKOUT
AUGUST 2008

The opening was small but it would do.

Danny knelt on the cement floor and peered out to get his bearings. He could see a narrow ledge running just outside the hole and the interior prison yard down below. He looked behind him, along the corridor toward the guard station. All was quiet. A half-dozen inmates crowded round in anticipation, waiting for Danny to decide. He tied his long, black hair into a bun on the top of his head and took a deep breath.

"I'm gonna go," he said.

He pushed a leg through the hole and then twisted his upper body behind it, with his head and trailing leg coming last. His heart was pounding and he tried to steady himself to keep his breathing in check. He was outside now, standing on a ledge that ran along the interior of the recreation yard about ten feet above the ground. He could feel the warm evening air and smell the prairie grass. Directly above him was a surveillance camera that kept watch on the yard. Below the ledge and across the yard were large windows; patrolling guards could pass them at any moment and see Danny if they looked up. The late summer sun was fading into a dark sky and the prison floodlights had not yet come on. Preston, Danny's little brother, knelt down and passed a jacket and some blankets through the hole.

"Hurry up," Preston whispered.

Danny draped the blankets over the razor wire coiled on top of the wall and began his climb. It was only five feet up from where he stood. He scrambled over the bricks, gripping the metal bars on the windows to pull himself up. Then he picked his way through the razor wire, doing his best to use the blankets to protect himself. In seconds he'd reached the top of the wall. On the other side, the ground was about fifteen to twenty feet down, but he didn't hesitate. He leapt, tumbling and sprawling on the grass upon landing. He stood up, gingerly testing his feet and ankles. Not broken, still able to run. He glanced quickly around. No sign of the guards.

Inside, Preston was next. A hundred thoughts were running through his mind. What if he climbed the wall and then got stuck? What if he was shot? The plan was to turn back if he had to, but would he be able get back down? His heart was racing. *I'm going to get caught*, he thought.

Preston followed Danny's route through the hole and up the bars to the top of the wall. He caught sight of Danny crouching below, waving, gesturing for him to jump. Preston took the plunge, falling through the air and rolling once he hit the grass.

The brothers waited a few moments to see if the others were coming. Ten seconds passed in anxious silence before they decided they couldn't wait any longer. The others would catch up. There are no watchtowers with sharpshooters at the Regina Correctional Centre, but guards patrol the perimeter. Danny and Preston swivelled their heads in every direction and could see no one. They jogged along the wall, staying in a half-crouch until they reached the edge of the jail building, then dashed for the nearest fence.

The fence was about twelve feet high and topped with barbed wire. Preston got halfway over before getting tangled up. Struggling made things worse. The wire sliced into him, catching his clothes and cutting his skin. Seeing his little brother in trouble, Danny chose a better spot to go over and then waited as Preston, frazzled by nerves, picked himself free and climbed over at a less treacherous point.

They ran further, scaled one final, shorter fence and then they were out. They had done it, but they were by no means safe. The Regina Correctional Centre is five kilometres outside the city and surrounded by tabletop-flat farmland, a topography that made them vulnerable. They wore grey prison-issued sweatsuits and were the only people on foot for miles in any direction.

They ran through the fields as fast as they could. Danny surged ahead while Preston struggled to keep up with his fitter, stronger, older brother. They ran for about five minutes heading east across the prairie before Danny realized that Regina was in the other direction. He and Preston made a U-turn in a field and took off west, cursing the time they had lost. The first burst of adrenaline was gone and the extreme stress was fast draining their reserves of energy. Preston began to falter. He watched Danny ahead of him, remembering how his brother had nagged him to exercise when they were preparing for the escape. He wished he had got in better shape. Danny eventually turned around and came back for him. They walked together awhile, then began to run again. They walked and ran on and off for a few kilometres, eventually making it to railway tracks where Cody Keenatch and Ken Iron, two of the four prisoners who had followed them out of the prison, caught up with them. The other two, Ryan Agecoutay and James Pewean, had already decided to go their own way on the outside, and shortly after reuniting with the brothers, Iron decided to split from Danny and company, thinking he'd be less likely to get spotted by himself.

As darkness set in, Danny, Preston, and Cody reached a gravel road. They stopped for a few minutes, unsure what to do. They talked back and forth, weighing different destinations, then decided to follow the railway tracks into Regina. As they entered the city three-quarters of an hour later, Danny was jubilant. He kept saying he couldn't believe they had done it. They wandered around the alleys of Regina's east end for a while as the trio considered their next move. They paused to drink from a garden hose in someone's backyard and regroup.

"At first we were going to go home to Okanese," Preston said, referring to the First Nations reserve about an hour's drive from Regina where their family lives. "Then we thought that wouldn't be good because [the police] would look there.

"I didn't want to call somebody in the middle of the night and say, 'I just broke out of jail, come get me.' Where are we going to go? What are we going to do? We were all discussing it. We didn't know."

With incredible determination and cunning, Danny had just pulled off one of the most spectacular prison breaks in Canadian history. A group of six gangsters – four of them locked up on murder charges, three of them members of the feared Indian Posse – were on the loose. Danny, who had already served a federal sentence for threatening to kill witnesses, had vowed to take out those who had turned against him this time. Once the implications of this breakout became clear, he would become the most wanted man in the country.

1

THE EARLY YEARS
1976–1988

Danny Wolfe was born in Regina, Saskatchewan, in June 1976. He was the second child of Susan Creeley, a First Nations woman from Saskatchewan's File Hills.

Danny came into the world small and weak and three months early. His mother was drinking heavily in the months before she went into labour and had already finished a bottle of whiskey that night when worried friends drove her to Regina's General Hospital. Danny survived his premature arrival and from his earliest days was an energetic, exuberant child, with a ready smile and a fierce temper. Years later an elder would bless Danny with a ceremonial name: Come Up Shouting at the Earth. It was a good fit, his mother said.

When Danny was three and his older brother, Richard, was four, Susan, tired of Regina and wanting to be closer to her older sister, moved the family to Winnipeg. Her partner and the boys' father, Richard Wolfe Sr., followed, and although they were more often apart than together in subsequent years, Susan and Richard Sr. quickly became fixtures in the boozy, combative, party scene in the city's urban core. As a result Danny and Richard had a lot more freedom to roam than most children their age. Their first brush with the law was when Danny was four and Richard, five. Susan was at home in their modest, two-bedroom apartment in a dingy, low-rise block on Sherbrook Street that smelled of cigarettes and beer. When night fell, Danny and Richard still hadn't returned. Normally she let them play around the street and they were fine, but this was very late. Finally there was a knock at her door. Susan opened it to see Danny, with a muddy and tear-stained face and a policeman's hand on his shoulder. The boys had walked more than a mile west and got lost near the Sargent Park swimming pool. Susan was relieved, but this scene – police at her door, the boys in trouble – would be repeated dozens of times in the coming years.

When Danny was about eight he and Richard and a few friends conspired to hide inside a downtown department store after closing time. They crouched under a table and among the jackets in the men's clothing department. Once everyone left they had the run of the place and marauded through the toy section. But it wasn't long before security spotted them and police were called. Once again, they were driven home in a squad car.

Susan remembers very little of these incidents, except to say that they happened regularly. She drank a lot in those days, sometimes day after day. One party would fold into the next and she didn't always come home. It would ususally be an aunt or a neighbour who would check on Danny and Richard to make sure they were fed and clothed. Richard Sr. was often on the street, living a more or less transient life, or locked up in jail.

When the boys reached school age the family moved to a neighbourhood just south of the Canadian Pacific Rail yards, a vast stretch of metal track and freight cars that in many ways defines the city and its racial and economic divide.

The North End is a tough, densely populated working-class neighbourhood that looms large in the city's mythology. It's where

Eastern European immigrants fought their way to establishing themselves in Canada beginning in the early twentieth century, and where socialist radicalism burst forth in the 1919 General Strike. In his 1957 book *Under the Ribs of Death*, John Marlyn memorably writes of the "howling chaos of the North End," a description which applied as much to Danny's youth as it did to the area one hundred years ago. While brawling and boozing were the story in an earlier day, shootings, fires, drugs, and prostitution became the stuff of daily life north of the tracks in the 1980s and 90s. The city to the south, by contrast, remained largely insulated from the roiling violence on the other side. But in the years when Richard and Danny were growing up, the poverty that plagued the North End crossed the bridge into the neighbourhoods they inhabited in the city's core.

The family lived on the upper floors of a large white house on Ross Avenue, a stone's throw from the rail yards. The boys attended Pinkham School, which was so close they could see it from their upstairs bedroom window. Danny was a quiet, live-wire presence, his former principal, Carolyn Loeppky, recalled. Both he and his brother Richard seemed to take everything in with cool detachment, rarely speaking and doing their best to stay under the radar, but with a furious energy boiling beneath the surface. They stuck to themselves mostly, she said, and didn't play much with others. Ms. Loeppky saw in their family many of the patterns common to troubled families in the neighbourhood: they moved around a lot, changing schools regularly. Their mother seemed to be in an alcohol haze most of the time, she said, and the kids, who were not well nourished, were often late for school. The school tried to engage Susan and help the family, but she seemed to doubt their motives and wanted to keep her distance, Ms. Loeppky said.

"They were enigmatic. They were hard to figure out, hard to reach and suspicious [about] the purposes of others," Ms. Loeppky said.

Danny was a very tiny child, she recalled. His skin had a yellowish tinge that suggested some kind of ill health. Ms. Loeppky said she thought he was probably destined for a difficult life. But there was something mysterious about Danny that stuck with her: "Behind that very quiet façade you thought there were all kinds of things going on in that little boy's mind."

Richard says he and Danny were often in trouble with their teachers. Susan recalls a lot of meetings with social workers and school administrators.

The final straw was a school fundraising drive for which each student was given a box of chocolate bars to sell. Richard and Danny were left out. They suspected it was because the teachers thought they were untrustworthy. Danny was incensed and claimed the teachers were racist.

"Danny didn't like it one bit," Richard recalled. "So we said, 'Screw this, let's break in.'"

Five young burglars – Danny, Richard, and three friends – broke into the school and started trashing the office. When one of the boys saw police lights out the window, they all headed for the door. On the count of three, Richard said, each of them should run in a different direction so they would be harder to capture. He opened the door and started running, but everyone else forgot the plan and followed in single file behind him. They all got caught.

After the break-in Richard and Danny both moved to different schools. Ms. Loeppky said she believes it was because their mother moved to a new house. The school authorities were so keen to get Danny to school that they paid for a taxi to pick him up at home every morning and to chauffeur him to his new school, which was across the bridge in the North End. Susan said she agreed to it because it kept the social services people off her back. They were constantly threatening to take her children away, she said.

Susan was an alcoholic. She was a regular at a bootleg operation on Sherbrook Street a few blocks away from home. They sold bottles of hard liquor at inflated prices, but it was convenient and social and they would extend credit to Susan, who was often broke and did not have a job. As soon as the welfare money arrived each month, she would use it to fuel more partying. Drinking twelve to twenty-four beers was fairly typical, she said.

The parties went on all night. People they didn't know stayed to the wee hours pounding back beers and then passing out on the floor. Bottles were strewn all over the house. Richard and Danny started sneaking out to get away from it. They would climb out a second-floor window of the house on Ross to the roof of an adjoining garage, then slide down to the lane below. They were out there on the streets most nights from about the age of eight or nine. Richard would steal blankets from clotheslines and the two of them would sleep in an apartment stairwell or in a play structure at a neighbourhood park, hoping to escape the fear and alienation they felt at home.

There was rarely food in the house. Danny, even as an eight-year-old, was constantly hungry and would yell and scream and ask his mother why they had nothing to eat, Susan remembers. Sometimes she would shoplift at the grocery store by stuffing refrigerated meats inside her clothes or filling a duffel bag and walking out. She wonders if the store employees just chose to look the other way.

"I was good at stealing," she said, "[but] I think people knew."

Richard and Danny were driven to distraction by hunger, and often staked out the garbage bin behind a Kentucky Fried Chicken, waiting for scraps to be tossed out. Eventually, hunger led them to some of their first crimes.

In the summer Richard would survey the vegetable gardens kept by Portuguese immigrants in their neighbourhood. At night he and Danny raided their backyards, stealing carrots, crabapples, and tomatoes. From there, they graduated to testing the doors of parked cars to see if they were unlocked, and before long, smashing their windows, to get the loose change from cup holders. At first they used the money to buy food at a convenience store – a bag of chips, candy, sometimes a loaf of bread and some bologna, Richard said. And then it got a little more serious.

Discovering they could fend for themselves fed the boys' sense of adventure. Danny was a risk taker, always pushing a little further than Richard. Once, Susan got a phone call from police in Ontario saying they had Danny in their custody. He was only about eight or nine and had snuck onto a freight train carrying new cars. It was late autumn and cold outside but he and a friend, exploring the rail yards, had climbed aboard, found a key in the ignition, and started the engine to keep warm. The train had rolled all the way across the provincial border, a two-hundred-kilometre trip, before the boys were discovered in Kenora.

Far from being chastened by his brush with police, Danny was emboldened, and Susan's attempts at discipline had little impact. When he was ten, Richard was sent to Saskatchewan to live with his aunt for a year. When he was reunited with Danny, his younger brother taught him how to shoplift and break into cars, skills he'd picked up from older boys in Winnipeg.

One night the Wolfe brothers and a few others were walking downtown. They used to roam the streets freely in those days, ranging miles from home. They were near the Towne Cinema in the Exchange District when Danny broke away from the group and started snooping around a rental car lot. Thin as a whippet, he was able to sneak through the gate. He got a set of keys somehow, either from the office or a drop box, and then scurried around the parking lot trying to find a vehicle that would accept them. They got a van.

The boys all jumped in and decided they should head to Regina, about six hours away on the Trans-Canada Highway. They knew the route from having driven it many times with family. At one point a police cruiser pulled up next to them at a traffic light, but the cops didn't notice it was Danny's twelve-year-old cousin at the wheel.

The crew of preteens drove all night and arrived in Regina early the next morning. They went straight to their aunt's place. Another one of Danny's cousins came out to greet them.

"Where's Auntie?" she asked.

No adults, just us, the boys explained. Their cousin's jaw dropped. When her father came home Danny and company had to confess the van was stolen, news that was not well received. His uncle insisted they leave and return the vehicle. Instead, the boys went to stay with another aunt.

They settled in and started exploring their new surroundings. The new city offered great opportunities, particularly for stealing bikes, and soon their aunt's garage started to fill up with bicycles of all descriptions. Danny became obsessed with gathering more, rather than just enjoying what he already had. When they needed food the boys went to the store and stole some. But after three days of larceny they got caught. Danny and Richard had taken the van out for a drive. Danny, too small to operate the pedals, did the steering while his brother was on the floor, working the brakes and gas. They jerked the van back and forth across the road. This time police caught on – Danny could barely see over the dashboard – and pursued the brothers as they drove to their aunt's place. Once they stopped, the police pounced, sirens blaring. Danny jumped from the van and tried to run but was quickly caught in the backyard. The police waited for the other boys to show up at the house before hauling them all off to the station. Danny was too young to be incarcerated so he was taken to a state-run boy's home for the night. Richard and the others ended up in cells at the police station. They were held another day in Regina before the police flew them back to Winnipeg. They were so young that they weren't charged.

Today Susan is a sober, responsible woman who has worked at the health centre on her reserve for more than a decade. But when Danny and Richard were young she was only sporadically the kind of parent she wanted to be. More often she was lost in a fog of drugs and alcohol. She remembers those days with a mixture of happiness and sorrow. Despite her troubles, the boys' childhood also brought moments of love and laughter captured in family photos, like playing with action figures, stopping at the side of the highway to pose with the Welcome to Manitoba sign, and taking the children to a petting zoo. She also recalls taking foolish risks. She once got Danny, who was about seven, to drive a car for more than an hour on the highway into Regina, because she was blind drunk.

"I sat him on my lap like that and let him drive," she said. "From Balcarres to Regina [nearly 100 kilometres], he drove all the way."

Susan lives in a neat, two-bedroom house on the reserve. It's a small prefabricated home with windows that look out on the expanse of trees beyond her back door. On a late autumn day she sits at her kitchen table in the dazzling light of a setting sun, leafing through photographs. Her memories are patchy but the photos help.

She used to have more photos, she said, but Danny and Richard were playing with matches one night and started a large fire that destroyed their apartment. The boys had to be plucked from the flames, and most of Susan's mementos were lost. She still has some photos from their school days, though.

Danny, in his first school photograph, is an impish, dimpled six-year-old, who sits for his portrait with eyes sparkling, smiling at the camera. In the class photo, though, it's hard to spot him. "That's him at the back, pulling the face," Susan says. She points to Danny, who has deliberately crossed his eyes and pulled his mouth into a goofy grin, the only student who failed to stand at attention and smile. Susan can't help but laugh.

Richard's first photo is of his 1981 kindergarten class at John M. King school on Ellice Avenue in Winnipeg's inner city. He sits in the front row, hands neatly folded, his wispy dark hair parted on the side and falling over his ears. He appears eager to please, forcing a smile by jutting his lower jaw toward the camera.

By the time he's nine, Richard is already posing with a red bandana tied around his forehead, which would later become an Indian Posse gang symbol. That same year, he produced a class assignment that included a photo of himself, his characteristics and ambition. He wears a black hat in the image and the headline is "Richard – Wealthy and Powerful."

Susan wanted the boys to get a good education, to be able to grow up and get jobs, even if she and their father set a far different example. But her own experience at school made her distrustful of authority, and when the boys were in trouble at school, more trouble arrived on her doorstep in the form of Child and Family Services. She can't remember when Danny and Richard were first taken from her and placed in foster care. She knows nothing of any of the families or group homes they stayed with or what happened to them. They used to run away from those foster homes as soon as possible, never finding a situation that was stable or likeable. At the first opportunity they always made their way home to the mother they loved.

At her kitchen table, Susan ponders her few surviving photographs. She picks up a photo of Danny and Richard and another boy in front of a Canadian flag. Richard is showing off a cast on what must be a broken wrist or arm; Susan doesn't remember how he was hurt. In another photo she's sitting on a couch with Danny, holding a bottle of beer as her son leans in to smile. "That's the life I showed them."

She pauses with a photo of herself in her early twenties. She has a bright, round face, a huge head of permed hair, and oversized sunglasses that shield half her face. But even the large sunglasses can't conceal the bruise that covers her left eye and cheekbone.

"That's how I used to live." She seems disgusted and puts the picture down. She clears her throat, then begins to tell a story of driving in Regina one day in recent years. She looked out the window of her car and saw a little boy. He was about three or four and was running after his mother, a young First Nations woman. The mother was striding away, leaving the boy behind without even looking back. Susan watched the boy's face fall as his run slowed to a walk and he began to realize that his mother wasn't coming back for him. Susan instantly placed herself in the scene and allowed herself to spiral into the darkness of her past. She remembered a time when Richard and Danny were about the same age. They were running after her and she just walked away and didn't come back. She wasn't even sure someone would look after them. Maybe her sister would, she thought. Or maybe not. *They'll fend for themselves.*

"That's what I did. I didn't look back to see if my sister took [them]. I just went to the party and got drunk. I didn't give a shit. I did that because I didn't have love in my heart and I didn't have parenting skills. I lost all these things in the residential schools."

At the age of six, Susan was taken from her parents by a government agent and placed in the Prince Albert Residential School, several hundred kilometres from her home, under a government policy that has since been described as an act of cultural genocide. Its aim was to remove indigenous children from their homes and school them in the ways of the white settlers, and to ultimately extinguish their language, religion, and cultural identity.

Susan later attended the Gordon's Residential School near Punnichy, Saskatchewan, which was the site of countless horrors of sexual and physical abuse that destroyed hundreds of young indigenous people in the very years that she was there. One former teacher was accused of molesting more than one hundred pupils. Every year new children would arrive and more would become victims of sexual assault, preyed upon by teachers and fellow students. Aside from the sexual violence, there was the danger of physical abuse. And there was the very simple and profound pain of being rounded up by the agents of government and forcibly removed from their homes. Susan can still remember the dread that came with the end of summer and the knowledge that she would have to go back to the school.

In August 2012, Susan walked into a law firm on the fourth floor of a downtown Winnipeg office building. In 2008 the Canadian government recognized the massive scale of the residential school tragedy with an official apology to all its victims, delivered by Prime Minister Stephen Harper from the floor of the House of Commons. It was the beginning of what was hoped would be a process of reconciliation with Canada's indigenous peoples. As part of the legal settlement of the huge number of residential schools lawsuits, the courts established a process for hearing and compensating claims of sexual and physical abuse. Susan had put off this moment for as long as she could, reluctant as she was to raise these horrible spirits, but the deadline for making a claim was just days away. She was unusually quiet beforehand. She had spent the previous evening at the casino trying to take her mind off the upcoming testimony but could only manage a few losing rounds of slots before a sleepless night in the hotel. A lawyer invited her into an interview room and she followed, raising her eyes to the ceiling. The office was decorated with several pieces of aboriginal art and Susan nodded at a sculpture of an owl on her way past. A messenger, she said. The door closed behind her and Susan began to tell her story.

An hour later she emerged and walked straight past a small clutch of friends and relatives waiting in the reception area, tears still on her cheeks. She was too overwhelmed to say anything. She doesn't want what she went through to be public, she said, or catalogued in every detail. She was torn from her parents. She lived near some of her siblings at the school but was not permitted to talk to them or go to them when she was hurt. She was sexually abused. She was physically abused. It was awful, horrible, painful. What more can she say?

Danny and Richard were undoubtedly affected by her experiences. They were also stung by their father's absence. He, too, was a residential school survivor and an alcoholic, far more likely to be on the street or at a party than at home with them. When he was around, violence was not far behind. Richard Sr. used to beat Susan and sometimes the boys too. Richard said he and Danny would get clobbered without explanation, and he was afraid that his father would kill their mother.

Susan was unwittingly re-creating the life she thought she had left behind. Her own father, Bill Creeley, had been chief of their home reserve, Okanese, and a respected leader. He had served in the Canadian military in the Second World War, as had his father, Leonard, in the Great War. But Bill became an alcoholic, prone to rage at Susan's mother, Irene Thomas. There were many nights when Susan and her sisters would hide in the cupboards or flee the house. To this day, she keeps her shoes near her bed in case she needs to run in the middle of the night. She suspects much of his anger was a result of what he had been subjected to in the residential schools a generation earlier, although he never talked about his experiences. One summer

Susan came home from residential school and found her mother had simply left the family. Susan did not know where she had gone or why. Not long after, Susan was taken from her home by Mormon missionaries and placed in a home in Calgary. She suspects this was approved by her father, but within a year Bill came to collect her, and they hitchhiked back to Okanese.

Susan said she lived in fear at the residential school, fear of being hit and of the sexual abuse. When she was twelve, Susan and a friend decided that they'd had enough, and they fled. They made it to Regina, and eventually back to the reserve at Okanese. Her father was happy to see her, but his drinking and violence terrified her. When things got really bad, her older sister would take them out of the house and they'd spend the night sleeping rough in the bush.

Later that year Bill moved the family to Regina. Susan can't remember why, but shortly after she ran away. She's never been able to explain why she ran away, even to herself, but it was an important step in a very difficult life. She met friends in the city who were old enough to buy liquor and she started drinking, and later got into drugs, to kill the feelings of shame that used to overwhelm her.

As a young teenager Susan ran into some mild trouble with the law and was made a ward of the state. She got locked up in a kind of juvenile prison for runaways, which she hated. When she was sixteen and back on the street she met Richard Wolfe, who was three years older than her. She had known about him when she was at school because he was one of the best hockey players on another residential school's team. He was handsome, with a chiselled jaw and a thick head of dark hair that he swept up in a pompadour. He also had a reputation for being a good hunter, which to Susan meant that he would be a good provider. In retrospect she's not sure it was love, but it was exciting. They hung out and partied together and in no time Susan was pregnant. They lived for a while with his mother on his home reserve.

Susan remembers a cold winter with plenty of moose meat, but one night Richard beat her up, and she left soon after.

She was seventeen in 1975 when she gave birth to her first child, Richard, named after his father. A year later she gave birth again, this time to Danny, whose name, Daniel Richard Wolfe, was just the inverse of his father's and brother's name, Richard Daniel Wolfe. Susan even had the initials RDW tattooed on her arm.

She was drinking heavily at that point and Danny's premature birth was most likely triggered by excessive alcohol consumption. She said she believes that Danny suffered from fetal alcohol spectrum disorder (FASD), an affliction that impairs judgment. Danny's elementary school principal, Ms. Loeppky, said she suspected the same. Although he never had a formal diagnosis of FASD, Danny certainly exhibited signs of impulsiveness and poor decision making that would go on to shape his life in important ways. In later years he was described as having suffered from failure-to-thrive syndrome, a broad diagnosis that can be related to the emotional deprivation of a parent's withdrawal, or to poverty and malnutrition in the first years of life. After Danny was born, Susan made a trip to Okanese and left him with her sister. A short time later Danny became sick and ended up in intensive care at the hospital, before being placed in foster care. Susan sobered up enough to get Danny back when he was about six months old, but then she and Richard Sr. split up again. Richard Sr. took Danny with him to Saskatoon, but a few months later Susan got a letter saying that Richard had been jailed and Danny had been placed in foster care. By the time Susan got her younger son back for good, he was about eighteen months old and walking and talking, she said. The disruptions that Danny suffered in those years would mark him forever.

After Susan's third child, Murray, was born in 1977, Susan's family suggested it would be too much for her to raise three boys aged three and under by herself. For his welfare and hers, Murray was given to another First Nations family that had raised one of Susan's sisters. Susan approved, although it was heart-wrenching to let go of her baby. In the early 1980s she had two more sons whom she gave up for adoption because she knew her addictions to drugs and alcohol made it unlikely she could properly raise them. Today she is still trying to build a relationship with those two sons, each of whom feels some anger toward her, she says.

"It's tough," she said. "But they grew up in good homes."

Susan is candid about her failings. She was not a good parent, she says, and did not know how to be one. But the intergenerational effects of the residential schools in her life are easy to identify. Her father, a residential school student, was an alcoholic who beat her mother. Her mother, also a residential school student, left her family when Susan was a child without saying goodbye or carrying on much of a relationship afterward. Most of Susan's childhood was spent away from her own parents, during which time she was physically and sexually abused and inadequately educated. After fleeing residential school, Susan says she drank and used drugs to ease her pain and to forget what they had done to her. She became a mother when she was very young and completely unprepared.

"I was so sick. I didn't even know how to be a parent," she said. "That residential school really did a number on all our people."

When they were old enough to realize the degree of dysfunction in their lives, Richard and Danny tried to decipher its causes.

"We talked about it a few times, me and Danny. We have a good idea of what mark [the residential schools] left on our relatives. Hitting the bottle that hard, they're just trying to forget about it. But at the same time they're not thinking about what they're doing to us young kids around them. We were watching them," Richard said. "Why was there drinking in front of us? Why wasn't there food in the fridge? All that didn't just happen spur of the moment. Something had to have happened to her for her to act like that."

Susan's years with Richard Sr. were tumultuous and their relationship ended for good with a beating that landed her in hospital. Visiting her bedside made a memorable impression on young Richard and Danny. Her head bandaged, jaw broken, feeding through a straw, she was almost unrecognizable to them. Their father didn't come around anymore after that. His violence, as well as his absence, stoked a sense of anger inside the boys.

"Every time after that I tried to find out where he was, people said he's on the street or he's drinking," Richard said.

Shortly after her release from the hospital, Susan started seeing a new boyfriend, Clarence Buffalocalf. On their first dates she drank beer with a straw because her broken jaw was still wired shut. Unfortunately, this new relationship was also violent. Susan says they fought one night and as he was beating her she picked up a hammer and swung it at Clarence's head. He ended up in hospital and she was charged with aggravated assault.

It was not Susan's only criminal charge. On another occasion she was in Regina visiting her family when she witnessed her brother-in-law bashing her sister with a teapot. Susan instinctively picked up a knife from the counter and slammed it into her brother-in-law's gut. He survived, but she went to jail. She kept the tiny news clipping from the *Regina Leader-Post* as a souvenir. "Woman Charged," says the headline. Susan has no idea where seven- and eight-year-old Danny and Richard were during this chaos, or where they stayed while she was in jail.

By the time they were about ten or eleven years old, Danny and Richard were quite accustomed to raising themselves. They had no regard for conventional rules or morality. They saw themselves as survivors and were prepared to do whatever it took to make it.

—

In 1988, Danny's life was at a turning point. He was twelve years old, had been in and out of foster care, and was regularly apprehended by police. Out of the blue one day he bumped into his father in Winnipeg. He hadn't seen Richard Sr. in several years, though he had often wondered where he was. They were walking along the same street heading in opposite directions, and it was only as they neared one another that Danny recognized his dad. They both said "Hi" and exchanged a few words, but Richard Sr. said very little. And then he just walked away.

Danny was dazed, and this encounter became a moment he would mull bitterly for the rest of his life. *That's my dad*, he thought to himself. *He hasn't seen me in years. And that's all he has to say? Why doesn't he even want to talk to me?* Danny was angry. The encounter marked the death of his original family. But it was only a matter of months before another family was born.

2

BIRTH OF A GANG
1988–1994

Richard, Danny, and their two-year-old brother Preston Buffalocalf moved with Susan to a tall, white house on Beverley Street in the summer of 1988. The house sat on a tree-lined street in the heart of Winnipeg's downtown, a short walk from Portage Avenue and near the University of Winnipeg. The rent was manageable and Susan considered it a step up in the world.

Shortly after arriving in the new neighbourhood the boys started hanging out with some kids who lived nearby on Langside Street. At the time, Langside was a notorious address, the site of a disproportionate share of the city's violent crime. The houses were rundown and the residents, many of them indigenous people, were desperately poor. Drinking and drugs were obvious social problems, and many children in the area, like Danny and Richard, had little supervision.

The brothers formed a small, close-knit clique with a big, strong neighbourhood kid called Lawrence, among others. Even though he was the youngest of the group, Danny was "a mischievous little guy," according to Richard, always the one to test limits and encourage the others to join him. He was the first to smoke, the first to drink, and the first to try marijuana. The others followed, and soon they were all smoking, drinking, fighting, and stealing. They broke into garages, stole coins from cars, and shoplifted. They called themselves Scammers Inc., a local nuisance, but not yet anything more than a crew of petty thieves.

The atmosphere in Winnipeg in the summer of 1988 was tense, as relations between indigenous people and the police reached a disastrous state. For years there had been accusations of racism and differential treatment; then, in March, indigenous leader J.J. Harper was shot and killed by a policeman. Although Harper didn't match the description of the suspect the officer was pursuing, the officer stopped him to ask for ID, which Harper refused to provide. The standoff escalated, and in the physical struggle that ensued the officer fired a fatal shot into Harper's chest. It was a tragic, senseless killing made worse when Winnipeg's chief of police, Herb Stephen, immediately cleared the officer of wrongdoing. Native leaders accused the police of racism, and the Manitoba government called an inquiry into the treatment of aboriginal people in the justice system.

The Indian Posse began to take root that summer when Richard and Danny's little clique ran across another group from Langside who claimed the first block south of Portage Avenue as their turf. The other group was led by Raymond Armstrong, known as Ray Ray, who disliked Richard and his crew at first. But when Ray Ray noticed that one of his rivals had several attractive sisters, a truce was struck and the two groups got together. The Indian Posse's founders were now in place.

In late summer of 1988 a group of them were hanging out at the Wolfe house on Beverley. The basement, where twelve-year-old Danny and thirteen-year-old Richard slept and where their mother rarely ventured, was the boys' space. "The basement" is a term the gang still uses when talking about the Indian Posse's origins. Seven young men were present that day, including Danny, Lawrence, and Spencer

LaPorte, who years later died after a drug overdose. Richard won't reveal the identity of the others because it's a gang secret. (Ray Ray Armstrong was named as a founder in a book by Gordon Sinclair.)

Up until that point they were just a group of teenagers hanging around and getting involved in small-time crime. Richard and Lawrence, though, had started to chafe at their roles in the group. Some of the older guys in Scammers Inc. treated them as errand boys, they felt, getting them to make drug deliveries or do small tasks. They didn't treat Danny this way. So, with bigger ambitions on their minds, Richard and Lawrence decided to form their own gang. In the late 1980s, street gangs were just beginning to gain prominence in Winnipeg aboriginal popular culture. Gangster rap was growing in influence, and the boys had already been impressed by the first aboriginal gang to assert its presence in Winnipeg, the Main Street Rattlers. Richard's cousin dated one of the Rattlers in the mid-1980s and Richard admired the way they oozed a menacing cool. "I remember looking up to them," he said.

As they lounged in the Beverley Street basement, the boys tried to come up with a name for their gang and flipped through the pages of a hip hop magazine looking for ideas. They wanted something that announced who they were. They were invisible people, they felt, and they wanted to make a name for themselves. They were all either First Nations or Metis but the word *Native*, the politically correct term of the era, just didn't feel right. "Syndicate" was considered but rejected. Richard liked "Indian" and its straightforward hostility. To him it meant the down and out, the addict on the street corner who drank rubbing alcohol and household cleaners. That's what an Indian was to the mainstream white society, he said.

During this time the word *Indian* was still used in the legal definitions of indigenous status, but, often seen as derogatory, it had fallen out of use in most other contexts. Like the hip hop groups that reclaimed the N-word, the Beverley Street boys flipped *Indian* to express something they held in common: a feeling of poverty, of being looked down upon, and of resentment. To their minds, the world held nothing for them. They weren't going to finish school and find jobs. Still, they wanted what the rest had: cars, homes, and money, and they were prepared to take those things by force if necessary. The only way to survive with the odds stacked against them was to bind together. With their parents either drunk or on drugs, fighting or in jail, the boys decided that day in the basement to form a family – a posse – of their own. They became the Indian Posse.

"We just wanted to make sure we stuck with each other and watched each other's backs," Richard said.

The Indian Posse quickly grew to a group of twelve or fifteen, and included all of the boys in the Langside clique, even those who weren't present "in the basement." Like any smart organization, the group focused on establishing an identity and a reason for being. The Posse wanted to protect themselves from other gangs; they wanted to control their neighbourhood; they wanted power; and they wanted cash. At night they roamed the streets looking for ways to make a quick score.

"We'd just break into cars, stuff like that. Fight people," said one early member. "We were just kids but people were scared of us. Even men. They would get beat up too. We were fearsome. We were kind of crazy."

There was no shortage of muscle. All the boys had grown up in tough environments and fighting was something they knew how to do.

Lynn was one of the first girls to join the Indian Posse and became one of Danny's closest friends. She remembers Danny was in the middle of a fight the first time they met, wrestling his friend Sam-Boo for a video game controller. She ignored them, picked up the controller, and started playing the game they had abandoned.

Danny released Sam-Boo from a headlock. "Who the hell are you?" he asked. "I'm Lynn," she said. He was impressed by her audacity, and from then on, they were friends. Lynn came up with many of the ideas for gang colours and symbols. The enduring choice was the red bandana, which the gang believed symbolized power, the spilling of blood, and their identification as indigenous or "red" people.

The branding was effective. The Indian Posse represented a kind of raised fist of rebellion for teenagers desperate to be connected to something bigger than themselves. Kids were attracted to the gang in ways that even its founders struggled to understand. Something – perhaps the name or the colours or the idea of belonging – obviously touched a chord within indigenous youth in the city. It was hip hop and urban at a time when those trends were taking off in music and movies. Though they barely had time to establish many rules, there was one that they immediately put into effect: only indigenous people could join. Aboriginal teenagers clamoured to get in and the gang grew quickly.

"Within a year the numbers climbed into the hundreds. I have no idea why that happened. I thought we were just a bunch of kids hanging out together. But all of a sudden there was members everywhere," said one original member.

For the gang's leadership structure the founders chose the circle, a symbol of central significance for indigenous people that represents life, the sun, the nest of a bird, the medicine wheel, among other concepts. The Indian Posse would be governed by a leadership council, or circle, a body of five to ten people that would make all the major decisions on the basis of consensus, another concept imported from indigenous governance models. Consensus gives equal weight to every voice, at least officially, and decisions are made collectively, not by majority rule. Unlike most other crime groups, which value a clear, top-down decision structure, in the Indian Posse no single person was chosen as top boss. That was by design.

It was an unusual but potentially wise choice for boys still in their teenage years. A gang is vulnerable to losing its leaders, either to jail or to attacks from rivals, and having a pool of leaders mitigates that risk. A relatively flat leadership structure also cuts down on rivalry for the top position, although there was still intrigue and regular jockeying for position among gang members.

As time went on the Indian Posse adapted to the likelihood that members would spend time behind bars by making prison experience mandatory in order to rise in the hierarchy. To reach the gang's highest levels, to get full-patch status or hold a coveted position on the leadership council, a member had to serve time in a federal penitentiary. This new tenet created a bizarre incentive in the gang to be caught by police. Why would criminals encourage getting arrested? Well, in part because the gang's ability to control and indoctrinate members was strongest in the closed environment of the prison system, but the rule also served to embolden the ambitious. Taking a worthwhile risk for the good of the gang that led to an arrest was not disastrous. The arrests helped them gain legitimacy in the criminal underworld, and the arrested members would get out eventually. In the meantime, they could help consolidate the gang's presence in the prisons, where much of the recruiting took place. Getting arrested also entrenched the sense of commitment that was required from members. The Indian Posse was for life.

Each prospective Indian Posse member had to earn his way into the gang. He waited to be given a first mission or task, which could involve a robbery, collecting a debt, or transporting drugs. Once the prospect successfully completed several missions, he was eligible for his first gang tattoo, the G-money, usually a small G stylized to look like a dollar sign. This tattoo represented status as a striker, the rank of the basic foot soldier who always does as he or she is told. Usually a group of five or six strikers reported to someone a rank above them, often called a full-patch or a member, who in turn was identified by a tattoo of a shield, usually in the neck area, or by arm bars, a large tattoo on the forearms. For a long time the full patch, a big back tattoo, could only be earned after a stint in federal penitentiary, although that rule has relaxed somewhat over the years.

In the gang, Richard and Danny found an acceptance they hadn't found anywhere else in their lives. School was a disaster, family life the same. With the Indian Posse, they had people who cared about them. The older guys struck them as solid, dependable, and devoted to them.

It was these older guys, those in their late teens and early twenties, like Spencer, who started pushing the idea of making serious money, one of the originals remembers. Richard's first enterprise was stealing car stereos. He would walk the city's back lanes at night looking for unlocked garages, then he'd punch through a car's side window with a screwdriver and use the tool to pry the stereo out. He could get four or five a night without much trouble. They were worth about $400 or $500 and he'd sell them to a guy in Chinatown for $100 apiece. Danny did a similar line in hubcaps.

Within a year, the Wolfe brothers graduated from robbing garages to houses. Houses were a riskier proposition, but they were also more exciting. Richard would roam all over the city on foot or on a bike, descending on residences that appeared empty. He loved finding a place with nobody home and then digging through strangers' stuff for things he could steal – jewellery, electronics, cash, and CDs. Anything that could be quickly resold.

"We didn't think about [the people we were stealing from] being victimized or traumatized. There was none of that," Richard said. "I wanted what they had."

The boys were young and prone to slip up, though. Once, when they were getting tired and had been out late, Richard and Danny broke into a home before dawn and found a well-stocked pantry. Richard decided to make himself a big breakfast of fried eggs and toast. He ate and then fell asleep, eventually waking up face down in the food to the sound of the owner returning from his night shift.

Danny's first conviction was for a break and enter, and he was found guilty on January 18, 1989, at the age of twelve and a half. He was sentenced to one year of open custody, essentially less stringent rules inside the youth correctional facility, and a year of probation.

This brush with the law did absolutely nothing to change Danny's direction in life. A few weeks after his fourteenth birthday he was convicted of theft. Lynn says she remembers him getting arrested for taking rims off cars and selling them for $400 a set.

In the early days of the Indian Posse a small number of women had a role in the gang. That changed in the early 1990s, when, according to Richard, the leadership decided that the girls were too vulnerable and were getting muscled for their money on the street. It's not clear if this was true or just an excuse to get women out of the way. The council of male leaders decided girls could hang around, advise on decisions, and commit crimes with the guys, but membership would be restricted to men only. Many of the women at that point were in relationships with the men in the gang, so some remained on the scene; others drifted away as they grew up and their relationships changed.

One woman who was there in the early days said Danny dreamed of giving all the kids who had been messed up by their parents a home base, a chance to have something in life, and a way to learn to make money and feed themselves. She said Danny taught her how to steal and how to be his driver as he moved money and product between gang houses. She knows those things were wrong, but at the time they seemed necessary. She said she and many others had no structure, no sense of purpose, no home, but Danny provided those things for them, moulding them into a unit and showing them a life that was both terrifying and exhilarating.

As the gang grew larger it developed something of an aura. Indian Posse graffiti appeared on the walls of houses and garages from the downtown core to the North End of Winnipeg. Members would walk through the streets in groups, announcing their presence as Indian Posse to those they encountered.

These early members were tough, hardened by their family circumstances, unafraid of violence, unsentimental about their neighbours or even their friends. They could be brutal and callous. Taking what didn't belong to them became their way of life, and they knew that separated them from other kids. Every now and then the contrast would be reinforced when a new person from a more conventional background tried to get down with the gang.

"Once in a while we would have the silver spoon kids come and hang with us but they wouldn't last," Lynn said. "They had everything: meals, parents who cared they went to school, clothes, chores. I never had that. Danny never had that. We were just running around all the time at all hours."

The gang's code was drawn up in these early years. Every crime group needs to regulate the behaviour of its members, but those members are often some of the most difficult people to control. The Indian Posse rules were straightforward: no hard drugs (defined mainly as cocaine and heroin); never talk about anything to anyone (a strict code of silence enforced by violence); and blood in, blood out: new members would be accepted only after a gang beating of a predetermined length, usually a minute or two. These "minutes," as they're called, involved three to five established members smashing the prospective recruit with fists and kicks. Over the years, a few were nearly beaten to death. Getting out of the gang was also deliberately made difficult. Some of the leaders believed no one should ever be allowed to leave alive; others said a severe beating was required. The rule was never uniformly enforced, but it's certain that people have been shot, beaten, and in some cases killed for trying to quit the Indian Posse. As Manitoba's provincial justice minister put it some twenty-five years after the Indian Posse was founded, joining a gang can be a life sentence, and it can also be a death sentence.

By their mid-teen years, from roughly 1990, the pace of Danny and Richard's criminal education accelerated. Richard started carrying a gun to school when he was thirteen. It was a .22 calibre pistol that he bought from a friend for about $200. He would tuck it into the back waistband of his jeans. It led to his first youth conviction, which was for carrying a firearm.

Susan remembers police raiding their house on Beverley during this time and emerging, to her astonishment, with televisions, stereos, and other equipment she had no idea was under her roof. While she had been off drinking, her sons were committing dozens of crimes. One day her youngest, Preston, found more than $1,000 in cash hidden in the home and brought it to her. She didn't ask Danny or Richard about it; instead she kept the cash for herself and used it to buy clothes for Preston and more booze for herself.

When the gang started to move beyond breaking and entering, stealing cars was next. Spencer LaPorte was particularly good at breaking into and starting a locked car, and he passed his skills on to the others. Soon, car theft became rampant in Winnipeg. Indian Posse gang members would steal four or five a night, taking them for joy rides or using them as getaway cars for other crimes, particularly armed robbery. They regularly raided gas bars in the North End at gunpoint for cash and cigarettes. These were serious crimes that brought in a lot of money, but also a lot of heat from police. The gang decided it needed a more reliable, less risky source of income.

When Richard and Danny were about fifteen and fourteen respectively, they graduated to dealing drugs and pimping. And that's when the money started pouring in.

By 1992 the brothers were living in their own house, paying $866 a month in rent. Their lives were by no means stable: they were frequently in and out of jail and always on some kind of probation. Richard said he used to steal cars to be able to make it to his probation sign-in on time, and would leave the stolen vehicle running while he dashed inside to check in with his probation officer. For his part, he was making thousands of dollars a month, the bulk of which came from drug sales, and getting a taste of the glamour of gang life.

With its growing membership and bolder criminal activity, the Indian Posse staked out its turf, primarily around the Lord Selkirk Park Housing Development just off Main Street in the North End. It was a sprawling complex with a mix of townhouses and drab apartment buildings populated almost entirely by First Nations and Metis people, though about half of the units were empty, either because they were too rundown to live in, or because the area was so undesirable it drove away potential tenants. Unemployment in the housing project and surrounding blocks was among the highest in Canada. The people in the neighbourhood had low levels of income and education and their surroundings bred dysfunction. In short, it was a ready-made market for drugs.

Richard would deploy teams of kids, many of them residents of the housing project, to sell drugs to their neighbours. They called the area "Little Chicago." Its poor design gave drug dealers vantage points that allowed them to spot police, while simultaneously preventing police from seeing what was going on inside.

Drug sales were strong across the city. The gang started with marijuana, hash, and LSD and worked their way up to cocaine.

Richard used to meet with rival gangs to rig prices and reduce competition. It was usually fairly easy to negotiate a fixed price with other dealers, he said. It wasn't in the Indian Posse's interest to undercut anyone. The going rate was about $15 a gram for pot, and the margins were relatively slim, but dropping the price to gain market share was not something Richard wanted to do. As someone on the low end of the drug business, who had to buy from a supplier, he never had enough product or margin to justify such a move.

"We'd say to them, we know you're selling over here. How much for? They'd say $15. We'd say, Okay, we're going to go over here and do the same fucking thing. That way we're on the same page . . . As long as everybody was making money everyone was happy."

That kind of diplomacy in a sixteen-year-old is remarkable, and it was one of Richard's strengths. If there was a particularly valuable skill that he brought to the gang it was the ability to sit down and win the confidence of potential rivals. He described it as being able to "talk to the room." In a street gang it's often the person with the wildest, worst tendencies who rises to the top, because no one can match his ambition or appetite for violence. But, for this brief moment at least, it was different in the IP. Richard attributes his growing role then to his cool temperament. Danny, by contrast, was a hothead, and did not have as prominent a position in the gang. Richard tried to talk to his younger brother about his temper but it was pointless, he said. Although D-Boy (as Danny was known on the street) was often easygoing and loved to laugh and joke, he was a hurricane when he lost his temper.

Keeping the peace in the drug-selling underworld during this time wasn't easy. Drug turf tends to be contentious, and as the number of gangs in the city ballooned, conflicts erupted. In 1992 Winnipeg police said they knew of only one youth street gang; a year later, they said there were eighteen. On June 1, 1993, the Indian Posse was mentioned for the first time in the pages of the *Winnipeg Free Press*. Police had been called to break up a fight between the IP and a group described as "the skaters" at the Unicity mall on the western edge of the city. Nearly three hundred kids, many of them IP or members of other gangs, showed up carrying knives, baseball bats, and other weapons, the paper reported.

The IP's first notable conflict was with a gang called War Party. War Party wanted to make inroads on Indian Posse drug turf, and the IP wasn't going to allow that. The leader of the rival gang thought he could discuss a merger, with himself in a leadership role and his gang's name intact. The IP leaders were having none of it.

"We told him we wanted to sit down and make a deal with him, talk to him," Richard said. "We showed him two pounds of weed. We told him we've got more of this for you and your crew but we need to talk about it. Come for a ride. He bit on the bait, sure enough."

They started out up Main Street, travelling through the North End and Old Kildonan. It was just before Hallowe'en and the storefronts displayed ghoulish skeletons and ghosts. As they continued into the countryside and the street lights faded in the distance, the War Party leader thought this was just another drug deal. In reality, he was being set up by the Indian Posse.

They turned onto a side road, stopped the car, and the five of them – four IP members and the War Party leader – piled out and made for a wooded area off to the right of the highway. It was dark and cold. There was no one around for miles, the only sound an occasional car zooming down a distant road. It became clear that this wasn't a drug deal at all. It looked like an execution.

"He didn't cry at first," Richard said. "He just kept asking, 'Why?'"

No one answered, letting the tension build. Alone and confused, the rival gang leader pleaded for an explanation. Eventually someone spoke.

"One of the brothers told him to 'shut the fuck up and start digging.'"

He was handed a shovel. Richard had seen this trick used before by bikers, and it was devastatingly effective. The shovel clanged on the hard mud; the earth was already solid in the late autumn cold. Their rival repeated the action tentatively, going through the motions because he didn't know what else to do. He started to cry and beg for his life. The IP guys made him squirm for a few minutes. Finally one of them spoke up and laid out the terms of surrender. War Party would patch over to join the IP, and the IP would be in charge.

"You guys are with us now."

The War Party leader leapt at the offer.

The IP took back the shovel. The shaken War Party leader did his best to stay cool, while the Posse leaders enjoyed their display of power.

The gang grew by a dozen or so as the War Party members were incorporated into the Indian Posse. It was by no means all of the rival gang, but the numbers weren't crucial to the IP leadership. Adding new members could have a destabilizing effect. Would they attempt to take over the Indian Posse from the inside? Would they pay their share of the gang tax to the IP leadership? For a gang that had been eliminated, and in some ways humiliated, that kind of reaction from the former War Party members couldn't be discounted. The advantage, as far as the IP saw it, was the elimination of a rival.

Over time the Indian Posse concentrated its strength in the North End. Danny and Richard got an apartment on Redwood Avenue. A gang clubhouse was established on Pritchard Avenue. The Merchant's Hotel on Selkirk Avenue became one of the key locations for their drug dealing. Selkirk Avenue was once a primarily Jewish and Ukrainian-Polish commercial district; today only Gunn's Bakery remains as a vestige of an era when the street catered to immigrants from all over Eastern Europe. From the 1970s, as thousands migrated to the city in search of more opportunity than existed on the reserves of Manitoba and Saskatchewan, the neighbourhood became increasingly aboriginal. With its smaller homes and lower rents, the North End was the city's natural landing spot for newcomers.

The Merchant's Hotel, built in 1913, sat at the heart of Selkirk Avenue, the legendary centre of commercial and community life in the North End. It had a dingy, roughneck bar that drew people at all hours of the day. In a community crippled by poverty and addiction, the Merch, as it was known, was a magnet for those looking for some temporary relief from their troubles.

The Indian Posse, a new kind of merchant in the local economy, established itself as a leading drug distributor at the hotel around 1991. The street corner outside became an open-air drug market where low-level Posse members stood around waiting to sell customers dope or LSD. They would do their deals quickly through car windows, particularly in the cold Winnipeg winter. To shield themselves from the elements they often ducked into the bar or the laundromat across the street. Prospective clients could identify the dealers with no trouble – teenagers with darting eyes who wore a flash of red, either a bandana hanging from a pocket or a red baseball cap or T-shirt.

By looking to claim the heart of the North End as its own turf, the Indian Posse put itself in the crosshairs of rival gangs. Their attitude, according to one veteran police gang investigator, was that they just didn't care. They weren't afraid of anyone or anything.

The IP ran up against a gang called the North End Brotherhood, NEB for short. The NEB was in many ways similar to the IP, albeit smaller. Their crew was only about thirty strong, and the Indian Posse was already four or five times as large. Still, the NEB had a pretty tough reputation, and a claim to the Merchant's Hotel. Wanting that turf for themselves, the IP drew a line in the sand.

Richard told the NEB, "We make good money here. Either you guys go with us or we can go to war."

The IP leadership was reasonable enough to know that a conflict was best avoided. There were members, though, Danny among them, who were enthusiastic about a shooting war. But before any violence could break out, the NEB leadership acquiesced, deciding to wrap up the old name and fly the red flag of the Indian Posse. The IP name was starting to resonate in the city and momentum was on their side.

This kind of takeover became common as the gang swallowed its smaller rivals, but peace was temporary. The addition of the North End Boys brought a group of tough, ambitious thugs into the fold and they soon began to transform the gang into an even more ruthless and violent force. Hostilities between the Indian Posse and another rival group, the Overlords, eventually broke into open war. On the night of February 9, 1994, the temperature hovered around minus 30 degrees Celsius, or minus 22 Fahrenheit. An Overlords member crept through the snow to an Indian Posse house on Magnus Avenue in the North End and fired a shotgun through the kitchen window. The blast hit the ceiling but none of the gang members inside.

It took the attacked gang just a few hours to retaliate. Richard Beaulieau was an early member of the Indian Posse, and at seventeen years of age, he had significant status in the gang. He and a fifteen-year-old sidekick loaded shotguns and got a car ready. The trouble was that the only car at their disposal had to be driven by the fifteen-year-old's mother. Somehow, the two Posse members convinced her to drive past a house on Alexander Avenue, where they knew an Overlords member lived. As they rolled by, Beaulieau and his sidekick opened fire, sending five shots through the front windows. Blasts of return fire came from the house and an incoming shot hit the mother at the wheel in the hand. Later, when she went to hospital to get her wounds treated, suspicious hospital staff contacted police, which led to the arrest of Beaulieau and his accomplice. While investigators were still at the hospital another group of Indian Posse returned to the same home on Alexander Avenue and opened fire again. By this time their intended targets had beaten a retreat, leaving the home empty.

The rise of the drive-by shooting was, in many ways, consistent with the way the young gangsters mimicked the American gang life popularized in hip hop music and films. They wore a uniform of baggy jeans, lumberjack shirts buttoned at the collar, black-and-white Adidas track suits, and baseball hats riding high on their heads, with the requisite red bandana draped from a pocket, just like their counterparts in the gang wars of Los Angeles. They adopted the language and gestures, too, particularly hand signs that signified Posse or IP. Pat Olson, a sergeant with the Royal Canadian Mounted Police (RCMP) in Manitoba who spent many years leading gang investigations, said although most gang members are not very literate, there was one book that turned up consistently in raids on gang houses and in police stops: *Monster*, the autobiography by Sanyika Shakur, a member of the Crips gang of Los Angeles, was treated like a bible. It became required reading for police officers, too, as a window into the mind of the new kind of criminal they were pursuing.

When Richard Beaulieau landed in court a few months later in April 1994, the press reported that these were the first drive-by shootings to be prosecuted in Winnipeg. Since he was seventeen at the time of the shootings, Beaulieau could have gone to court as a youth, but he asked to be tried as an adult, which meant he would face a much longer sentence. A longer sentence was worth more to Beaulieau because it would put him in a federal penitentiary and elevate his status within the Indian Posse. That kind of perverse logic was a reflection of the value the gang placed on serving time in adult jails. Beaulieau smiled throughout, even as Judge Susan Devine rejected the sentencing recommendations from the Crown and the defence for being too lenient. Drive-by shootings were a new phenomenon that had to be stopped in their tracks, she said. Even though no one was injured in Beaulieau's attack, save his accomplice's mother, she sentenced him to four years in prison.

"It is in my view incumbent to the court to tell these gangs that behaviour like this will not be tolerated," Judge Devine said. "The fact nobody was injured was pure chance."

The stiff sentence did nothing to slow the growth of gangs in Winnipeg. If anything, it signalled the end of the beginning – not the beginning of the end.

3

YEARS OF MAYHEM
1989–1994

From the age of thirteen, Danny spent a significant portion of his life – as much as two-thirds of it – locked up in institutions. But he didn't do his time quietly, nor did he ever stop thinking of escape.

He and Richard developed an eye for business early on in their prison lives. When he was a teen locked up in the Manitoba Youth Centre, Danny sold drugs for the Indian Posse. It was a small market but still worth exploiting, as it is in any jail, because the extreme scarcity drives prices higher than in the outside world.

A pastor who worked in the youth jail and knew Danny, Richard, and most of the other young Indian Posse members, describes Richard as the most thoughtful in the group, saying he would often mull over discussions of the bible and contemplate the rights and wrongs of his actions. Most gang members are difficult to work with and come from terrible family situations, the pastor said; in his experience, many have been abused and preyed upon and in time they learn to be predators themselves, always looking for an angle, or a play, some way to exploit a situation. Richard was different. The pastor was convinced that he, at least, would eventually turn his life around.

"Richard always had that ability to be honest," the pastor said.

He believes that Richard and Danny's hunger for the love and purpose of family led them to create the gang as a substitute. In his view, they never anticipated the gang would become such a violent force.

"[Danny] was very impressionable," the pastor said. "He didn't have the smarts Richard had."

In those days Danny was not yet a leader and looked up to Richard as a role model and the primary influence in his life. But before long the gang became everything to Danny. He seemed less willing than his brother to see being a member of the gang as only one potential avenue among many in his life. The idea that another future was possible never seemed to cross his mind, the pastor said. Danny was also more prone to turbulent mood swings. He had an edge to him.

In early 1994, Danny took part in a period of murder and mayhem that forever changed Winnipeg and cemented the presence of street gangs in the city. In March that year, another drive-by shooting happened in the North End, outside an Indian Posse house on Redwood. A man named Justin James was standing in front of the house at 9:00 a.m. when he was shot in the buttocks, according to the local press. The shooter was a member of the Overlords gang, and James just had time to turn his back to the onrushing yellow Camaro as his attacker leaned out the window and opened fire with a handgun.

Shortly after the *Free Press* broke the news of the shooting they received a call from the Headingley Correctional Centre. The caller, who identified himself as a member of the Indian Posse, told the reporter the Posse would have to retaliate. "There's going to be a lot of stuff happening. We're going to hit back," the caller said.

The gang was proactive about calling the media to get a message out or to correct inaccurate reporting. Even though they were barely out of their teens the IP leaders sought to manage the media for their purposes. Because crime reporting is heavily informed by police sources, it was useful to the gang to put their own spin on events.

Though drive-by shootings were becoming commonplace in the city's gang wars in 1994, Danny didn't like them. He found it hard to aim from a moving car, but he also had a philosophical problem: he wanted his targets to know he wasn't afraid. So when the time came to hit a rival gang, Danny always advocated a walk-by. Walk-bys were aggressive, direct. They involved more risk and the younger Wolfe wanted to be seen as fearless.

By his own estimate Danny was the triggerman in fourteen walk-bys and drive-bys in the early 1990s. Many of them were not reported to police, as the homes being shot up belonged to rival gangs who, out of pride and devotion to the gangster's code, wouldn't call 911, so it's hard to know how many people Danny shot. There were also times when other, younger members confessed to crimes that Danny committed, in order to spare him and to prove their devotion to the gang.

"I know a lot of guys went in for Danny, to the youth centre, for break and enter and assaults," Richard said. At one point Danny was caught on camera beating someone and a younger gang member stepped forward and successfully took the fall for him, Richard added.

In July of 1994 Danny was convicted of escaping lawful custody at the Manitoba Youth Centre. It was his second conviction for escaping the youth jail. The first time he used a tent pole from a ceremonial teepee to vault the fence; this time, he just snuck away from his escort while attending his grade 10 classes at a special education program outside the jail.

Though Danny was under eighteen at the time of the escape, the judge still gave him his first adult sentence at the Headingley Correctional Centre, a provincial jail just west of Winnipeg. Headingley was a cesspool of gang rivalry and violence that was bursting at the seams as the Posse and a rival gang, the Manitoba Warriors, competed to recruit the most muscle. Inside, Danny was reunited with Richard, who had also gotten himself moved to the adult prison a few months earlier, because the gang needed a steady hand to run their drug smuggling operation; by then, the gang was adept at manoeuvring through the prison system. The drugs were crucially important inside because they represented currency and power. A steady drug supply kept members happy, and helped lure recruits. Danny acted as Richard's loyal lieutenant and enforcer.

Getting contraband into prison, whether tobacco, marijuana, LSD or harder drugs, was never an insurmountable problem. "We had some people on the payroll that would bring us what we wanted," Richard said. It was quite common for the Posse to target certain corrections workers for smuggling purposes, and sometimes the corrections workers would offer to bring drugs in themselves, for a price, or look the other way at the appropriate moment. Throwing the drugs over prison walls, for example, was a common Indian Posse delivery method. They would slice open a tennis ball, place the drugs inside, and then glue the ball back together. A ball has the added virtue of being easy to throw, so it could travel the necessary distance over the prison wall into the exercise yard where inmates retrieved it and quickly hid the drugs. If the guards were being paid to ignore what they saw, it was much easier.

While Richard had his eye on doing his time and making his money, Danny made a name for himself in prison combat. He intimidated potential opponents with his indifference to danger, which was his way of compensating for his small stature. When he first landed at Headingley, Danny weighed little more than 120 pounds. Although he followed the gang stipulation to lift weights, and even tested positive for steroids at one point, he struggled to add bulk. Nevertheless, he was brutally effective with his hands, thanks to a combination of speed and vicious cunning.

"I saved a lot of foes from being killed [at] the hands of D-Boy," Richard said. "We fucked up a lot of people."

The drugs, violence, and gang recruitment that were tearing Headingley apart would later play a major role in the growth of the Indian Posse across Canada. For the moment, though, it was all part of a long, difficult summer that saw gang crime jump to the top of the public agenda.

In September of 1994 the police announced they were targeting the Indian Posse with a two-week sweep specifically intended to lower violent crime rates. It was reported that robbery was at an "all-time high" in the city, and the gang, which specialized in armed robbery, was at the root of the problem.

Inspector Ron Gislason, the officer in charge of the Winnipeg police tactical unit, made an incisive point about spikes in certain kinds of crime, particularly armed robberies, which he said could be linked to times when the Indian Posse was recruiting new members or when veteran Posse members returned to the streets from behind bars.

"It seems the first experience of going through the justice system isn't getting through to them," Inspector Gislason told the local media. "So what's going to happen is either they're going to learn after the second or third time, or they're not . . . If they don't, then I'm afraid we're going to have a very young group of career criminals."

His remarks would prove prescient.

The rising public alarm over the Indian Posse and gangs in general had an impact on Richard, who was following the news from Headingley. When a reporter from the *Winnipeg Free Press* inquired about getting an interview, Richard said he'd be willing; he wanted to explain to the public what the Indian Posse was about. This was a dangerous decision. No one in the gang had spoken publicly like this before.

Richard sat down with reporter Paul Wiecek at length at the Headingley jail and even posed for photographs. The interview was part of a major series in the paper; a telling glimpse inside the gang's culture that described youth gangs as a multimillion-dollar crime problem sparked by as few as three hundred young people. Crime rates were falling in the rest of the country but rising in Winnipeg, Wiecek wrote, and gangs were part of the difference.

Richard identified himself as a founder of the Indian Posse, which made him the gang's only publicly recognized leader and a focal point for the anger and fear many civilians felt about gang violence. He also revealed a great deal about the gang that others in the leadership circle would have preferred to keep secret. For example, Richard said the gang had bank accounts in which it kept money for criminal lawyers, should they be needed.

He even gave the *Free Press* some pieces he'd written in prison to explain the Indian Posse ethos, in which race and pride were important themes. These included a poem that served as a kind of Indian Posse manifesto. When he described his childhood, he repeatedly said, "We were looked down on." It was a feeling most of the gang shared, he said, a feeling that they were separate from and outside society because of their race. The gang was what they had created to provide for themselves, and they defined it in racial terms. Richard was conscious of using warrior imagery to position the IP as part of a struggle to restore indigenous pride and self-sufficiency, which had been decimated by colonization.

Our color is red and it's here to stay, some of us have something to prove
    and some of us already have.
But all in all we are the Indian Posse and together we stand tall.
We are a breed that has seen it all and had its better days, but in the end
    we will learn our true native ways.
We don't mean to disrespect our elders, but we want to stand proud like
    they did in our hearts.

We are warriors and in our mind we will survive the war path.
In the days of old, our people used to fight and kill each other and, as they
   did, we will if there is no other way.
We hold our heads high because we are not scared to die for one another,
   for we will join the Great Spirit in the sky.
Call us what you will, but it is your racist blood we will spill.
Brothers Forever: Indian Posse.

The next-to-last line cuts to the heart of a deep historical wound in Canada, one that many non-indigenous Canadians understand and fear. *Call us what you will, but it is your racist blood we will spill.* Most non-aboriginal Canadians understand that indigenous people have suffered since the arrival of Europeans: the deaths of tens of thousands due to starvation and disease brought by settlers, the loss of their land and way of life, treaties that have been dishonoured, the forced removal of children to the residential schools, the deliberate extinguishment of language and culture – the list goes on. Their grievances, although not well understood, are widely believed to be genuine and sincerely felt. The possibility that those grievances could fuel racial violence has preoccupied national police and spy agencies over the years, and here was the Indian Posse, in its first public statements, promising to spill racist blood.

To place this moment in historical context, it was only four years earlier, in 1990, that Mohawk warriors took up arms in Quebec to prevent the construction of a golf course on a sacred burial ground. The standoff led to the killing of one Quebec police officer and a long, tense summer of hostility and blockades. At the same time, a rising tide of aboriginal activism had helped torpedo the Meech Lake constitutional accord, which failed to recognize Canada's First Peoples as full partners in Canadian affairs. Manitoba's Aboriginal Justice Inquiry made clear that the justice system had a disastrous and unfairly disproportionate impact on the lives of aboriginal people in the province. The occupation of Ipperwash Provincial Park by native people in Ontario, which led to the killing of protester Dudley George, was just a year away. The rise of the Indian Posse could have been perceived as the most violent and dangerous aspect of a tide of resistance among indigenous people in Canada.

Although Richard's intention was to explain the origins of the gang, his language touched a nerve. The city of Winnipeg was in the midst of transformation at the time, as the province's aboriginal population migrated to the city in large numbers. From the 1950s to the mid 1990s, the number of aboriginal people in the city had grown from a few thousand to more than 45,000 – roughly 7 per cent of the population and growing rapidly. Richard's race-based rhetoric raised the prospect of an armed aboriginal underclass bringing chaos to the city, while the *Winnipeg Free Press* series ensured the Indian Posse was known to everyone, from national criminal intelligence services to ordinary citizens.

It didn't take long for the gang to decide that Richard should be disciplined. In the view of some other leaders he had said too much to the media and brought too much unwanted attention to the Posse, which would inevitably mean more targeting by police and more arrests. Within hours he was summoned to face the prison gang committee, which was led by an old friend. Richard walked into one of the small cells at Headingley and found three members waiting for him. Word had already been passed down the range that he would face a disciplinary board, or d-board in gang-speak, and he knew what was coming.

There was no hearing and Richard wasn't asked for an explanation. He never got the chance to say that he thought it was important to explain why they had created the gang, and that their message of resistance was as vital as the gang's business interests.

As he stood there, in the centre of the cell, three IP members closed around Richard. They threw blows at him from all angles, hitting him in the back and side primarily; then they took aim at his head and face. He fought back a little before crumpling to the ground. He had been lucky it was just fists and kicks. Richard was bruised, but he would be fine.

When they finally left Headingley, Richard in November 1994 and Danny sometime thereabouts, the brothers walked back into the world with more power and status. The gang was a significant player on the streets and Richard took on an important task, even if it was one he didn't much like: he was given charge of the gang's prostitution racket, according to his parole documents.

Prostitution was becoming a big business for the gang. Demand for the sale of sex on the street ran to thousands of dollars per day, and the Posse quickly moved in on the prostitutes working the areas around Main Street, the Lord Selkirk Park Housing Development, and an area called the Low Track, near the rail yards in the North End.

Richard ran an operation consisting of roughly ten girls. Many of them had been working for another pimp, but he convinced them that working for the Posse was to their advantage. He upped their take to 40 per cent of proceeds from 25 per cent, and promised them more protection. Pay increases for the women were not really much of a cost to the gang, since many were addicts whose earnings were spent buying the gang's drugs.

Richard also brought in new women who had been recruited by his friends or by the girlfriends of other leading Posse members.

"I treated them with respect," Richard says of the women he pimped. "I didn't look down on them or anything. They were the friends of our girls. They'd see them at the parties and they'd say, 'You're always sleeping with this bro or that, why don't you get paid for it?' And they'd see the play and say, 'Okay.'"

Richard is reluctant to discuss this aspect of his work for the gang because, years later, he's deeply ashamed by it. It was wrong, he now says. In his 1994 interviews with the *Winnipeg Free Press* he made a point of emphasizing that one of the few Indian Posse rules dictated there would be no pimping of underaged girls. There is no evidence to indicate he encouraged underaged girls to work the streets, but some were certainly doing so, and possibly doing it with the protection of the Indian Posse. While Richard was in Headingley earlier that year a police sweep caught girls aged twelve and fourteen, the youngest girls the vice squad had ever come across, trying to solicit undercover cops on Main Street. Richard was aware that young girls were working, but he said it wasn't on his watch and they weren't working for him.

Richard said, "I remember seeing little girls, one ten years old, working around Little Chicago, and I was shocked. I jokingly asked her what she was doing out there and she said, 'Fuck off, I'm working.' And I said, 'What?' She said, 'I'm ten years old. I can do what I want.' We didn't allow anything like that. You had to be sixteen, seventeen, eighteen. I was just [a teenager] supervising these girls. But we made sure they were taken care of."

In those days he made $3,000 to $5,000 a night in cash from prostitution alone, he says. His parole documents indicate he was making somewhere in the region of $15,000 a week. Police officers are skeptical of those figures, however. They say that even with a crew of ten women or more, his daily proceeds were probably closer to $1,000 than $5,000, given the low price of sex on the streets of Winnipeg at that time.

Over the months of late 1994 and into 1995 Richard and Danny enjoyed some of the best times of their lives. There was a lot of money around, they had a decent place to live, the Posse was growing, and they were both in love for the first time.

Danny met Crystal at school when he was fifteen or sixteen years old. She was a year younger and the mother of a newborn girl. She lived in the North End in a big white house just off Salter Street, a main thoroughfare that ran south to downtown, and attended R.B. Russell, a vocational high school whose student population was about 90 per cent aboriginal.

Colleen Simard, Crystal's cousin, is a freelance journalist who was around in those days when Danny and Crystal were dating. She remembers Danny as a sweet, respectful boyfriend, and far from intimidating. He and Crystal used to hang out on the couch, cuddling. Danny was very affectionate with Crystal's young daughter, whom he treated like his own.

"They were a sweet couple. Inseparable. They'd be just sitting there, their thin builds with matching long black hair and matching black clothes. Walking down the street you couldn't tell which was which," Simard said.

She remembers that Danny talked about the Indian Posse as if it was a native warrior society, but Simard was skeptical of his grandiose claims. She remembers Danny producing a bag of jewellery one day and the glitter of gold wowed her two little sisters, who were bowled over when Danny offered to let them each choose a ring. Of course the jewellery was almost certainly stolen and they probably shouldn't have accepted, but there was a grand generosity in his gesture. Years later, in a column for the *Free Press*, Simard wrote: "Daniel Wolfe is a dangerous criminal . . . But I still remember the skinny kid who was a fixture in our family for a while almost two decades ago; who seemed respectful and one day gave two of my sisters each a gold ring from his bag of loot, like some kind of twisted Robin Hood." Danny would have enjoyed the comparison.

Another girlfriend from that period fondly described the wild parties the Indian Posse used to hold, with walls of beer cases, massive bricks of hash, sheets of acid, "and enough weed to supply Cuba." She painted a picture of Danny as a gallant, fun, and caring boyfriend who always took care of her, always made sure she had money in her pocket and her drugs for free, always gave her rings and jewellery (which she kept in a safety deposit box at the bank), and always wrote to her when he was locked up in the youth jail. They had a wild and fun romance that included many nights of Danny sneaking in her basement window so as not to alert her grandmother that he was there. Or they would break into houses still under construction and sleep in a half-finished building site, Danny looking at her with his "beautiful, dark, soul eyes," and covering her up with his coat. When the night was over Danny would reach into his pocket for his thick roll of cash and peel off a few bills to pay for her taxi home. In quiet moments, when he felt safe, he would talk about how he hoped his mother could get clean. He also spoke of his dream of leading a huge gang that stretched from coast to coast.

"He thought he could handle everything. Made you believe it, too," she said.

Richard had fallen for someone, too. Her name was Colleen. He had met her walking down the street. His approach with girls was to invite them to a party, saying they could either bring booze or bring themselves. It was a litmus test. Girls who thought they need only show up were too impressed with themselves, in Richard's view. Colleen brought a case of twenty-four beers as well as a bottle of liquor, and she and Richard soon fell madly in love.

Colleen was always willing to wait for him when he got sent back to jail, Richard said, which in those days seemed to be every few months. She also knew to get out of the way when business had to be done, which earned her the respect of other gang members.

By the time Danny joined Richard on the streets in late 1994 the Indian Posse was sending emissaries south to Indian reservations in South Dakota, trying to establish ties with American native gangs to facilitate the movement of drugs. Richard said they bought a lot of pot south of the border. He didn't like going to the U.S., though – the border presented too big a risk for getting caught. He preferred making trips to the West Coast, to British Columbia, to get pot, cocaine, and LSD and magic mushrooms. He and Danny would grab a car and head west, often accompanied by their friend Sam-Boo.

The Posse got into drug dealing at the bottom. They were street dealers and distributors who sold drugs in units that went for about $10 or $15 a piece. This kept the gang relatively low on the criminal food chain, and below motorcycle gangs, like the Los Bravos, who ran Winnipeg's drugs scene for a time, and the Hells Angels, who controlled the supply.

The Indian Posse was always fiercely independent, said Nick Leone, a veteran gang officer with the Winnipeg police. They never formed an official affiliation with a more powerful crew, such as a motorcycle gang. In fact it was quite common for them to buy from one mid-level supplier one week and then rob him for his drugs the next, burning bridges at every turn.

The frustration of being at the mercy of bigger suppliers started to boil within the gang's leadership. Selling drugs at the street level is the riskiest end of the business. Indian Posse members would get shot at, robbed, and arrested, and when they were in custody there was the possibility they'd implicate the higher-ranking members of the gang. All of these potential complications contributed to the gang's desire to move up the ladder for a bigger share of the profits.

"Back then we were always doing it through a middle person. Even the council [members] were saying 'What the hell, why aren't we just going straight to the main person? What the fuck's the problem?'" Richard said.

Solutions were hard to find. The motorcycle gangs and Asian crime syndicates remained the primary sources for drugs and they weren't about to allow their own customers to cut them out. The Indian Posse was stuck.

In the early 1990s crack cocaine was only just making its way into Winnipeg, having taken over the drug scene in most American cities several years before. Richard and Danny caught their first glimpse of it at the home of a biker gang associate who was their usual source for drugs. The biker had called Richard and asked him if he'd be willing to do a job. At the biker's house, the biker held up a tiny rock and handed it to Richard, who passed it on to Danny. The biker said, "You know this stuff?"

Danny said, "Yeah, I know what that is."

"You guys think you can get rid of it for me?" he asked.

Richard looked over at his younger brother. The money would be great, he thought. But did the Indian Posse want to sell crack, which had been demonized in the U.S. war on drugs? "I got a lot of it," the biker said. He went into the kitchen for a moment, and when he came back out, he was carrying a huge plate of the stuff.

"He just brought it out. Boom," Richard said.

Richard and Danny looked at each other. This was a new frontier. Crack had the aura of a deadly street drug, one that would enslave its users instantly. The brothers were wary.

"I don't know, man," said Danny, breaking the silence. "Just for that right there how much time do you think I'd get?"

"Fifteen to twenty years," said the biker.

"Yeah, that's what I was thinking," said Danny. He was motivated to make enough money for himself and his friends to have whatever they wanted, but crack cocaine was too risky, not only for him but for those who worked for him. He pushed the plate back across the table. "Not for me," he said.

Getting to know the motorcycle gangs eventually led the Indian Posse to other opportunities. Although the street gang lacked experience and didn't have a strong criminal network, they had a lot of bold, ambitious members who acted like they had nothing to lose. It was a perfect underworld workforce that the motorcycle gangs coveted.

Richard said one rare but lucrative sideline for the gang was to execute armoured car and ATM robberies that were planned and set up by the bikers. While those paid well, drug dealing and prostitution were still the main sources of income. The gang produced enough profit to allow Danny and Richard to rent houses and apartments for themselves, to gamble on sports, and to buy whatever they wanted. They had all the gangster trappings: the stereos, the Nike shoes, the baseball caps, the red-and-black checked jackets favoured by West Coast rappers. Richard walked around with hundreds of dollars rolled in a fist-sized wad in his pocket. He and the Posse had earned the kind of money and respect they were seeking when they formed the gang, but they were now being closely watched by police.

"I always thought Richard was one of the most dangerous guys on the street . . . He was a force to be reckoned with," said James Jewell, who worked as gang investigator for Winnipeg police during that period.

Richard said he was stopped and searched regularly, often for no apparent reason. A police officer would pull up in a cruiser, get out, and demand to see what was in his pockets. Richard had learned not to carry any weapons or drugs, but there was always the cash. How could he explain it? He claims that it was not unusual for police to seize a little less than half the money he was carrying, usually a few hundred dollars.

"They'd ask, 'How much you holding?'" Richard said. "I'd say, '$1,200.' They'd grab half and say, 'It looks more like $600.'"

There's no way to verify Richard's claim. He never made a complaint, and the cash he carried was obviously money obtained by crime, so it's not as though he had any recourse. Still, he wondered why it was always a consistent take, usually about 40 per cent, and rarely more than half. He treated it like a tax of sorts.

The Wolfe brothers hated the police. Richard said there were times the police picked him up and took him to the edge of the city and left him to walk home in the cold weather, a practice known as a starlight tour. It was long whispered about among aboriginal people but little known until a suspicious death in Saskatoon, when seventeen-year-old Neil Stonechild died alone on a freezing cold night in a field near the city limits. His death was initially treated as a case of misadventure, but years later a public inquiry concluded that he had been in police custody the night he died.

Richard said he was taken twice by police and dumped at the edge of town, though he was able to make it home safely both times. After the second incident he was angry and he wanted revenge. He said he had been left in the industrial area at the edge of Saint Boniface, about five miles from where he was staying in the North End. When he got home he went for his gun.

"I wanted to go shoot a cop," he said.

Danny went with him, along with a friend whom Richard didn't know well. They had only gone about four or five blocks when they came upon a police cruiser with an officer inside, parked on a North End street. They snuck up on him from between two houses.

"I was creeping along on the ground when I turned around to check on my brother and he's gesturing at the other guy, saying basically, 'What about him?' My brother didn't really trust him."

If he went ahead and shot the cop, would this acquaintance stay silent? Richard reconsidered.

"I'm glad I didn't do it," he said. "My anger was getting the better of me."

Danny, by contrast, was not always the type to think before acting. There were times when that quality played to his advantage. In the Indian Posse his propensity for violence made him seem bigger and tougher. But at other times it led to unnecessary trouble.

"I don't know why but that's his way of solving things – send bullets flying everywhere," Richard said.

About a year earlier Danny had come back to the house they were renting on Stella Avenue looking as though he had been beaten and tortured. His face was swollen and bloody.

"He looked worse than Rodney King," Richard said.

Danny told Richard he had been jumped by a rival gang, the Crips (named after but not affiliated with the more famous L.A. gang of the same name), an incident that gave rise to a lifelong grudge. He was angry and looked to his brother for support.

"Let's get the guns," Danny said.

Wearily, Richard agreed.

They didn't find the guys they were looking for that evening. But a few nights later Danny and Richard were drinking with some others at the Merchant's Hotel. When it was time to leave they sent two guys to collect the guns that they had stashed nearby (they typically stashed guns in yards or garages to avoid the risk of being stopped with a weapon). While they waited for the guns to come back, Danny noticed a Trans Am driving by.

"That's the one that rolled up on me," he said, referring to the gang that had jumped him a few days earlier.

When the guns arrived Danny and Richard each grabbed one and ducked down the alley to an adjacent street. They waited. The next time they saw the Trans Am it had turned its lights off.

"Sure enough they'd seen us and they came peeling around the corner," Richard said. "One pulled out a little handgun and started popping off."

Richard dove behind a tree. Danny, meanwhile, stood his ground and returned fire right there on the street.

"I screamed 'take cover' and he wouldn't take cover," Richard said. "Danny's just standing up, letting 'em go. *Pow! Pow! Pow!*"

The Trans Am stopped a little further up the street and the firing continued. Richard jumped out from behind a tree on the boulevard and pumped his shotgun, but the shell jammed. Danny screamed at him as the car drove away.

"What the fuck's your problem? Why aren't you pulling the trigger?" Danny asked, according to Richard.

Richard held out the gun for Danny, to show him that it was jammed. Danny grabbed at it and pulled. The shell popped out sideways.

"That's all you had to do," Danny said.

One day, the brothers drove out to the countryside to practise shooting. Richard had brought his prized weapon, an AK-47. As he fired, his mind drifted to other thoughts of loyalty and vengeance. He thought of the van rides, the term the gang used for an execution, that were central to Indian Posse lore and a threat that lurked in the thoughts of many gang members. If you had to take a van ride, there was no coming back.

Once, some of the older guys set Richard up, as though they were taking him on a van ride. A senior leader showed up at his place unannounced and pointed to a waiting van at the curb. Inside the house other IP members quietly held their breath, wondering what was going on. Richard played it cool; if this was the end he wasn't going to beg for mercy. He said, "I'll get my coat. Let's do this." The senior guy laughed and patted him on the back. The tension dissolved. But there was a message there for Richard and the others watching. Anyone was expendable. The gang was a living organism, volatile, unpredictable, and prepared to kill to further its interests.

Out in the countryside that day Richard fired a few bursts with the AK-47. Thinking of Danny's propensity for violence he looked at his little brother and asked him a serious question. If the family, meaning the Indian Posse, asked him to take out his own brother, would he do it?

"[Danny] looked me right in the eyes and said, 'Yes, I would. For the family.' We made this family and no matter what happened we would do what was right."

"My answer was the same for him," Richard said.

For the sake of the gang, the Wolfe brothers were willing to kill one another.

4

RICHARD LOST, DANNY ALONE
1995

In April 1995, Richard and Danny and about ten other Indian Posse members were hanging out at a gang house on Stella Avenue. The police knocked and Richard was about to answer it when the cops broke down the door.

They were looking for a thirteen-year-old boy who had been reported missing and was known to hang around the Indian Posse. The cops blanketed the area with officers as a precaution, since they knew the Posse would have weapons either in the house or nearby. Some officers went to the front door; others circled around the back. Hearing the shouts of "Police!" the young man they were searching for – the thirteen-year-old, who was actually in the house – tried to escape out the back door but ran smack into the police. Richard was trying to slink away through the front entrance hall to the back of the house, but he was blocked. Danny, meanwhile, was frozen to his chair in the living room.

"How'd you like to take a seat?" one of the officers shouted. He directed Richard and his girlfriend Colleen to the living room and they plopped down on the worn couch next to Danny. There was a wooden coffee table in the middle of the room and it was covered with dozens of small squares of tinfoil. There were two clear plastic baggies, both empty, and eleven bundles of marijuana. Elsewhere in the house police found a machete and bows and arrows, but no guns – those were stashed in a neighbouring yard. It was clear that Richard was the focus of the cops' interest; Danny seemed to have flown under the radar.

"Well, Richard, whose drugs are they?" the senior cop said.

"I don't know. There's lots of people here," Richard said.

The drugs were actually Danny's. He had been sorting them into gram-sized packages just before the police barged in. When he heard the door come down he dropped the stuff on the table and left it there. Now it was obvious that someone would be charged for the drugs, and Richard was wrestling with what to do. He had just picked up a foolish drug charge a few weeks earlier by selling some weed to an undercover cop outside the Merchant's Hotel and he didn't need to rack up another one.

Danny was still under eighteen, though, and could go to youth court, where he would get a lighter sentence than Richard. But Danny had taken a charge for his older brother before, for posses-sion of stolen property, and Richard had never repaid the favour. Richard had a protective instinct when it came to his little brother and he felt he owed Danny. All of this was running through Richard's mind as the police officers waited for someone to take ownership of the drugs.

"I looked at Danny and he wasn't saying nothing," Richard said.

Meanwhile, Colleen was staring daggers at Richard, urging him to throw Danny under the bus, Richard recalled. He didn't know what to do – save himself, please his girlfriend, or protect his brother? He chose to protect Danny.

Richard held out his wrists to accept the handcuffs. Colleen cried out, and started pleading with the officers, saying the drugs were hers.

As the officers flanked Richard on their way to the squad car she ran after them, shouting, "They're mine. I'll take the charge."

It was an emotional scene, but a grateful Danny accepted his brother's gift. The officers put Richard in the back seat of the cruiser next to Danny, who was taken into custody briefly but not charged. Shortly after, Richard was released to await his court date.

At this point, Richard's hold on power within the gang was growing more tenuous. Then, two weeks later, on May 14, 1995, a watershed moment arrived for the Indian Posse.

Richard says the story begins with an unpaid drug debt owed to the gang. The news that he was being played for a chump was circulating via the criminal rumour mill, he says, although the debt, somewhere between $30,000 and $60,000, wasn't actually owed to Richard but to Spencer LaPorte, who had died of an overdose six months earlier, leaving Richard on the hook for collecting it. He says the outstanding debt was a big deal because it was a challenge to his credibility, which is crucial in the drug business. If threats of violence don't work, actual violence has to follow – otherwise no one ever pays. The unpaid debt kept getting raised by one of the biker drug suppliers that Richard met with, he said, and it had to be dealt with. None of this featured in the police investigation, and there are many reasons to question the account, but Richard swears it is true, and when he later confessed, the national parole board concluded it was the true explanation for his actions.

It was a Saturday night and Richard and Colleen were walking through the North End when they dropped by an apartment that belonged to a woman named Christa and her boyfriend Darryl. It was not uncommon for people in the North End to drop by and use their neighbours' phones (lines were frequently cut off for non-payment and cell phones were still rare), so Christa and Darryl weren't surprised when Colleen, a junior-high classmate of Christa's, showed up unannounced.

Colleen told Christa that they were going to order a pizza and holdup the driver for his cash. Christa was intimidated and didn't dare say no.

Richard got Colleen to phone and tell the owner that this order was for Spencer. That would make it clear, he said, that, as he told the parole board, he was collecting a debt from people at the pizza shop. They also ordered some Hawaiian pizza and RC Cola for the sake of appearances and supplied an address on Pritchard Avenue near Main Street, a dark and isolated corner near the Lord Selkirk Park Housing Development that they chose for its tactical advantages.

The call came in to the Jumbo Pizza shop on Isabel Street at 11:48 p.m. The shop's owner took the order, which came out to $31.50.

Maciej Slawik, a forty-three-year-old father and recently arrived immigrant from Poland, had been working as a delivery driver at Jumbo Pizza for just two weeks. He worked a day job in a hospital kitchen and was taking these delivery shifts to help his family get established in the new country. It was a slow night for a Saturday and his boss told him he could go home early at midnight, but then there was this one last order that needed to go. Would he mind making a delivery on his way home? At first Slawik refused, saying he was tired.

"Just take it. It's a few minutes. Not far and that will be your last one," his boss said.

Slawik finally agreed, then grabbed the pizzas and stuffed them into the red thermal delivery bag. He slid behind the wheel of his ten-year-old Hyundai Stellar and headed north, crossing over the bridge to the North End. Slawik rolled slowly along the street, trying to pick out the house numbers in the dark. His destination was at the end of the block, and as he drove toward it, he passed a tall aboriginal girl on the sidewalk. When he found the house on Pritchard, he was surprised to see no lights on. He looked around and noticed that the tall aboriginal girl had disappeared. *Strange.* Feeling a little uneasy, he pulled up to the curb and left the car running, in case he had to make a quick getaway.

Slawik bent down to get the pizza from the back seat and heard the sound of footsteps running toward him. Richard stormed out of the shadows, his face covered by a black balaclava, while his accomplice had a red Indian Posse bandana tied over his face. Richard gripped a sawed-off shotgun at about waist height.

"Give us your fucking money," Richard said.

The driver was still trying to process what was happening when Richard opened fire. Slawik felt a gust of wind rush past his face as the shot thundered over his head. Richard had been crouched in the dark waiting for some time, so now he was jacked up with nerves and excitement. He thought the debtor was going to deliver the cash himself, and with his mind clouded by anger, he planned to teach him a lesson.

As the driver tried to back away around the rear of the car, Richard pursued him. Slawik picked up one of the two-litre bottles of cola in the back seat and hurled it at Richard, who ducked as it sailed overhead.

Slawik said he heard Richard call to his accomplice: "Grab the pizza, get in the car, and drive away." The car, although it was a cheap import, meant a lot to Slawik, and he didn't want to give it up. He made a quick appraisal of the kid, who wasn't holding a gun and looked scared. Slawik stepped toward the teenager – then heard the click of a shotgun pump. Richard fired again.

Slawik spun into the street from the force of the blast. He looked down, and what he saw sent him into shock. His torso was blown open.

Richard bolted. His teenage accomplice did as he was told and drove off in the car with the pizza bag. Richard ran through the alley, intending to dispose of the gun.

Richard knew he had screwed up, and he worried the police would be on him quickly. The officers would trace the order back to

Darryl and Christa, who would deny ever making the call. But would they give up Richard and Colleen?

Slawik, meanwhile, lay in the street in shock and struggling to stay conscious. He remembered that a Polish church was just a few blocks away so he got up and staggered in that direction, but he was losing blood and slowing with every step. He made it a few metres before his legs gave way and he slumped to the ground, crying out for help. A family that lived nearby called 911.

Richard ran back to Redwood Avenue, where he kept a place in a rundown low-rise building called the Micheal, curious for its unusual spelling, and where Danny also shared an apartment with another IP member. Richard sat on the steps for a moment. He later opened the pizza bag and realized the $30,000 to $60,000 he was expecting wasn't there. He hadn't even bothered to rob Slawik, who had been carrying $500 cash, and who had nothing at all to do with the debt.

Just then Christa and Darryl were walking up the alley, on their way home from a late-night meal at a diner. They were curious to hear about the planned pizza robbery, and as they walked they bumped into Richard's teenaged accomplice. He had ditched the stolen car and was carrying the empty thermal pizza bag.

"Something went wrong," the teen said, then hurried inside to dump the bag. Then Colleen arrived. They asked her what had happened.

"I don't know," she said. "Richard told me to just take off."

The three of them walked around to the front of the building together, jumpy and out of breath. Richard was sitting on the front steps, visibly upset. He told the others they should leave right away. He was already worried about Darryl and Christa and what they might say to police. He knew it was only a matter of time before police traced the order and started asking questions. "You guys both know what to do when they show up?" he said menacingly to the couple, more of a statement than a question.

He also said he'd somehow lost the butt of the shotgun: "I just hope my prints aren't on it."

He and Colleen went up to the apartment, where Danny was waiting. "I fucked up," Richard said. "I have to bounce." He explained what had happened. Danny couldn't believe what he was hearing. He kept shaking his head, trying to make the bad news go away.

"You fucking guy," Danny said in frustration. "You should've got somebody else to do that. We don't have to do that stuff no more."

Richard said little in response. He kept muttering to himself about the butt of the shotgun, and ran through a mental checklist of all the other things that might trip him up. At least he was wearing a balaclava, he thought. He and Danny talked things over, then Richard focused on cleaning himself up to remove any traces of physical evidence. He stripped out of his clothes and jumped into a bath, scrubbing his hands over and over to rid them of gunpowder residue. Unable to sit still with a potential murder charge hanging over his head, Richard paced in the little apartment. It felt too small. He needed fresh air.

"Let's go to your place," he said to Colleen.

They went downstairs with Danny, then Richard walked around to the back alley with his younger brother. Richard had a feeling he would probably have to go away for a while.

"If I don't see you again, keep your head up and be strong," Richard told Danny. "The people who live where we used the phone, I don't like them. I think they're shady. If you don't remember the names, this is the place," he added, describing for Danny where they lived.

Danny was upset. "Are you sure? Do you think they're going to roll over on you?" he asked. *If you don't trust them, why wait*, he wondered. "Do you want to go see them now?" Danny asked.

Richard said no. He hoped the police would need a few days to put the pieces together. He and Colleen walked through the streets past Christa and Darryl's place in the early morning darkness and saw that police cruisers were already outside. *Shit*, Richard thought.

Detective James Jewell had been awakened that night by his supervisor, Sergeant Bob Marshall, and by 4:00 a.m., he was at police headquarters. He and a partner were immediately detailed to stake out the Micheal apartments. At 6:30 more officers arrived to provide backup, and shortly after they decided to go in.

Danny and Richard were gone and their apartments were empty, but once the police were inside they found the thermal pizza case. Somehow the brothers had forgotten to dispose of it. Then the police, well aware of Richard's associations and habits, knocked at the door of Colleen's parents' house, where they suspected he'd be hiding. Colleen's mother allowed the officers inside and four of them clambered down to the basement where Richard and Colleen were sleeping in a corner. They ordered Richard out of bed, gave him a moment to get dressed, then handcuffed him and led him upstairs. They told Colleen she was also being arrested in connection with an attempted murder.

"That wasn't me," Colleen cried.

As she was being led out of the house she shouted to her mother: "Call me a lawyer, a good one."

The police knew Colleen well because of her relationship with Richard, and the two of them were considered the first couple of gang crime, according to the lead investigator, Detective Jewell. The police hoped that Colleen was the weak link and that they could convince her to talk.

"They had almost a Bonnie-and-Clyde reputation," Jewell said of the couple. "Not a lot of women were trusted in the gang but Colleen was Richard's right-hand girl. She participated in a lot of the crime, which was unusual."

Detective Jewell is a tall, accomplished officer with a self-assured manner. He sat down next to Colleen in an examination room at police headquarters and started with some basic questions. *Where were you last night? Who were you with? What do you know about the shooting?*

"I don't know what you're talking about," she told him.

"We're talking about a robbery where we believe Richard shot a guy. That's no joke. That's about as serious as it gets," Jewell said.

"Is the guy going to die?" Colleen asked.

"It appears he will survive but his injuries are very serious."

She asked, with sincere concern, whether the police were also holding Richard's teenaged accomplice. He was young and she cared about him.

"Yes, he's here," Jewell said.

"What's he being charged with?"

"At this point I would guess robbery, attempted murder, and the use of a firearm," Jewell said.

"Attempted murder? [He] didn't do it," she pleaded.

"He may not have been the trigger man but we believe . . . he played his part in it."

"I don't want him going to jail. I'll take the rap for him. I'll take the charge," she offered. Her eyes were welling up with tears.

"Look, Colleen, we just want the truth," Jewell said. She sat quietly. Jewell continued. "We have information that you made the phone call to set up the delivery man and it went from there."

"OKAY, I made the call but I wasn't there for it," she blurted.

"For what?" Jewell asked.

"The robbery," Colleen said, aware she had said too much.

"Where were you when it went down?" he asked.

"I don't think I should say any more."

Meanwhile, Richard was being held in another part of the building. While Colleen agonized over her own fate and that of Richard's accomplice, Richard was worried about her. He didn't want her to go to prison. If she was convicted, she could be looking at a sentence of more than ten years.

When it was his turn to be interrogated in the interview room, where cameras and audio recorders capture every statement, Richard said nothing. But the officers said that when they went to remove him from his holding cell he told them, unprompted, that the shooting had been an accident. They said that he admitted he shot the driver and was adamant that Colleen had had nothing to do with it.

Richard denies ever making that statement. It is odd that this confession took place when it couldn't be captured by recording equipment, because officers know the value of such statements and want to get them on camera. Richard could have been testing to see how they'd react. He later alleged that the officers threatened him by saying, "We should take him under a bridge and get a statement from him." In other words, that he should be beaten until he confessed, an allegation the officer denied and a judge later dismissed.

The police felt fairly confident at this point that they had the case wrapped up. But Danny Wolfe wasn't prepared to give up on his brother.

Early that same morning police dragged Danny in for questioning. Predictably, he said nothing. But the criminal education he'd obtained in youth and adult jails allowed him to assess his brother's situation, and Danny was already plotting how to help. First, the weapon was hidden and unlikely to be found, Richard had told him. Second, identifying Richard would be almost impossible for the delivery driver, and for all Danny knew, the driver might die in the next few hours. Finally, Richard had scrubbed himself and changed his clothes to limit the possibility of incriminating physical evidence. The key to the case then, Danny knew, would be Christa and Darryl and what they said to police. If they stayed silent it would be difficult to connect Richard to the crime scene. Of course, Christa and Darryl would also want to clear their own names.

The next evening, after Danny was questioned and released, he got a message from Richard. It's not clear whether Richard was able to call Danny or whether a message came through another prisoner. The older Wolfe told his brother that the police had shown him statements from Christa and Darryl that would effectively sink him. Danny had to take care of the situation.

This was a pivotal moment for Danny and he was reeling. For his whole life Richard had been his foundation, the one person he relied upon and looked up to. When he was just a hungry little kid Richard was the one who fed him, and when he was running from foster homes Richard was the one he ran to. He was Danny's protector as well as a source of status and strength. And now he could be going away for life. Danny sparked a joint and swallowed a hit of LSD to calm his nerves, something he and Richard liked to do together.

He was upset. The gossip mill was already churning within the gang and Richard was being torn to shreds for his poor judgment. The night before, as he paced in the apartment, Richard had assured Danny it would be a few days before the police would make an arrest. Instead, it had taken only a few hours.

Danny gathered six Indian Posse members and headed to Christa and Darryl's basement suite on Flora Avenue. His right-hand man, a teenager, slipped a black balaclava over his head, a 12-gauge sawed-off shotgun dangling at his side. The four others circled the house as Danny and the armed teenager knocked.

Inside, Christa was lying on the couch, watching television. Darryl was already asleep. Hearing the knock, she noted the time, ten to midnight. She walked up the stairs from the basement to the back door.

"Who is it?" she asked.

"Gertie," a voice replied. She knew the word was slang for something but couldn't remember what it meant.

"Who?" she called again.

This time there was silence. Christa was getting nervous. She had a feeling this was about the robbery and the statements she and Darryl had made to the police. She didn't think the Indian Posse would find out this quickly, but she knew they would be at her door eventually. Could she talk her way out of trouble? Maybe.

"Fuck it," she said. She faced her fear and opened the door.

It was dark but she recognized Danny immediately. She saw the man beside him with the gun, too, and eyed it anxiously. Danny stepped inside without asking permission and Christa retreated.

"Who ratted out Colleen and Richie?" Danny asked.

Christa stammered, trying to find the words to explain that no one had ratted. She backed away down the stairs. Darryl, hearing the exchange and recognizing Danny's voice, bolted out of bed to come to Christa's aid. He passed her on the stairs and went up to meet Danny at the door.

"Danny, come in here," he said, doing his best to sound calm.

The teen with the gun stepped inside too but stayed at the top of the stairs. Danny walked downstairs with Darryl, telling the men outside to check the sides of the house.

Darryl tried to reason with Danny by saying they had only given statements to the police because the cops already knew Richard was behind the robbery. He begged Danny to try to understand, saying he and Christa were starting a family and they had a kid on the way.

"You're a liar and a rat!" Danny shouted. "You guys better not show up in court." He climbed the stairs to grab the shotgun from his accomplice and pointed it at Darryl and Christa. Darryl cowered and said they would do as Danny demanded: they would not testify.

"I don't want to see my brother go to jail. So don't go to court, or we will be back to shoot you," Danny said. He turned and went back up the stairs. "Do not go to court," Danny repeated, before leaving with the teenager.

The whole exchange lasted less than five minutes and Danny felt he had completed his mission. What he didn't know yet was that he had pushed Darryl and Christa further into the arms of the police.

Shutting down witnesses through intimidation was an important tool of control for the Indian Posse, as it is for many gangs. It's a relatively cheap and effective way to minimize risk. Gangs tend to operate in poor neighbourhoods where citizens have few resources and are unlikely to be able to move elsewhere for their own protection. Many already distrust the police. In Winnipeg's North End, where accusations of police racism were common, conditions were ripe for a campaign of fear.

As soon as he had closed the door behind Danny, Darryl realized his life was forever changed. The police detective had told him less than twenty-four hours earlier that the gang might come after him. *If they do, call me*, the detective had said. So Darryl picked up the phone and called 911.

The police wasted no time. Darryl and Christa were placed in a witness protection program that night and immediately moved out of the province, taking with them just what they could carry. The next day they were in Regina, Saskatchewan, told to return only to testify against Richard, Danny, and the Indian Posse.

5

JAIL
1995–1996

From the moment he was arrested for the shooting of Maciej Slawik, Richard's position in the gang was under threat. Although he was a founder and leading figure, his stature had taken a hit and his judgment was being questioned by other members of the gang.

The shooting of a blameless pizza delivery driver was plastered all over the newspapers and treated as an outrage by the press and police. It was a miracle that the man was still alive, and Richard was lucky not to be facing life in prison. His act contributed to a further ratcheting up of the anti-gang rhetoric that was beginning to dominate the civic conversation. In the ensuing months a special police gang unit was created and much more aggressive investigative techniques were brought to bear. The additional scrutiny threatened to curtail the gang's efforts to make money.

Richard was initially jailed in the Remand Centre while he awaited trial. Anxious to keep up with news from the streets he used his phone time to call Indian Posse gang houses and check in on an almost daily basis. He also tried to maintain a confident posture with police. "This will never come to court," he bragged to the investigators. "You'll see – we'll fix the rats."

The police were happy to have him behind bars, particularly after his public boasts about the size and strength of the Indian Posse just a few months earlier. Despite Richard's telling the *Free Press* the gang had a war chest to hire serious lawyers for its leaders, when his case came to trial he had a legal aid lawyer. He did his best to mount a defence. He claimed he had stayed at home on the night of the shooting, that he was watching TV and playing Yahtzee (which he actually had done with Colleen's parents after the shooting). But the flimsy alibi collapsed when it turned out the shows he claimed to have watched weren't on that night.

The gang did make one further attempt to rescue Richard. Several months after the shooting, as he awaited trial, the gang tracked down Darryl and Christa despite the fact they were in witness protection. Danny's closest friend, Sam-Boo, confronted the couple, threatened them again, and then sweetened the pot by offering a few thousand dollars for their silence. Richard's fate was in their hands.

Because Richard didn't want to take his chances with a jury, especially not in a city fed up with gang violence, the trial was by judge alone. The Crown argued that Richard had a simple plan to rob the pizza driver that ended in gunfire, and made no mention of Richard's story of a drug debt. Richard, who denied any knowledge of the crime, held on to the hope that Darryl and Christa would be too frightened to testify. Unfortunately for him, both showed up for the trial and gave damning evidence. Christa said she had seen Richard in the alley behind his apartment building not long after the shooting and that she heard Richard say that the delivery driver had tried to run and he'd accidentally shot him.

The judge found Richard guilty of attempted murder.

One question remains: Why would a high-ranking gang leader who was making thousands of dollars a week be interested in a minor score like robbing a delivery driver, as the Crown's theory suggested?

Richard didn't rob the driver after he shot him, even though he was carrying a considerable amount of cash. Richard maintains that he planned to collect an unpaid debt that was an embarrassment and a threat to his credibility. But if he intended to collect the money, why didn't he allow more time for the exchange to take place? Rather than check if the money was there, Richard charged out with his gun drawn and opened fire. He says he needed to send a message to anyone who might owe him money in future.

A week later, shackled and anxious, Richard returned to court for sentencing. None of his family was present. His mother did not even know he was on trial; his father was in jail in Prince Albert, Saskatchewan, and Danny was locked up for making threats on his brother's behalf. Richard's other family, the gang he had built, did not send a single representative to court that day.

Normally an attempted murder conviction results in a sentence in the range of seven to fifteen years. But this was a different case. Covered extensively in the local press, it was seen as a symbol of the rise of gang violence and the threat it posed even to citizens who had nothing to do with gangs. Richard remembers the court being packed with police officers eager to see him put away for a long time.

The judge handed Richard one of the longest sentences anyone present had ever seen for attempted murder – nineteen and a half years. As Richard left court in chains he claims that one of the police officers spoke to him: "See you in nineteen years, Wolfe."

"This ain't over," Richard replied.

He launched an appeal but eventually dropped the case, either because he couldn't pay for it or couldn't find a lawyer to take on the challenge. Richard decided it was wiser to adjust to the new reality, namely spending the better part of the next two decades behind bars.

In some ways it was predictable. Richard's life had always been subject to state control, either in foster care or in custody. When he was young he was surrounded by violence and moved from group home to group home. He would run away and then get caught, and run away again. He graduated from group homes to youth prisons, and then the provincial jail. Now it was the federal penitentiary.

If he had one thing to look forward to, it was a reunion with his brother Danny.

6

ARRIVING AT THE MOUNTAIN
1995–1996

The note of warning that preceded Danny Wolfe's arrival at the Stony Mountain penitentiary was spelled out in block capitals. It distilled what the justice system knew of Danny on September 20, 1995, the day he set foot inside "The Mountain" for the first time: "HIGH-RANKING INDIAN POSSE GANG MEMBER."

The note was handed to the sheriffs who transported Danny by van from the Remand Centre (where prisoners await trial) in downtown Winnipeg, and the sheriffs then passed it to the guards at the penitentiary when they delivered Danny to his new home later that morning. It's not clear whether the block capitals were for ease of reading or emphasis. It might have been difficult to convince the sheriffs that this quiet nineteen-year-old, who weighed about 120 pounds, was to be treated with extreme caution.

Danny was arrested the day after he threatened Darryl and Christa in May 1995. It didn't take long for police to find him, as they'd been questioning him in connection with the attempted murder barely twelve hours before. He submitted quietly. He was charged with obstruction of justice and using a firearm in the commission of a crime – a small price to pay, in his view, if it helped set his brother free.

Bail was set at $10,000, a sum he could have raised but didn't. In those days prisoners on remand were given credit of two days of time served on their eventual sentence for every day spent awaiting sentencing.

When he walked through the gates of the federal penitentiary, his peers treated it not as a failure but as an achievement. By receiving federal time he had reached a senior level in the gang. Danny was a founder, of course, but that had never been enough to guarantee a position at the top of the gang. It had to be earned.

On arrival, as part of the intake process, Danny submitted to a battery of psychological tests and interviews that revealed a great deal about him. Among gang members, particularly those still in their teens, bragging about rank and status is often overblown. Danny, however, tried to sound as humble as possible when speaking to the psychological assessors. He downplayed his status, telling his interviewer that he wasn't a high-ranking member, despite the intelligence reports to the contrary. He was just one level above a striker, he said. Both of those statements are probably true. Danny wasn't on the gang's council, its highest rank, in 1996, but he was no mere foot soldier either. He was one level below the top. In the gang world that meant he could "earn" by taking a portion of what more junior members made selling drugs or committing robberies.

Still, prison officials were skeptical of Danny's story. In their eyes he was an Indian Posse leader and his mere presence posed a threat within the institution. During his first lengthy interview, Danny explained that leaders could be easily identified because they had the right to speak on the gang's behalf. He did not have that rank, he said. But then he raised eyebrows with a frank statement about what he intended to do once he was admitted into the prison population.

"He states that when he enters the Stony Mountain population he will go and talk to other members of the gang and find out what they are doing (i.e., selling drugs, taking programs, etc.). He states he will then do what he thinks is good for him and he does not care if the other members want to follow him or not," the interviewer wrote in his prison file. That's not typically how things work in prison, a highly regulated world where those who break norms place themselves at risk. Danny's attitude was taken as proof that he enjoyed what they called "the privileges of a high-ranking senior member."

Over the next few months the psychologists and psychiatrists who met with Danny compiled a long list of issues he needed to confront. His life story, as they summarized it, read like a guide to building a sociopath: His parents were absent and their relationship was abusive and dysfunctional, creating an absence of family ties in childhood. Some of his family members were criminals. He was socially isolated and easily influenced by others, and had mostly criminal friends who abused substances. He didn't use hard drugs because the gang forbade it, but he sold drugs for profit. They described the area where he lived, the North End, as "criminogenic," meaning likely to cause criminal behaviour. Danny had no bank account, no credit, no collateral, and no hobbies, and his relationships were described as predatory.

A prison psychologist who spent some time with Danny described him as a "high energy" individual who showed signs of underlying anger and anxiety. Danny had relatively low ego strength, the psychologist wrote, which partly explained his impulsiveness and inability to deal with frustration. The family history of abuse and neglect was a contributing factor to his difficulties forming attachments.

"Somewhat nervous," the psychologist noted in a looping scrawl. "Likely to 'get involved' in [the prison] population."

Stony Mountain is Manitoba's federal penitentiary, a medium-security jail about twenty-five kilometres north of Winnipeg. It is also the de facto seat of government for the Indian Posse. The prison council inside the jail is home to the gang's senior leadership, sometimes referred to as "the circle." In theory, the circle at Stony Mountain calls the shots.

In the four months of dead time before he was sent to Stony Mountain, Danny began to step out from Richard's shadow. He organized an extortion racket in the Remand Centre, where he forced prisoners to either pay him protection money or face a beating, according to a prison intelligence report. He also ejected some members of the gang by "rolling" them out – in other words, by initiating a vicious beating. Danny got so cocky that he walked around with the Indian Posse logo painted on his jail uniform, a provocation that resulted in a formal disciplinary procedure. He might have seemed quiet, the disciplinary report suggested, but he was dangerous, and extremely influential behind the scenes. He was becoming a leader in his own right.

Three months after his twentieth birthday, on October 6, 1996, Danny met with prison psychologist Richard Howes in a private room at Stony Mountain for an extended evaluation. The purpose of the meeting was to see whether Danny could qualify for early release. Dr. Howes began with Danny's early life. He asked him when he had last seen his father. Danny provided a very specific answer: It was in 1988, the same year the gang was founded. He told Dr. Howes about not having seen his father in years and then bumping into him on the street, only to be ignored. The psychologist described it in his notes:

> After greeting his father and a brief exchange the father moved on with a rather lame "See you later." The 12-year-old Mr. Wolfe thought to himself, "That's my dad. Why doesn't he even want to talk to me?" and in fact he never talked to his father or even saw him again. It is relatively easy to see the attraction of a gang to a young boy who felt so hurt and neglected by the one man who should have cared about him.

Mr. Wolfe has been described in previous reports as a "street orphan", and I have no doubt the neglect and inadequacies in his childhood led him to willingly join his older brother in the founding meetings of the Indian Posse, which he says took place in his mother's home when he was just 12 in 1988.

"We had nothing," Danny told Dr. Howes. He and his friends were raised in impoverished, broken homes surrounded by alcohol and violence. Dr. Howes recorded his observations that the Indian Posse had provided "a sense of 'strength in aboriginal unity'" for Danny and "friends that loved one another."

Dr. Howes concluded that forming a gang, given Danny's circumstances in life, was perfectly understandable. But his membership in the gang made it much likelier that Danny would live his whole life as a criminal. He had surrounded himself with people who held selfish, exploitative criminal values and "who live in an undisciplined, hedonistic fashion" that Danny embraced. "For as long as he chooses to maintain [his place in the gang] he is unlikely to pursue any sort of conventional life, for such would be the antithesis of all he has experienced and practiced," Dr. Howes wrote.

Danny wanted the psychologist to understand that there was something different about the Indian Posse, that it was more than a typical street gang. "When we first started it was all crime," Danny told him. But as the gang members grew up the Posse became a source of aboriginal spiritual teaching, a way for kids raised without their families' stories to understand their place in the world. Together they attended sweat lodge ceremonies, smudged with sweet grass, and carried medicine bundles, or at least they did when they were in Stony Mountain, where these services were provided for indigenous offenders.

Dr. Howes was doubtful. There was no evidence among the gang members of any direction, other than a pattern of escalating crime and violence. But he noted that Danny "does seem to genuinely believe something healthy and enlightening can emerge from the gang. One might skeptically and perhaps realistically conclude that he is simply deluding himself if he believes this, but I was left with the sense that he is not committed to the gang simply because he prefers criminal associates."

The gang, of course, was the primary reason Danny was in jail, but his crime was not merely an attempt to protect another gang member. He intended to protect his brother. That led Dr. Howes to wonder whether Danny was actually committed to using violence to achieve his goals, or whether his threats were empty.

His psychological tests were consistent with anti-social personality disorder, which Dr. Howes described as no great revelation, considering Danny was the founder of a street gang and convicted of threatening to kill witnesses. His level of moral development was described as adolescent, "which is what one would expect given the major influences in his life."

Tests showed that Danny was of about average intellectual ability and that he presented a below-average risk to reoffend. Though he was significantly short of the threshold for being deemed a psychopath, there were several reasons to be cautious about letting Danny back into society: his substance abuse – alcohol, marijuana, and LSD mainly – his unstable lifestyle, his habit of escaping custody, his criminal history, his comfort level with a criminal lifestyle, and even his school adjustment problems (the prison had seen evidence that Danny had been diagnosed with attention deficit hyperactivity disorder as a child) and the early experience of the separation of his parents.

Despite the fact that Danny presented a below-average risk to reoffend, Dr. Howes recommended he be denied early release. He described him as a young man with many good intentions who would never act on them. Finally, he offered a perceptive observation that cut to the heart of Danny's devotion to the Indian Posse. Danny's risk to the community would only be reduced substantially if he became mature enough to walk away from the gang and stop believing these "idealistic notions of what this gang is or might become."

Prison officials who met more regularly with Danny also concluded that he was unlikely to change his ways. They did not hold out hope that the programs they offered would have much impact on him, according to a note on his file. Trying to convince him to leave the gang was pointless, they concluded.

A few days after his interview with Dr. Howes, Danny made a special request to a prison caseworker. Danny hadn't had a single visitor in more than a year. His own mother hadn't come to see him. His father was in jail in Saskatchewan. But his brother Richard was, like Danny, being held in the Stony Mountain penitentiary. Richard, though, was being held in isolation from the other prisoners because he'd been deemed too great a danger for general population. He was kept in solitary confinement for months while awaiting transfer to a maximum-security facility in another province. But Danny's request to see Richard was turned down. He was told that they would be allowed a short visit before Richard's transfer.

7

BURNING DOWN THE HOUSE
1996

Richard had been given an unusually long sentence for attempted murder, a sentence based on the evidence. But nothing occurs in a vacuum, and it may well have been influenced by a transformative event that occurred on April 26, 1996, right in the middle of the trial, and just before he took the stand in his own defence.

Located about twenty minutes outside the city of Winnipeg, Headingley Correctional Centre is the provincial jail where prisoners serve sentences of two years or less. The gangs had grown very quickly behind bars and the correctional system was struggling to adapt. Headingley is where those tensions came to a boil. It was overcrowded and restive in the mid 1990s – in large part because of the growing influence of the Indian Posse and other gangs, particularly the Manitoba Warriors – and it had earned a reputation as one of the nastiest prisons in the West.

The gangs ran a thriving drug trade in prison. Their methods for smuggling the drugs past the security net varied, but as one guard revealed, many successful attempts revolved around the soft drink vending machine in the visiting room. Visits took place in the evening from 7:00 to 9:00 p.m. in a large, open area where inmates and visitors sat together at tables. There were only two guards to watch a room that had as many as thirty to forty people meeting simultaneously. A visitor would buy a drink from the pop machine and on the inside of her palm there'd be a balloon or condom filled with drugs. As the visitor reached down to collect the can from the machine's bin, she would deposit the drugs in one corner of the vending slot. Shortly after, an inmate would also buy a can of pop and surreptitiously collect the drugs. Typically the inmate would not be obviously associated with the gangs but someone who had been coerced into working for them.

"[The inmate] would suitcase it. He would insert the drugs in his rectum," one guard told a public inquiry. "Quite often we'd search and we'd find the rear end of their pants would be sliced and their underwear would be sliced and they would do it sitting right at the table. As rude and crude as it sounds that's the culture we're dealing with. And this may be a well-educated blond-haired blue-eyed kid. But he was going to do it or he was going to get a terrible licking when he got back to his range. So he took the risk and he did it."

By 1993 the gang situation had deteriorated to the point that a unit manager approached his superior to tell him the gangs had mushroomed beyond the institution's ability to control them. They were too powerful. "I'm getting guys [inmates] beat up on a daily basis in there," the manager said. "It's almost to the point we're scared to go in the blocks 'cause these guys are so confrontational."

A new administrator named Larry Krocker had taken over at Headingley that year and he had new ideas about how things should run. He wanted a more open policy that would allow prisoners greater freedom of movement, and he wanted guards to eat their meals with the prisoners. A committee of guards and administrators had recently been created to deal with gang issues, and before it had even met,

Krocker said there was no gang problem, citing as evidence his contention that there had been no serious gang beatings. Guards were unhappy with the new direction, and scoffed at the notion there was no gang problem – they could see it. The more relaxed attitude to prisoner movements, in their view, allowed the Indian Posse to recruit more easily, as they were able to talk to and intimidate prisoners in all areas of the jail.

On April 26, 1996, a nurse arrived for her shift at Headingley at 7:30 a.m. and made her way to the prison's medical ward on the first floor, where she encountered a lone inmate snooping around the ward. There were no guards around. This inmate was normally housed in the basement, known as the "predator block," the range reserved for the most violent criminals. No one knew he was upstairs.

"I came from the basement. I'm one of the predators. I came to see you," he said to her. He asked the nurse if he could have some Epsom salts, which were commonly used to mix street drugs. For prison officials this alarming security lapse was the first clue that something was wrong. They were soon to learn that a large shipment of drugs had made it into the prison just the day before. A few hours later, inmates started making unusual purchases at the cafeteria that suggested they were trying to get as much liquid currency as possible, another sign that drugs were on sale. Later that night the guards, having concluded that drugs were indeed inside the prison, decided to search the cells in the basement – the predator block – where the gang members were getting rowdy.

The inmates, already well into the drugs when the guards arrived, knew that a search would mean giving up the large shipment they had just obtained. They had also beaten up an inmate that night, and he was in bad shape in his cell. They had been warned earlier that another beating would mean trouble for the whole unit: they would be locked down, essentially confined to their cells, for up to two months. They didn't want that. So feelings were tense when the guards began the search.

The guards did not count the inmates before they entered, and so didn't immediately register that one prisoner was missing. By omitting the count they failed to pick up on the high level of risk to themselves at that moment. This unit was a powder keg: the inmates felt they had nothing to lose by rioting. As the guards cautiously went from cell to cell on their search they eventually found the victim, who was badly beaten and bleeding. One guard immediately took the victim upstairs to the medical unit. Moments later, the inmates launched a full-blown attack on the guards, who were outnumbered roughly twenty to six. They radioed for reinforcements but were overwhelmed in a fury of advancing inmates who rained blows down on them.

A guard named Earl Deobald fell to the ground; the prisoners grabbed a set of keys from his belt. He suffered a "severe and savage beating," according to the independent review of the riot. A nurse who worked with him for ten years couldn't recognize him when she saw him lying on a stretcher, his face was so badly disfigured.

"Once they get the keys we're fucked because there are so many more of them than us. They just ran rampant after that," one guard told the local paper.

The keys the inmates snatched included a master that allowed the twenty or so gang members access to anywhere in the jail. They immediately headed for the medical unit where they could get more drugs. From there they unlocked the unit where inmates in protective custody were kept, many of them sex offenders or those who had informed on other inmates.

The protective custody inmates were force-marched down a dark stairwell. Armed with bats, broomsticks, and blocks of wood, the gang members lined the staircase to beat their victims in a vicious gauntlet. They lit fires, broke windows, and settled scores. The inmates maintained control of the prison overnight as police and fire crews tried to calm the situation from a distance. But as the situation spun further out of control, some of the inmates turned to torture. The newspaper headline captured the horror succinctly: "Jail a burnt out shell: Fingers amputated, castration attempted in orgy of violence."

Eight guards were hospitalized. Three or four inmates had fingers cut off. Several attackers tried to castrate some of the sex offenders. Another person said his attackers celebrated after scalping him, parading clumps of his hair as a trophy. One man offered the rioters the chance to cut off his index finger because he feared the alternative was death. When the finger couldn't be severed by the rioter's dulled blade the victim tried to appease his attackers by snapping it off himself. "He was jabbing at my finger but I guess he couldn't get through the bone," the victim said later in court. "It was just hanging there and he said, 'When I come back that finger better be gone.'" Another inmate slit his own wrist to fake death. In all, thirty-one inmates were treated in hospital. It was an utter disaster, the jail reduced to a smouldering, blackened shell. The riot leaders revelled in their victory and taunted crisis negotiators who tried to end the siege. They eventually allowed the most severely injured inmates to escape the barricaded prison, in exchange for pizza.

In the aftermath, inmates had to be moved to other jails. Many were released early, including one who committed murder a short time later. Many people were charged following the riot, some of them members of the Indian Posse, others attached to the Manitoba Warriors. The provincial minister vowed the inmates responsible for the riot would pay – that they would be made to rebuild the jail themselves. For obvious reasons of safety that didn't happen and the suggestion was ridiculed.

The tone of the media coverage that followed the riot made clear what many felt: gangs were out of control, which pushed the gang issue even higher up on the public agenda. The gangs themselves, and the reason for their sudden explosion, were central to the final report on the Headingley riot produced by Judge Edward N. Hughes. But for officials working in corrections, the riot drove home how dangerous the concentration of gang inmates could be. Fear of having too many Indian Posse members in one institution, and a greater understanding of the violent threat they represented, led corrections officials to start moving the gang members around the country. The gang couldn't have asked for a better opportunity to expand.

8

THE BROTHERS PART WAYS
1997–1999

By early 1997 Richard had been shipped west from Stony Mountain to the Edmonton Institution in Alberta. Edmonton Max, as it is known, is a maximum-security prison, and Correctional Service Canada had been sending many of its high-profile Indian Posse inmates there over the previous year or so.

Near the end of his time at Stony Mountain, Richard had begun having doubts about his involvement in the gang. Edmonton Max intensified those doubts. He was anxious. He remembers feeling the first twinge of apprehension soon after they set out from Stony Mountain, as he looked around at his fellow travellers, a dozen or so of the region's most violent criminals, all being shipped by bus across the prairie – like a scene from the recent movie *Con Air*. He was shackled to the floor and surrounded by tall plastic shields that shut him off from the other inmates. His wrists and ankles were chained together and attached to another chain that ran through a steel loop on the floor. His arms were tied so tight he strained to lift a sandwich to his mouth to eat. He was considered too dangerous to even eat lunch – could he really handle nineteen more years of this?

And, even after a few months, Richard hadn't adjusted well to the Max. One former Manitoba Warrior described what he considered the worst part of his experience at the prison: the times when he awakened to the sound of "metal on metal." Attacks on inmates occurred in the morning when the cells were automatically opened and a sleeping inmate could be caught unprepared by inrushing attackers; the horrible screech of metal crashing into metal announced that a shank, a homemade knife, had penetrated all the way through a body and smashed into the bed frame below.

There were other Indian Posse members in Edmonton when Richard arrived, including his close friend and IP co-founder Lawrence, as well as more recent inductees to the gang, serious criminals who had committed murders and had long sentences. They didn't know Richard but they didn't like what they had heard. Hostility toward him had been brewing before he'd even arrived.

Lawrence said that people started bringing up the lengthy interviews Richard had done with the *Winnipeg Free Press* in 1994. They thought he talked too much, citing how during his trial he had said, "Brothers do what I say." His swagger rubbed them the wrong way, Lawrence said. Who was this kid, they asked? Would he expect *them* to do as he said?

"The old guys that I had [recruited in prison] would say 'I'm loyal to you, I know you, but I'm not doing what this fucking punk kid tells me,'" Lawrence said.

There was also a troubling line that had appeared in one newspaper story, which said Richard had two convictions for sexual assault. That history would make him an outcast in prison, where "skinners" are despised. Richard denied being convicted of sexual assault (his adult record showed no sign of it at the time), and he believes someone confused his father's record, which did include sexual assaults, with his.

Lawrence and Richard were the original partners in crime who had come up with the concept of the Indian Posse back on the streets of Winnipeg. By the time Richard arrived at Edmonton Max, however, Lawrence was the higher-ranking figure in the gang. Having been among the first of the IP to hit Stony Mountain, he was by now a hardened criminal with years in the penitentiary behind him. He stuck up for his friend Richard, but it was hard to convince the others. Sometimes it seems long-term inmates have nothing to fill the hours but to gossip and plot against one another. Richard was in the crosshairs and Lawrence struggled to keep tensions from escalating.

Lawrence's early life was different from many of the other gang members'. He says he came from a stable family and grew up with both parents, but he rebelled, taking off and leaving home with Richard for weeks at a time. He preferred the camaraderie of the gang to the stability of a normal family life, and eventually the Indian Posse became his family of choice. Richard was like a brother to him.

"I did everything with Richie," he said. "He would come with me and pick up stuff, whatever we were told to do . . . That's when I got into all the fights, the beginning of gang school."

They marauded through the city with seeming impunity in those days, he recalled fondly.

"We did a lot of bad stuff. We'd say, 'Let's go to work.' We'd jump in a stolen car, do a break and enter, go to a party with all the stolen stuff and then make friends at the party and sell all the stuff . . . At eleven I was already on my own stealing car stereos, doing my own thing . . . Winnipeg was open season. Child welfare and cops, there really weren't that many around then and they weren't so serious about everything like they are now."

Lawrence is built like a brick, with the massive arms and chest of someone who has spent years in prison weight rooms. In his glory days he could bench press 550 pounds and his fists are like giant soup cans. He's tough, but he's also well-mannered, articulate, and shrewd.

He says that although there was a lot of alcoholism, drug use, and physical abuse among the parents of Indian Posse members when they were young, he doesn't blame them or anyone else for the rise of the gang. It was the thrill, the lure of a fast, exciting life, the kind they'd seen in the movies, that drew everyone to the gang. Nothing else on offer could compete. "It's all about the hype," he said.

"People say it's because of the North End. Parents are alcoholics. It played a part, sure, but that's not all of it. The choices I made, those were my choices," Lawrence said. "I know Susie [Danny and Richard's mother] is always so hard on herself, saying it was her fault that she neglected us and whatever, but I disagree. I always had someone I could go to. Between us we probably had six or seven mums and someone at least would be there for you."

Lawrence wanted to be there for Richard when he got to Edmonton Max, he says, but he didn't have the power to move the rest of the gang. When he had first landed at Stony Mountain some older inmates had taken him under their wing. They had protected him, treated him like a son, explained how things work in prison, such as when and how you use violence, what you can learn to live with and what you have to fight. He had learned to pick his battles, and at a certain point he realized he couldn't protect Richard any more.

"You got to stay in the shadows and he exposed himself," Lawrence said, shaking his head regretfully.

While Lawrence was facing a painful reckoning in his friendship with Richard, Richard was doing some soul searching of his own. A few months after he was sentenced there had been a shooting in the North End and a young boy was killed. It was one of those crimes that's described in the media as a watershed, and it affected him profoundly.

In the early morning hours of July 23, 1995, Joseph Beeper Spence, a popular thirteen-year-old, was hanging around the corner of Robinson Avenue and Flora Street. Beeper was a bright kid whom Richard and the other IP members used to let hang around when they were all out on the streets. Beeper wasn't in the gang, but he looked up to the older guys in the way many local kids did, and he was treated almost like a mascot.

It was a little after 2:00 a.m., which was late for a thirteen-year-old to be out but not uncommon on a summer night in the North End. Earlier that evening, unbeknownst to Beeper, some IP members had beaten up a member of a rival gang, the Nine-Deuce, whose territory was in the West End. Conrad Johnson, Fabian Torres, and Kami Pozniak, teenaged members of the Deuces gang, were bent on revenge. They got in a van and drove to the North End, where they were sure they could find some IP members to attack. As their van rolled toward the street corner where Beeper was standing, rap music blaring inside, Johnson said, "If we find any IP, bang."

He reached for the 12-gauge shotgun as Torres passed it up to him from the back.

"Are you going to scare him?" Johnson was asked.

"No, I'm going to shoot him," he replied.

Johnson, just fifteen years old, unwrapped the gun, which was covered in a jacket, and put gloves on. He wiped down the weapon a few times with his gloves and then took a shell from his pocket, which he also wiped before loading it into the shotgun.

"I'm ready," he said.

The van pulled up at the corner and Johnson looked out the window. "Who you repping?" he asked the boy standing on the corner.

"IP," Beeper replied proudly. "In full effect," he added, despite the fact that he was not actually a member.

Johnson raised the gun through the open window and took aim. Beeper turned to run.

"Bust a cap in his ass," said Torres from the back seat.

Johnson opened fire, hitting the little boy in the back and killing him.

The gangland hit was splashed all over the news. Richard followed the coverage from jail and felt deep remorse for his role, however indirect, in getting a young boy killed. Things were out of control. The gang had become the monster he had feared it might be.

"[Beeper] wasn't down with IP. He just wanted to fit in. Just saying [Indian Posse] ended up getting him blasted in the back with a 12-gauge," Richard said. "It was really [a turning point]. That was when I actually started thinking about [leaving the gang] a lot."

But Richard was already in prison, a pressure-cooker environment where he couldn't afford to let his guard down. No one could know that he was struggling with being part of the gang. If word got around that he was going soft, he'd be finished. "I had to try and hide it. Especially making decisions on things that were happening in prison. I couldn't show any weakness because then red flags would go up on me."

Over time, though, he wore down as his commitment faded. This gang that he and his brother created was attracting so many young people, but if a kid like Beeper could be killed just for aspiring to join, where would it end?

"I wanted out," he said. "That Beeper thing was laying heavy on my head."

Richard met with the three highest-ranking members of the gang in the prison, all of them members of the council or soon to rise to that level. They went to the office dedicated to the native brotherhood, an organization for First Nations inmates that was also an effective cover for Indian Posse activity inside prison. Richard, though he knew it was a risk, told the others that he wanted to leave the gang. He hoped that his years of service, and his role as a founder, would get him a kind of honourable discharge. After hearing him out, the three members left the room. Richard sat with an elder, discussing books on native culture, but keeping half an eye on the craft room where the three were discussing his fate. They came out with poker faces, and then consulted some other members, casting glances in his direction. Richard's heart was pounding as his life hung in the balance. He knew the bitterness over his media interview a few years earlier and the doubts about whether he had two sexual assault convictions still rankled some of them.

A senior gang member pulled him aside. He was going to be disciplined, get a beating, and then that would be it. "They came back and said, 'Alright, if you don't do this and don't do that, everything's good. You can walk,'" Richard said. "Some disagreed with it and said they should wipe [me] right out."

His sense of relief was brief. A short time later an old friend, one whom Richard had recruited personally in Winnipeg, pulled him aside. This guy was a huge man, well over six feet tall with arms like cannons. The friend said he was sorry to have to tell him this, but the council had ordered him to put a hit on Richard and take him out permanently. The man said he couldn't do it, out of loyalty.

"I said, 'Alright. Step aside brother. If it's going down then it's going down. I ain't going anywhere,'" Richard said.

He might have talked tough, but Richard was alarmed. He had been handed a death sentence. He couldn't spend the next seventeen years running from the gang that controlled most of the prisons in the West. They would come for him. So he kept two shanks close to him at all times and he never went out to the yard to exercise. When he ate he sat with his back to the wall. "I wasn't going to make it easy for them."

One day Richard was playing cards in his cell with another inmate. It was a small space that looked almost like a university dorm room, with photos on the walls and a poster that read "North Side – Winnipeg." One of his friends had sent him a photo of the intersection of Selkirk Avenue and Isabel Street, a corner where the IP used to ply its trade. "You must be homesick. Here's a picture of the North End," the accompanying note had said.

Richard got up to use the washroom. When he returned his opponent had taken his spot on the wall, forcing Richard to sit with his back to the door. Richard was puzzled but didn't think much about it and sat down.

At that moment someone rushed up from outside and entered through his open cell door, then grabbed him around the neck and squeezed his windpipe. The inmate Richard was playing cards with began punching him in the face and body. He struggled to reach for his shank. His attackers swung the door closed and put a blanket over the glass in the door to conceal what was going on. A punch to the back of his head knocked Richard down to one knee and when he tried to lunge at his attackers, he had one set of arms around his neck and another on his arm holding him still. Then he saw the flash of a blade. He tried to kick out to defend himself but it was useless. He felt a series of sharp punctures as the shank plunged in and out of his body five times – in the back, in the side, and in the arm. Then his attackers ran out of the cell, leaving him near death on the floor. He was still conscious when the guards arrived and found him, a spluttering, bloodied mess.

"Is he dead?" he heard one guard ask.

Richard was lucky. He had been able to block some of the blows with his arms and none hit a vital organ. One IP member claimed the attackers weren't intent on murder, but in an assault like that it's difficult to know whether someone will live or die. Another gang member recalled that the order was to kill. He said Richard survived only because the hit was badly executed.

Richard was treated in the prison's medical unit, and while he convalesced, Lawrence visited him at his bedside. Richard's long-time friend had a duty of friendship to him, but Lawrence also needed reassurance that Richard wouldn't talk to police. Some of the other leaders were afraid that the older Wolfe brother would iden-tify his attackers. The gang insisted that its code of silence apply even to those members it tried to kill. Lawrence said he personally vouched for Richard as a "solid dude" who would never talk. Others were less confident.

Lawrence leaned over the hospital bed. He knew there was a chance that prison authorities would be monitoring their conversa-tion, and he wanted to make sure whatever he said would be heard by the guards and police.

"You know what's up eh," he said, giving Richard a deliberate look. This was one of the moments when the power of the gang would be tested, and Lawrence didn't know what to expect. Richard was an Indian Posse founder who had been nearly murdered by the family he created. He was injured and he was angry. If he gave even a hint that he would bring down his attackers, Lawrence knew the gang would go after him again, and he didn't want that.

"I asked if he saw who did it," Lawrence said. "He just looked at me and he got the play. I said, 'We'll get those fucking white boys.'"

There was a pause as Richard thought for a moment; then he nodded. "Yeah. One was a short white boy," he replied, buying into the lie.

Once he was released from the medical unit Richard was placed in segregation for his own protection, which he opposed. He wanted to show the council and his attackers that he was not afraid to go back into population. The council offered Richard a chance to stay in the gang at a lower rank if he carried out a hit on their behalf. He declined, and about four months later he was sent to Drumheller

Institution in rural Alberta. In a way, he was starting over there. He didn't know many people and there were no gangs there yet, save for a chapter of the Aryan Brotherhood.

Richard's psyche was fragile. He was through with the Indian Posse, but he couldn't be sure that the Indian Posse was through with him. He had given up whatever power and status he had once had and now was trying to make it on his own. Then he received a letter from one of his old lieutenants in Winnipeg who was still on the street, warning him to be on the lookout, that the gang was manoeuvring to have a hit man transferred to Drumheller to finish him off. It would be someone Richard didn't know, a new recruit from Alberta.

Paranoia started to gnaw at Richard. As the months passed he thought the delay was part of the plan, and he told himself the Posse wanted him to drop his guard. When word got round that a new busload of inmates would be arriving soon, Richard's mind went into overdrive. He created a profile in his mind of the would-be assassin: someone young who probably began his time in Edmonton, then got recruited and transferred to Stony Mountain, and now would be heading back to his home province near the end of his sentence. The hit on Richard would be the recruit's chance to prove himself.

A few days after the bus arrived Richard decided which of the new arrivals was the assassin. He was an inmate from Alberta, some-one the rumour mill said had done time in Edmonton and Stony Mountain, just as Richard had anticipated.

"I think it was probably three days just waiting, deciding what to do. Then I thought, you know what, I'm not going to wait any longer 'cause he might get me. So I went to go get him," Richard said. He wasn't even sure if the new arrival was an Indian Posse member.

Richard was in the middle of a card game when someone told him the newcomer was in his cell, alone. Richard got up from the table and went back to his own cell. He emerged with a bandana covering his face and a shank in his hand.

The victim never knew what hit him. Richard attacked him in his cell with a feverish intensity, stabbing him several times. The newcomer survived, though, and Richard got caught.

A prison official brought him in for a meeting. Puzzled, he wondered why Richard had suddenly turned violent after years of good behaviour. Richard told him it was a pre-emptive strike. His victim planned to get him, Richard said, and he had moved first to avoid getting hurt. But why? the official asked. Richard made up a story about a card game, saying the victim had accused him of cheating and had left to get his shank. It was all a lie, but he tried to assure him that this incident wouldn't be repeated.

Richard continued to worry, though. He assumed his instincts had been right, that the gang was going to pursue him until he was dead. It wasn't until several months later that the details of his victim's life started to come out. Richard finally realized that the newcomer was not a gang assassin, nor had attacking Richard ever entered his mind. Richard regretted the attack, but the stabbing added another two years to his sentence, making it almost twenty-two years.

Word of the stabbing got back to Danny in Stony Mountain; he was worried about his big brother. Richard had no backup network in Drumheller, no old friends or other Indian Posse inmates to rely on. Danny wrote to him, asking if they needed to get someone transferred to Drumheller right away.

Richard didn't ask for any help in his reply, saying only that he had been sure the gang wanted to finish him off. But could he be sure of his own brother? After all, Danny had told him he'd be willing to take him out for the sake of the Indian Posse. Richard was walking away from the gang with a lot of secrets; it was only natural to think that they would want to eliminate any risk that he might talk in future. Or that they might just make an example of him to keep the others in line.

Danny told Richard that he was overreacting. He had checked with the leadership, and the gang was not coming after him. "Get over it, man, you're fucking paranoid," Danny told him.

9

GANG EXPANSION, POLICE RESPONSE
1997–1999

As Richard turned away from the gang, Danny embraced it even more fervently. The Indian Posse was their own creation, something the brothers had built into a surrogate family and viable criminal enterprise. It had helped lift them out of poverty and given them a sense of pride. Along the way they had discovered hundreds, even thousands, of young aboriginal people who had led similar lives marked by poverty, abuse, and the child welfare and justice systems, who flocked to join. Danny truly believed the gang was the only place he belonged, and he was puzzled by Richard's withdrawal from it. He idealized the raised fist of resistance and native pride that he believed the gang represented, which made Richard's decision all the more difficult to accept.

Danny was not apparently involved in any of the gang deliberations over Richard's fate. Although he had said a few years earlier that he would be willing to kill his brother for the sake of the gang, his resolve was never tested. Afterward, he seemed to refuse to accept that his brother's stabbing represented a stern rejection from the rest of the leadership. He lobbied to keep Richard in the gang, even if it meant his brother's accepting a much lower rank.

He wrote a letter to Richard in Alberta from Stony Mountain in November 1997. He beat around the bush for a while, getting to the point only at the end, where he says, "Word in here is that you can't be high ranking but you can still be down."

10:48 p.m.

Rich,

What's up? Me not much the "man" put the big bad Wolfe back in the hen house! And they still can't keep me down! Fuck them they'll never break me. Anyways, yah, I had fun when I was out. Party here, party there you know how it is. I even went to the Rolling Stones. Fuck that was good . . . Hey when I get out of here and my time is up just let me know where you are and I'll be there bro. Don't let the man get to you. And about [Colleen] don't even let that shit fade you. I'll hook up with some chicks but you have to send some pictures of yourself and bro not naked fuck! . . . I have three old ladys but I have to tame them first. There too wild for me . . . So how is it out there? Well word in here is that you can't be high ranking but you can still be down! And for me I'm try to keep things cool. I did to much things for the name now it's time to do my own thing and kick back and see what happens. Well bro I hurt my wrist in a football game so I can't write that much so keep in touch and take care of yourself.

Love your bro, D.Wolfe

p.s. I miss you to but I'll be there for you soon! So stay strong!!

The letter was sent shortly after Danny was sent back to Stony Mountain. He had been caught on a parole violation just a few weeks after he was released from prison in September 1997 after serving two-thirds of his three-year sentence.

His release conditions had said he was to live with his aunt Connie Bullbear in a house she rented on Pacific Avenue near the CP rail yards, not far from where he grew up. Connie's husband had died twenty years earlier and she was in failing health, unemployed, and living on social assistance. In an interview with Danny's parole officer she explained the difficulties Danny faced as a child, particularly the violence he'd witnessed between his mother and father. By the time Connie moved to Winnipeg in 1991, Richard and Danny were so far gone in the gang lifestyle there wasn't much that could be done, she said. Although she made no excuses for the Indian Posse, she said most of its members were exactly like Richard and Danny, young people from dysfunctional families. She said she would welcome Danny into her home but would not allow Indian Posse members to visit.

Danny's parole officer concluded that Connie was not a naive woman and that she understood what she was getting into. There were no illusions about how difficult it would be for Danny to stay out of trouble.

Danny did his best to live it up for the short time he was free. Less than a month later, though, on October 7, 1997, he got nabbed. Four men kicked in the door of a North End home and pulled shotguns on the people inside, saying they were looking for drugs and money. It was a classic drug rip-off, a staple of the Indian Posse's criminal diet, where a drug dealer's house is targeted for a quick score.

Police responded to a neighbour's 911 call and swarmed the area, led by officers from the street gang unit. They were looking for four men who had been spotted running from the house. A couple of blocks from the scene they spotted Danny and two other men sitting, or hiding as the police described it, on the front porch of a house. The cops approached in force and asked what they were doing. Danny told them he had just stopped by to say hello to some old friends. The officers were skeptical. They knew Danny as Richard Wolfe's less notorious little brother. While they couldn't tie Danny directly to the robbery, they could prove he was in the company of known gang members, including one who had been charged in the Headingley prison riot a year earlier.

Danny was dressed "in full gang regalia" according to the police report, which included a black hat and red bandana with feathers tied to each side, and a "gang lighter," which was not described. When the police pointed out that he was carrying Indian Posse symbols, Danny proudly agreed, but that was not a crime in itself. He said he had known these two friends since 1988 and couldn't just ignore them if he bumped into them, even if the court ordered him to do so. The police were unsympathetic and Danny was sent back to prison for violating the condition that he have no contact with known gang members.

Danny didn't appear too distraught over his return to prison. He had only a year until his sentence expired so he quickly got to work moving up the gang hierarchy. Before Christmas that year, an internal prison investigation found a large accumulation of weapons – twelve shanks – on two ranges, or sections, in the prison. Danny, who was working in the metal shop, was the prime suspect in the manufacture and smuggling of the blades. Four months later another weapons cache was found. Danny was again identified as the ringleader, but the authorities could never prove it. From his letters to family and friends it's clear Danny delighted in his ability to avoid consequences.

The prison intelligence officers were alarmed by Danny's growing importance in the prison and began eavesdropping on his phone calls. Over four days in April 1998, Danny used another inmate's personal ID number to make phone calls to contacts outside the prison, hoping the prison would fail to monitor what appeared to be another inmate's call. The subterfuge didn't work, though, and the calls were still tapped, so the police were probably monitoring all the lines Danny was likely to use. Police listened as Danny organized a shipment of drugs into Stony Mountain. The plan was to have four men connected to the Indian Posse throw a ball stuffed with drugs over the prison wall. Unbeknownst to Danny, the telephone intercepts had prompted RCMP and Correctional Service officers to set up surveillance on the prison's perimeter.

At dusk on April 22, 1998, the RCMP surveillance team spotted the four men walking up the road adjacent to the prison. The men shouted something to the inmates in the exercise yard and then dashed toward the perimeter fence, trying to get close enough that the throw could clear the prison wall, which was set further back. At that point, prison officials broke off their surveillance and tried to chase down the four men, but not before they saw a black ball sail over the wall. Danny was seen running inside the prison yard like a wide receiver tracking a pass. The ball might not even have hit the ground. Moments later, Danny was seen running into the canteen area with the cargo cradled under his arm. Somehow he got inside and either hid or handed off the package before guards stopped him. He was strip-searched and skin-frisked but came up clean. The whole canteen area was searched but prison officials found nothing there either. Because there was no evidence that anything illegal was ever in his possession, Danny couldn't be charged. Somehow the drugs found their way into the prison's bloodstream and Danny and the gang grew richer.

It's an astonishing example of how difficult it is to stop shipments of drugs into prisons. Prison intelligence officers, as well as the RCMP, knew the drugs were coming on a given day at a given time. They watched the drugs arrive and saw them being thrown over the fence. They knew who was going to collect them and watched him run through the yard carrying something. Still, they couldn't stop it. Danny enjoyed his victory, but the celebration was brief.

The next day he was plucked from his cell and dumped in segregation. His presence in the prison's general population was "jeopardizing the security of the institution and the safety of others," he was told. Even though Danny had not been involved in any violence or convicted of any violations of prison rules, the prison raised his security level from medium to maximum. It was only because his release date was fast approaching that he avoided being shipped to a maximum-security jail.

While he had become a prominent bad guy in the eyes of his jailers, Danny had a charming side that tended to disarm even those long accustomed to dealing with serious criminals. Sandra Woytowich, his parole officer inside the institution, described him as "a very pleasant and likeable young man," resourceful and bright, who was capable of being a positive influence. Yet he had spent half of his twenty-one years behind bars and continued to focus all his energy on criminal enterprises, she wrote. She said it was clear that Danny had not benefitted from any programs during his time in the correctional system.

Danny, who hoped to upgrade his grade 9 level of schooling, was described as an excellent student in the jail's academic program, and planned to soon challenge a high school equivalency test. He was excited about poetry, according to the teacher, and asked about programs he could attend on the outside to further his education. She sent him some information on adult education centres in Winnipeg.

"I hope he follows up on this because he has a lot of potential," she wrote.

John, a First Nations elder, got to know Danny over several years in the correctional system through his work as a paid counsellor to indigenous inmates. He still works in prisons in Manitoba and has dealt with hundreds of Indian Posse members over the years, but Danny sticks out in his memory. He was very kind and respectful, John said, but something seemed to hold him back, as though he was forced to keep his distance from the elder. He wanted desperately to learn more about his native heritage and cultural practices but was clearly wary of appearing to get too close, John said.

"He had a certain image with the gang he had to keep," John said. "He always came and asked me questions and he wanted to go away quietly and think about it afterwards." The Indian Posse seemed to have a rule, John explained, that blocked its members from talking to him on a one-to-one basis. They always came as a group of seven or eight inmates. Paranoia and fear are rampant inside the gang and he suspects they're worried about what they might be perceived to be telling him. "They don't trust each other."

Danny was popular, that much was obvious, John recalled. He smiled easily, a trait rare enough in prison that John remembered it, and he observed that Danny never felt the need to bully anyone the way many of the other leading figures did. He was persuasive in other ways, which made him more likeable and magnetic as a personality. "He had a lot of savvy as far as gangs were concerned," John said.

As his mandatory release date approached in 1998, Danny wrote to Richard again. He passed on the news that their mother was wanted in Manitoba and Saskatchewan for writing bad cheques. He also talked about wanting to move west, possibly to British Columbia, to expand the gang's reach. "I'm too well known for my wild shit in [Winnipeg] so I gots to keep rolling," he wrote.

When he was released on May, 22, 1998, Danny headed for Saskatchewan and his mother's home reserve of Okanese.

10

THE COLONIAL LEGACY AND THE DEBT OF SACRIFICE
1870–1999

The road into the heart of the Qu'Appelle Valley descends from the Saskatchewan prairie through grass-covered slopes and wind-blown trees until it meets the picturesque lakes and rivers that snake for miles along the valley bottom. First Nations people lived here for centuries before the arrival of Europeans, surviving primarily off the buffalo hunt. In the early 1800s, as Europeans pushed inland in search of furs, a trading post was established at Fort Qu'Appelle.

By the 1870s life on the plains was changing rapidly. White settlers were arriving in large numbers and the buffalo were being hunted to near-extinction. The Cree and Ojibwa, feeling food shortages more acutely, in 1874 to meet in the Qu'Appelle Valley to negotiate a treaty with the Crown, from whom they secured the promise that they would receive schools on the reserve, tools, and assistance in making the transition to European-style agriculture, which they saw as a means to ensuring their survival.

Danny's great-grandfather Leonard Creeley was born in Moose Mountain, Saskatchewan, in July of either 1888 or 1890. He listed his heritage as Assiniboine and Cree and arrived in File Hills as a teenager, destined for the File Hills Industrial School, a residential school overseen with keen interest by local Indian Agent William Morris Graham. The school at File Hills became a kind of experiment in social engineering for Graham, whose job it was to oversee the local indigenous population on behalf of the federal government. The pupils at his school were prevented from speaking their own languages and practising their religion. Graham was determined that educating the aboriginal children to be like Europeans would ensure that they did not return to their old ways once they had left school. The students were given half a day of classroom instruction and half a day of practical skills, principally farming. Graham wanted to see his pupils established as farmers after graduation and procured land on the Peepeekisis reserve to create a colony entirely of residential school graduates. Graham even went so far as to arrange marriages between the students, to be sure they would carry on as they had been taught.

After he left school, Leonard Creeley married Lily Buffalo Bow. She was the daughter of Buffalo Bow, a prominent member of the Peepeekisis band whose claim to the title of chief was not recognized by the Indian Agent. In the 1911 census, when he was roughly twenty-one, Leonard is described as a labourer. Both he and Lily, who already had a one-year-old son, could speak and write English, according to the census, and they listed Roman Catholic as their religion.

Leonard was the "model" Indian whom Graham and the Canadian government wanted to show off to the world. When foreign dignitaries visited, they were brought to the File Hills Colony to be presented with scenes of "civilization" and progress, and Leonard seems to have been a leading member of the colony. There are photos of him posing with other members of the File Hills Colony band, a fifteen-member brass band that dressed in uniform and performed at fairs in other communities. He was also a member of the baseball team, which was photographed in caps, flannels, and knee socks after winning the McKenzie Medal, a proud W.M. Graham standing among them.

When wartime came, the young men of the File Hills Colony enlisted at a rate that was said to be the highest of any community its size, and Leonard was part of the first wave to volunteer. On October 5, 1915, a group of File Hills young men and their elders set out for Regina. The photographs of that day are of such historical significance that they are among the most frequently used to illustrate the history of First Nations service in the Canadian military. Leonard Creeley is photographed with Pimotat, who was the brother of influential chief Starblanket, suggesting that Leonard and Pimotat had some kind of nephew-uncle relationship and indicating Leonard's status in the community. The photographs are posed and formal. Leonard looks proud and serious, his demeanour fitting for what was seen as a great occasion. For Graham, the enlistment of his pupils in the King's Army was proof of the loyalty and reliability of the indigenous students raised at the colony.

Leonard's attestation forms listed his age as twenty-five years and three months. He was weighed and measured, and among the smallest of the group: five-feet-six-inches tall, with a chest that measured thirty-six inches when fully expanded. Eyes: black. Hair: black. Complexion: dark.

Leonard signed his name below his oath: "I Leonard Creeley do make Oath that I will be faithful and bear true Allegiance to His Majesty King George the Fifth, His Heirs and Successors and that I will observe and obey all orders of His Majesty, His heirs and Successors and of all the generals and officers set over me. So help me God."

He was assigned to the 68th Overseas Battalion of the Canadian Expeditionary Force. He was sent east to Quebec but didn't go overseas for another six months, departing in April 1916.

The details of Leonard's war experience are relatively scant. Some clues to that time are contained in a brief memoir written by

David Bird, another File Hills recruit who joined on the same day and was also assigned to the 68th Battalion. Bird said he played in the band until they landed in England, which made sense given his and Leonard's experience with the Colony brass band. They were then sent to the front, to the awful trenches at Ypres and then at the Somme, one of the war's largest battles, where Canadians fought for months at great cost. Based on the records of his injuries, Leonard was wounded in the leg early on, possibly at Ypres. After recovering in a military hospital he rejoined his unit and his Canadian comrades.

Returning to battle, Leonard was among the thousands of men who fell victim to the terrifying new chemical weapon unleashed by the German army: poison gas. He was at the Somme when the gas injured him. That might have been the last combat he saw, although it is possible he recovered enough to rejoin the Canadian Corps at Vimy Ridge, where his classmate Bird saw action, according to his memoir. Leonard returned to Canada in April 1919, landing at Quebec City. He was declared unfit for further duty and discharged.

Leonard travelled back across the country by train to the File Hills. He applied to the soldier settlement program and received a loan of more than $3,000 from the government to build a farm house and a barn and to acquire some animals. Leonard was more fortunate than other First Nations soldiers, some of whom got nothing. In fact, many reserves lost land to a federal government determined to give it to soldiers returning from the war.

On the confidential assessment section of his application, Leonard was described as steady and industrious, although he complained of lingering disability in his lungs from the gas attack. He had four children at this point, including Danny's grandfather Bill Creeley. Asked on the form why he was pursuing farming, Leonard responded: "Because I think it is the best occupation." The land, 320 acres, was described as favourable, "chocolate with clay subsoil," ideal for growing oats or wheat. The prospects for Leonard and his family were good.

But within a year or so Leonard's health took a turn and he developed tuberculosis in his already damaged lungs. Unable to work, he couldn't make payment on his $3,000 loan. His farm, his two-storey house, his animals, were all in jeopardy. The Indian Agent, Graham's successor, stepped in to arrange for Leonard's land to be transferred to another member of the band, a successful farmer named Joseph Bellegarde, who agreed to purchase the farm for his son William Bellegarde, and who was, like Leonard, a graduate of Graham's favoured school.

That decision was controversial and provoked a sharp letter from Duncan Campbell Scott, a senior Indian Affairs administrator in Ottawa, who was upset that this land transfer was done outside the normal rules. Bellegarde had not served in the military, and the purpose of the loan program was to help returning veterans. Graham, who had been promoted to a regional manager's post but still kept a close eye on File Hills, intervened to smooth the waters. His letter to Scott ensured that Ottawa approved the deal, and Bellegarde got the farm.

In their letters the Indian Agent and Graham suggested that it was Leonard who asked them to intervene for his own benefit. They make it sound as though he just wanted the burden of the debt off his shoulders. That's possible, but there is no documented record from Leonard indicating that was the case. He had missed a payment of $88 in November 1922, and at that moment he owed $2,200, having made substantial progress on his $3,000 debt. But it was also in the interests of the Indian Agent and W.M. Graham, who were keen to promote agriculture in the colony, to keep a valuable farm in the hands of former File Hills students, to ensure the success of their project. In 1946, when Joseph Bellegarde was still $1,971 in arrears, down only slightly from the debt of $2,113 he assumed in April 1923, the sale was cancelled.

What impact the loss of the farm had on the Creeley family is unclear from the record, though it's likely they were left destitute. Leonard's loyalty to the Crown and brave, physical sacrifice were quickly forgotten with a missed loan payment. No arrangements were apparently considered to keep the property within the family. Perhaps none was available.

The family's story through the middle of the twentieth century is uncertain. What is known is that Bill Creeley, Susan's father, was born at Okanese in 1914 and was still a young child when his father went to war. During this time, he was raised by his grandfather, and in a book of profiles of First Nations people in Saskatchewan, Bill recalls the day an instructor from the residential school, accompanied by an RCMP officer, came to take him away. "My grandfather cried when they took me from him, but he loved me so much he would come and see me every Sunday. Even in winter he came on horseback to visit and bring me sweets. The school burnt down, so I ran away, back to my grand-father." They built a small house, Bill wrote, and lived there together:

> We were poor; our house had no floor. The lectures I got from him are the ones I tell people now. I still believe them; I believe we have one God, one land, one sun, one life. There are four directions and four seasons. God gave each of us our body and our mind. He gave us hands and legs to work with if we want something so we don't have to steal. When I hear of any Indian ceremony, I try to be there to take part. Those people who keep to Indian customs, they are the ones who still love one another.

Bill's relationship with his father is less clear. It might have been that to reduce the burden on the family, Bill stayed with his grandfather and was raised by him, even after Leonard returned from the war. When the Second World War began, Bill volunteered. When he returned home he was chosen as chief at Okanese for a while. He struggled with alcohol, however, and was arrested many times. Susan's relationship with her father was complicated by his drinking. He died on May 31, 1984, when she was twenty-six.

Susan moved back to Okanese in 1998, not long before Danny arrived. After nearly twenty years in Regina and Winnipeg, she was determined to get her life in order by moving back to the reserve and quitting alcohol and drugs. She was volunteering as an addictions counsellor, a big step on her path to sobriety. Over the previous year she had immersed herself in spirituality and was learning about and drawing strength from her cultural roots, as Danny was doing in prison.

When Danny returned by bus, fresh out of jail, he hoped that after three years in prison, the quieter life would help him regain his footing. There is one photo of him and Susan from this period, an old Polaroid that has faded with time. They are standing in front of what looks like a rundown house with peeling paint and Danny is wearing a satin New York Yankees jacket. Susan has her arms draped around his neck in a joyous hug. She looks off-balance, as though Danny is the only thing keeping her upright. He looks slightly embarrassed. Years later, Susan chuckled ruefully at the memory as she held the photo up to the light: "Oh, I remember that one. I was so drunk." Though Susan was starting to get her life together during this time, the picture indicates it was not always a smooth process.

On May, 28, 1998, Danny met with his parole officer at the Harvest Fuel highway restaurant at Balcarres, Saskatchewan. In what was a major step, he brought his mother along and included her in the meeting. When he had been released a year earlier, there had been no mention of plans to see his mother, only his Aunt Connie. Danny and his mother had gone close to ten years with surprisingly little contact, and his juvenile prison records show that their relationship was often uneasy, as she missed meetings and he would get angry with her. She saw him only sporadically through his teenage years, ever since the Indian Posse had stepped in to perform the role of surrogate family.

The plan was for Danny and Susan to attend an in-patient alcohol rehab facility together, but Danny couldn't get a spot in the program. Instead, he was allowed to move into Susan's house, which she shared with her son Preston and a niece, provided he obeyed certain legal conditions, including a fifty-kilometre travel limit and random drug tests. Danny seemed amenable to the rules. He even asked his parole officer about enrolling in courses at school to complete his high school diploma and possibly to learn a trade. He was optimistic about his future.

That changed within two weeks. By the time his parole officer filed her next report, Danny wanted out of his mother's house. It was small and cramped with just two bedrooms, neither of which was his. He was sleeping on the couch and the four of them were in each other's way. The transition was perhaps a little too abrupt for him and Susan, after they had been so long apart. Danny wanted to move in with a cousin but the parole officer felt the cousin drank too much. Danny got angry, his parole officer wrote, but eventually calmed down and stayed with his mother.

Work was hard to come by, and Danny was a young ex-con with an empty resumé. He said that he planned to get a basic job, maybe working as a farmhand, but either nothing came up or no one was interested in hiring him, because he remained unemployed. In July he joined a local baseball team. His parole officer drove out on more than one summer night to watch him take the field with the FQ Motor Products team, playing not far from where his great-grandfather played in the flannel File Hills uniform seventy-five years earlier. "He gets on well with the team and he seems to enjoy the socialization," she wrote.

Danny had just turned twenty-two and was trying to enjoy what he could of his new freedom. He went to pow-wows and bragged about the number of women he romanced. He drank, smoked marijuana, and tried ecstasy. He was also clearly still in touch with the gang life, despite being banned from communicating with his old associates. He wrote to Richard explaining that he wanted to get some other gangsters out to the reserve so they could kick back and relax. The IP was still running the streets in Winnipeg, though, he said.

In the penitentiary, Danny's sentence and his work for the gang had earned him the right to get new tattoos, symbols of his rising status. Getting a back patch – in Danny's case, the words *Indian Posse* written across the back of the shoulders – was a big step up in the organization. It was also a very public declaration of loyalty: the gang's identity was now permanently marked on his skin. Danny wrote to Richard about going to the beach that summer and how, when he took off his shirt, everyone stared at him. He could feel the weight of his tattoos. They transformed his unimposing frame into a billboard that instilled fear. He enjoyed the feeling.

Still anxious about his older brother's place in the gang, Danny asked whether Richard wanted him to pass a message to the gang leadership in Stony Mountain. Danny said he had spoken to some "bros" but they didn't have much to say about Richard; as for Richard, he wasn't interested in them. In a sad aside, Danny wrote that he hadn't been able to find their father: "I haven't seen Dad yet, but that's nothing new."

Danny's ambition for the gang continued to nag at him and it wasn't long before he worked his way back into the street game. He hadn't found a job and had no income other than social assistance, so he gave up looking for work and gave up on going back to school. He went back to the life he had known, the best way he'd found to make money and survive. He travelled to Regina, determined it would become the new frontier for the Indian Posse.

Danny's task was to raise the gang's profile in Saskatchewan. The Indian Posse had already grown to more than one thousand members in Manitoba and the leadership wanted to expand even further. The first newspaper reports of its arrival in Saskatchewan had appeared in March 1996. Police said both the Indian Posse and their rivals, the Manitoba Warriors, had been recruiting heavily in the province. They were particularly focused on Regina, the provincial capital, a city of about 200,000.

Saskatchewan was fertile recruiting ground. Its population was very similar to Manitoba's: then as now, more than 10 per cent of the population was aboriginal, and also disproportionately young, more likely to be poor, and significantly over-represented in jail, to the point that 70 to 80 per cent of inmates were indigenous. Family breakdown, substance abuse, and a staggering number of children in state care combined to make the gang's job of luring young people easier.

Recruiting for street gangs is an imperfect art. Most people who join a gang tend to have little education, to come from troubled backgrounds, and to be inexperienced criminals. Given enough time, most will end up in jail. The kids who are susceptible to the gang's appeal are usually easy to spot, according to Richard. They're the ones out on the street alone late at night, with parents who might be abusive, addicted, or even incarcerated. Their lives lack structure, they feel unloved, and their sense of their own prospects is extremely limited. They're often tough kids, but they come with baggage. It would be easier if they were all smart and capable, but it doesn't always turn out that way.

"The smart guy can be a tough guy when the time comes, but not vice versa," Richard said. "The smart guys usually stay out of gangs though."

Danny was a good recruiter, charismatic and funny. He didn't need to talk as much as some, which lent his words an air of authority. Like many who've spent time in prison, he prided himself on being able to read people. He believed he could quickly assess a person's motives, as well as their vulnerabilities.

Every new recruit has the potential to upset the operation and is therefore also a risk. He might steal from the gang. He might plot against his fellow members. He might be trigger-happy and start costly wars with rival gangs. But there is a kind of capitalist hunger at the heart of the gang ethos; numbers mean power, so it's either grow or die.

One major advantage the Indian Posse had over other gangs was the strength of its identity. As Lawrence described it, the gang made its name by doing things other gangs wouldn't do, like using extreme violence to rob people, embracing drive-by shootings, and taking their level of criminality and violence a step further than their predecessors. They were feared, and their name alone had a defiant, in-your-face quality that appealed to teenagers. But there was also a political message that resonated with a frustrated and angry population.

The Indian Posse represented a violent rejection of Canadian society at the same time as it emphasized native spirituality, however superficially (meetings, especially in prison, included smudging to cleanse the spirit). That combination of transgression and spirituality had a powerful impact on those looking for an identity and sense of purpose. Indigenous blood was a requirement of membership and people of other ethnicities were banned (there were a few exceptions, and the restriction was later lifted in 2006 to boost recruiting). For many native kids raised without much sense of their own identity, the ceremonies, the attitude, and the slogans, like "Red 'til Dead," were a source of pride.

It was in this summer of 1998 that Danny met some members of AIM, the American Indian Movement, a militant group active in the

United States and parts of the prairie provinces. AIM was founded in Minnesota in 1968 and is best known for its connection to violent standoffs with authorities, including the 1973 siege at Wounded Knee on South Dakota's Pine Ridge reservation and the occupation and standoff at a park in Kenora, Ontario, in 1974.

There are few details about whom he met or what was discussed, but the encounter with AIM was an inspiration for Danny. He dreamt of turning the Indian Posse into a similarly coherent movement and described the meeting in a letter to Richard. "I ran into them [AIM] at a pow wow and they're like us," he wrote. "Into the militant stuff. And that's the kinda shit we need. We're like soldiers, but from the street." Before and after that meeting, Danny pushed the message of violent independence and resistance to mainstream Canada as a central tenet of Indian Posse membership. For him, someone with little formal education, AIM provided a structure of thought, a way of understanding the world. Richard once sent his brother a copy of AIM leader Russell Means's autobiography, *Where White Men Fear to Tread*. Inscribed on the inside cover was a note, the same words Richard spoke when they parted before his arrest for the pizza delivery shooting and when Richard was sent west to Edmonton Max: "Keep your head up and be strong."

In July of 1998, Danny went up to Prince Albert in northern Saskatchewan on a recruiting trip. The Indian Posse "had some bros over there" on the very large Peter Ballantyne Cree Nation, he told Richard, but the extent of their presence then is not clear. It was not unusual for large chunks of a reserve's young population to identify themselves with a gang even after only minimal contact with a gang member, let alone with the gang's leadership. Most recruiting was done through family ties: if someone had a younger cousin who could be trusted, he would be brought in as a striker; that striker might in turn bring in some friends. These young recruits might be too junior to have a recognized status but they would fly the gang flag by wearing red and taking on low-level missions such as drug dealing and debt collecting.

The Indian Posse spread like wildfire on the reserves. There are dozens of reserve communities scattered across the prairies, many of them small and remote. Alcohol addiction and drug abuse are, sadly, widespread, and it's not unusual to see unemployment rates in some places above 80 per cent. Drug dealing and selling bootleg liquor is a reliable way to earn a living in a place with few jobs, where typically less than half the adult population has graduated from high school. Many reserves have a local ban on alcohol intended to combat addiction problems, which serves also to inflate black-market prices for narcotics and booze.

Glen Ross, a former chief of the Opaskwayak Cree Nation in northern Manitoba, witnessed the speed with which his own community was transformed by the Indian Posse's arrival in the early 2000s. As he put it, the gang's symbolic values were alluring: money, power, respect – all of it on their own terms and in rebellion against the state. "There's pride in the outlaw," he said, "pride in fighting what they see as the government, the enemy."

Business on the reserves and in northern cities with large indigenous populations was very lucrative. Angus, a former Indian Posse member who was close to Danny and at times had a senior role in the gang, described how he profited from drug sales in remote communities. As a middle manager, Angus was in charge of his own network, which meant that unlike a foot soldier, who was paid by a higher-up, he had the power to earn serious money for himself, but also that he had to kick some of it back to the council, the gang's senior leadership. He said he typically returned 10 per cent of his profits to the council, which shows the gang was enforcing a much lower rate than the 30 per cent tax Richard described as the norm in the gang's early years.

Angus targeted the remote fly-in reserves, places so isolated that for six weeks in the winter they can be reached by ice road, and at all other times only by a small plane from the South. He was running cocaine into the reserves north of Lake Winnipeg via the regular mail service. He would buy a cheap stereo system or compact disc player and stuff the speakers full of plastic baggies of coke. A gram of cocaine could be broken up and sold in tenths on the reserve, usually for several times its value in the city. A gram of cocaine could fetch $100 on the street in Winnipeg, he said, but $1,000 on a remote reserve; marijuana that sold for $10 a gram in the city could be sold for $70 a gram. His relatives on the reserve would receive the drugs and handle the sales and distribution. He also had connections on the reserve police force tip him off when the RCMP planned to inspect incoming shipments. On average he made about $10,000 a week in gross sales. A large chunk went to pay his relatives and to buy more drugs, but he was earning a good living with manageable risk, he said. Typically he cleared $150,000 every six months.

This is the kind of network Danny was trying to establish in Saskatchewan, but it's not clear how successful he was. Before he tackled the smaller communities he needed to establish a foothold in Regina. He went about it with his typical panache.

"I made sure that our presence was there in Regina," he wrote to Richard. "We terrorized that place. Every bar we went to we got into some fights. But after a while they knew who we were."

By August of 1998 Danny had abandoned any sense of caution. On August 11, he and a friend went to a Regina Canadian Tire store and paid for a tire iron and light bulbs, while Danny pocketed some lug nuts from the automotive department without paying for them. A security guard saw Danny shoplifting and when he tried to stop him outside the store, Danny's friend attacked him with the tire iron. The security guard ran but Danny completely lost his cool and chased him down to beat him some more. They stole the guard's wallet, then took off running through downtown Regina until they were caught by police. Danny was charged with armed robbery, assault with a weapon, and theft under $5,000.

The robbery triggered what's known as a sensational incident report, which is sent all the way up to the federal public safety minister in Ottawa, mainly because Danny was a violent offender on parole. Danny was locked up for about a week in the Regina provincial correctional centre and then placed in a halfway house to serve the last two weeks of his three-year sentence for threatening the witnesses in Richard's case. Once that was over in early September he moved back to Winnipeg, the heart of Indian Posse territory.

Upon his return, Danny quickly moved back into an important role with the gang: armed robberies. They were always his specialty, and he always rolled with a loaded weapon. He told Richard his modus operandi was "Strap the gat and roll with the homies."

"He loved his guns," said Angus. "There were several houses he shot up."

That fall, as part of his new role, Danny was negotiating a significant drug buy with the Hells Angels, a group that was just beginning to move into Winnipeg. The Hells, who were engaged in a high-profile war for control of the criminal underworld in Quebec, were talking to both the Indian Posse and the Manitoba Warriors, to see if one of these gangs might become their puppet club. The aboriginal gang would do the low-end, street-level work and the Hells Angels would provide the drug supplies and direction. The Hells Angels were run by adults, men in their thirties and forties, and considered by police to be a more sophisticated criminal organization than the Indian Posse, which was viewed as a loose association of young, unsophisticated stick-up crews.

The meeting was set to take place at a hotel on Portage Avenue in Winnipeg. The motorcycle gang had rented a room for what was meant to be a preliminary meeting for the two sides to negotiate the size of the cocaine purchase. Danny, however, suspected that the Hells would have the drugs with them, and at the last minute, he decided to scrap the meeting and just rob them of the drugs.

Flanked by four other Indian Posse members, Danny walked into the hotel and headed for the elevator. They waited anxiously for the doors to open. Once inside they tied their red bandanas over their faces and rode up to the floor. This was a crazy idea, but Danny thought it would be so unexpected it would work, and to hell with the consequences.

"[Danny and his crew] had the guns out first," said one person with knowledge of the heist. "[They] just went in there, stuck a gun to them and asked them for their cash and their stuff and then left."

They made off with a few thousand dollars in cash and several more thousand dollars' worth of coke. A simple robbery, but one that was not well thought out. It sparked retaliation by the Hells Angels. Indian Posse houses were shot up in drive-bys and the Posse responded with drive-bys of their own, many of them led by Danny himself.

Angus describes Danny as someone the gang could rely on, a trusted leader. The people he worked with believed in him because of the generosity he showed them. He was dangerous, but he was a good person to have on your side, Angus said. "When things had to be done [he] would walk into houses, break down doors, stick guns to people's heads. If you need a vehicle he'll go steal a vehicle or if we're down [short money on a drug deal] he'll go make it up by doing a robbery or a break and enter. If somebody got caught doing a deal and got caught with the product Danny [would repay their debts himself.]"

In early October 1998, Danny got a call from a friend inviting him to a bar on Main Street, just north of the Indian Posse's territory in the North End. The friend said there were some girls he knew at the bar who had just been to see some male strippers and were looking for companionship.

Danny arrived at the bar around 11:00 p.m. in full Indian Posse mode: gold jewellery, sunglasses, hair down to his shoulders. A nineteen-year-old girl named Lisa pulled out a chair for him to sit next to her. She was slim with striking blue eyes, tanned skin, and curly, brown hair. "You sit down right here," she said with a smile.

She didn't know who he was, but she could tell there was something intriguing about him. She was instantly drawn in. "He had the long hair, the tattoos, the attitude," Lisa said. She'd also heard about the Wolfe brothers over the years as the Indian Posse grew.

She went to the bar, ordered four beers, and brought them back to the table, placing all four glasses in front of him. "Drink up," she said. "You've got a lot of catching up to do."

The group drank and talked all night and took the after-party back to Lisa's cousin's place. From then on she and Danny were inseparable. Danny was under the impression she was "some little white girl," she said. In fact, she was indigenous and had grown up in the North End during the burst of gang activity that gripped the neighbourhood in the early 1990s. Danny asked Sam-Boo if he knew anything about her. She was okay, Sam-Boo told him, but Lisa had her own troubled past.

"I have my dark side," she said. "I come from a long line of crazy shit."

Her father was heavily involved in crime and her mother was facing a narcotics-trafficking charge. Lisa was already a mother herself but had issues with alcohol and had lost custody of her child. She knew Danny's brother Richard had played an important role in the gang, so she had some idea of Danny's reputation. His whole family had a kind of aura about them, she said, and she was attracted to Danny. From the day they met, the pair embarked on a thrill-ride that was filled with drugs, sex, and robbery.

"My dad never wanted me to be with someone like that and that's exactly what I picked . . . [Danny and I would] sleep all day. He'd go out and come back with a [stolen] car and we'd go for a ride. It was one fun time," she said. "We'd go pick up some weed, pick up some beers."

Danny later estimated that he was drunk every day in this two-month period with Lisa, consuming somewhere between six and twenty-four beers per day. The relationship is a hazy memory, Lisa says now, but it was a fantastic time. Her dangerous new boyfriend had a lot of money and they did a lot of partying. She'd never had fun like that.

He kept his criminal activity mostly secret, but she could only assume that during their time together he was moving drugs and doing heists. She knew what the Indian Posse was about, and she also knew it was wise not to ask questions.

"I grew up in the North End," she said, as if that was the only explanation required. "All my friends were part of that [gang] situation. My dad always taught me to keep what you know to yourself."

About two weeks after they met, Danny and Lisa travelled to Regina, where Danny had some ongoing gang business. They stayed for two weeks, sleeping at a place that belonged to one of his relatives.

"He did his thing, but I didn't really know about what was going on . . . We kept all that on the down low so nobody could ask me anything," Lisa said. "I knew a bit [of the business side of the gang] but I didn't want to know. I wanted to be with him for who he was, not what he did or who he knew or whatever power he had."

Danny was charming, kind, and considerate. It was a relationship unlike any she had experienced before – exciting, passionate, and dangerous. Was she in love? She was too young to know what love was, she said. But she has only glowing things to say about him.

"It was the best. I had so much fun. I never up and left and went to a different province like that before. Or since," she said. "He was the most amazing person I ever met in my life. He had a wicked sense of humour. He wouldn't ever show me the gang side of him. He was such a real person. He wasn't fake. He didn't put on a show for you."

Her memories of Danny are obviously contradictory. She describes him as real and genuine, but also says he concealed the animating feature of his life: his gang membership. It's clear that Danny worked hard at being able to reconcile the two. He is described by nearly everyone as very pleasant, likeable, and polite. Teachers and parole officers wanted to believe in him. He was intelligent, at times deferential, even charming – but he was also a ruthless criminal who was prepared to do anything for the Indian Posse.

Lisa remembers Danny's pain and frustration over one particular incident that he felt he could have prevented. In 1998, a two-year-old child living not far from where they were staying on Toronto Street in the inner city was the victim of domestic abuse. A man who was angry with his girlfriend snatched her young son from his bed, beat him, hid the child in a randomly chosen van that happened to have been unlocked, and left him outdoors to die in freezing temperatures. The police searched for the child but they couldn't find him in time to save him. By coincidence Danny and Lisa had been in the area around the same time and hadn't noticed anything amiss. Danny was upset that he didn't save the child, to the point that he was haunted by it, Lisa said. Perhaps it hit especially close to home because of his own experience of violence and abandonment as a child.

The relationship with Lisa was intense, much like everything else in Danny's life. In December Lisa was feeling unwell and went to the doctor. She discovered she was pregnant. It was a surprise; another child was not necessarily what she had had in mind. She and Danny had been together for such a short time, barely two months – did she really know him? A child was a lifelong commitment. She was only nineteen and her life was not in the best shape. She was still trying to get full access to her daughter from child protection authorities. What to do?

Her head spinning with questions, Lisa went to Danny's Aunt Connie's house to find him. He wasn't there, but while she was there she got a phone call – Danny was under arrest. He had been charged with armed robbery and home invasion and he wasn't going to get bail. Lisa felt even more confused and alone.

That night Danny had been drinking with some of his Indian Posse brothers. They had been pounding back beers for a few hours, sitting around a table at the Concord Hotel on McPhillips Street. It was a grimy, dimly lit bar room with stained floors and a stage that advertised strip shows under the euphemism "Jamboree."

At closing time the group bought some more beer at the hotel's off-licence window and returned to the house on Toronto Street where Danny was staying. They drank some more until talk eventually turned to a drug debt that was owed to one of the three others. They decided it was time to collect.

The four of them, very drunk, piled into a van and drove a short distance to a house on Sherburn, a tidy street in a blue-collar part of town. Danny pulled a balaclava over his head. One accomplice slipped on a set of brass knuckles. Another held a sawed-off shotgun at his side. They knocked on the door at 2:45 a.m.

A man came to the door but, sensing trouble, he wouldn't open up. Undeterred, Danny and company kicked the door down and forced their way inside. The man turned and ran as the pack chased him through the house. They caught up to him in a back bedroom and punched him in the face, splitting his eyebrow under the weight of the brass knuckles. Then they delivered a blow that left a fist-sized imprint on his chest.

The four forced their way past him to find a woman, an admitted drug dealer and someone who owed the Indian Posse money. It's not clear if it was Danny who held the gun to the woman's head. The gang tied both victims up. Danny slipped the man's watch off his wrist and took a gold-and-diamond ring off his finger. Both went into Danny's pocket. Meanwhile, his companions ransacked the house, looking for valuables to collect. Danny went to check on their progress, issuing a warning to the man and woman before he left the room: "If he sticks his head out of the door I'll kill him. I'll shoot him in the head."

The four rounded up anything they could carry off and sell. Danny grabbed a television set in a bear hug and headed out the door. The others took three VCRs, a stereo, and a Sony PlayStation. It amounted to a little less than $5,000 worth of stuff, far less than would have seemed worthwhile, but the Indian Posse wanted to send a message: drug debts had to be paid.

Police, alerted by a 911 call, arrived on the scene within a few minutes and Danny was spotted carrying the TV set. The cops gave chase and Danny dumped the TV and started to run. Just before they took him down and placed him in handcuffs, the officers saw him throw the balaclava over a fence. When they searched his pockets they found the victim's ring.

Later that night Danny fell asleep in a chair while waiting to be questioned at the police station. He had already admitted to being an Indian Posse member, so he was handed over to the street gang unit for further interrogation. He sat across from a detective in the interview room and groggily answered questions. He displayed no sympathy for the people he had just terrorized. The victim was a drug dealer who deserved it, he told them.

"Business is business," Danny said. Debts must be paid.

Psychologists said Danny minimized the offence. He blamed the victims. He claimed it wasn't his intention to harm anyone, but he conceded the victims were "probably freaked out and terrified" (a report described their "high levels of psychological harm"). There was a lot of what the psychologist described as cognitive distortion in Danny's thinking. For example, he blamed the justice system for "labelling" him as a gang member. And, under the heading of "Motivation," the psychologist wrote, "subject identifies primary loyalty to a street gang."

Just talking about the crime afterward made Danny mad, he told a prison official, because it was stupid to get caught. His drinking and subsequent lack of judgment had cost him.

The evidence against him was substantial. Danny pleaded guilty fairly quickly, within two months of his arrest, and his sentencing hearing was held in Winnipeg on March 16, 1999. At the time, home invasion robberies were a focus of media attention and government concern, and stiffer sentences were being handed down, often to Indian Posse members, as part of a deterrence campaign. The Crown and Danny's defence lawyer agreed in a joint submission that Danny's sentence should be in the range of seven to ten years.

At the age of twenty-two, Danny stood before a judge as the details of his life were laid before the court.

"He has had a rather difficult upbringing," Danny's lawyer said, a significant understatement.

He read from a report prepared in 1991, when Danny was fifteen: Father in the penitentiary; mother and father separated because the father abused her and the children; both had serious alcohol addictions. Mother's subsequent relationship was also violent and marred by alcohol addiction. She was described as a binge drinker who sometimes became violent when drunk.

In his assessments, the psychologist concluded that "disruptions and deprivations suffered during the first two and a half years of life" had left Danny with only a limited ability to connect to people. He was often at a loss with his own internal regulation, the psychologist wrote, and needed intensive programming for his psychological issues. The report was submitted as a mitigating factor for the judge to consider.

"Seven years [in prison] is being asked for by the defence. That's a very significant period of time, on top of the three months of dead time that he's done. It seems to me that given his youth and given his record as it is, although not enviable, it's not the kind that's rife with violence or parole or probation breaches, that given that kind of background, that really the [sentence should be at the] lower end of the scale," Danny's lawyer said in court.

The judge asked for a ten-minute recess to weigh a sentence that could send Danny away for as long as a decade.

"In mitigation the accused is yet a youthful offender at twenty-two years of age," the judge said. "His background is, as unfortunately so many of the cases that we see in the criminal courts, indeed very unfortunate, replete with alcoholism, and violence and child abuse in his earlier years. A father in the penitentiary, drug and alcohol abuse, all of these common elements that so frequently contribute to the development of an antisocial young person who, for various reasons, then resorts to various criminal acts."

The sentence he ordered was in the middle range for comparable crimes but higher than Danny expected. The Crown asked that Danny be blocked from applying for parole, but the judge refused.

"I'm reluctant to predict the kind of person [Daniel Wolfe] will be in a few years time," the judge said.

Danny was sentenced to seven years in the federal penitentiary, time enough to change – or to become an angrier, more dangerous person.

time he reached adulthood, Ervin had a lot of experience manoeu-vring at the lower levels of criminality, selling drugs in relatively small amounts as an independent dealer. He was working at a bar in Winnipeg that was connected to the reserve in Pine Creek, Manitoba. The bouncers were given black satin jackets that bore the logo of the Pine Creek minor hockey team, the Warriors. An older guy joined the crew of bouncers and quickly went about organizing them into a gang. This guy was already big-time, with a drug network that extended all the way up north. He saw that the local drug distributurs were taking advantage of his young bouncer friends, who often had to pay too high a price for supplies and were then getting robbed of their drugs. The gang began calling themselves the Manitoba Warriors.

As they carved out a niche for themselves, the Warriors became part of the wave of gang crime that swept Winnipeg in the 1990s, unleashing more violence. They were at war with "pretty much every gang in the city," Ervin said. They started recruiting to cope with the needs of a growing enterprise. The new bodies were all at the lower rungs, strikers and hang-arounds, people who could perform debt col-lection, drug dealing, and intimidation. The gang had a policy that ran counter to that of the Indian Posse: they wouldn't recruit anyone under eighteen. Before long the Overlords, the gang that had been at war with the Indian Posse in central Winnipeg, began to make over-tures about joining forces with the Warriors. Most of the Overlords' leadership patched over to the Warriors in the mid 1990s.

By 1997, the Warriors were heavily involved with outlaw motor-cycle gangs and had adopted their leadership structure. Ervin was vice-president in 1998, joined on the gang's executive, police alleged, by president William Pangman and treasurer Izzy Vermette.

When they got involved in a bitter political struggle over control of the Waterhen reserve in central Manitoba, the Warriors became a much more pressing concern for law enforcement. Waterhen, a reserve of a few hundred people, is located three hundred kilometres north-west of Winnipeg. In 1996, the reserve's chief, Harvey Nepinak, was under constant pressure from a group of dissidents to open the band's books and explain its finances. In response to the growing tension, he moved his own supporters, at band expense, to hotels in the nearby town of Dauphin, leaving his opponents on the reserve. The federal government refused to intervene to end the stalemate, saying it was an internal matter. Into the mix stepped the Manitoba Warriors, brought in by the dissident faction to act as security. What they did isn't clear, but their mere presence in a political dispute set alarm bells ringing. Criminal Intelligence Service Canada warned that this event, in com-bination with their role in the rebellion at the Headingley prison, indi-cated that aboriginal gangs were gaining increased legitimacy in the community. As dissatisfaction with federal policies around native peo-ples was expected to increase, it could provide ideological cover for the gangs' illicit activities, Criminal Intelligence Service Canada said.

The rise of the Warriors and the Indian Posse presented an inter-esting problem for native leaders. The gang issue had become so per-vasive they simply could not avoid addressing it, yet they were resistant to what they saw as unfair labelling of native youth. If a dozen friends are together and commit a crime, is that a gang crime? asked national chief Ovide Mercredi. Were they being treated by the media and police as faceless gangsters, as people without names or motives or families or life stories, simply because they were indigenous?

Mercredi, national chief of the Assembly of First Nations from 1991 to 1997, was Canada's highest-ranking native leader. In October 1996, he requested a meeting at Headingley with the leadership of the Indian Posse and Manitoba Warriors. The meeting lent legiti-macy to the gangs and was a risk for a respected national figure like

Mercredi. Dan Lett of the *Winnipeg Free Press* wrote that Mercredi said afterward that he "was convinced the young aboriginal men representing these gangs were true leaders in their community."

It's a powerful phrase. The upper echelons of the Indian Posse, Danny included, undoubtedly displayed some of the characteristics of leadership. But they used their influence to further a criminal enterprise based on prostitution, drug dealing, violence, and intimidation. It was unexpected to hear them portrayed in those terms by Mercredi, who was a lawyer by training. He said that few were hardcore criminals, in his view, and that most were trying to find a real job away from the life of crime foisted on them by the extreme poverty in which they were raised.

Dan Lett wrote: "Mercredi said he found the gang members unexpectedly spiritual and fully fluent in aboriginal culture and prayers. Sessions in jail usually opened with a prayer and with the burning of sweet grass, he added.

"The gang members claimed they had banded together to create a sense of brotherhood or collective security against a world many of them felt had excluded them from basic opportunities to learn and work."

Years later, Mercredi said the gangs were undoubtedly a disastrous development that brought misery and destruction to countless lives, but that his first goal was to stop them from shooting each other. That's why he met with them. He hoped the gang and its leaders, who were clearly capable and disciplined, would redirect their energies from drug dealing and prostitution to combating racism and trying to lift their people out of poverty.

"I still think they have the capacity to help that cause," he said.

In 1996, Phil Fontaine was Grand Chief of the Assembly of Manitoba Chiefs, and he, too, got involved in the gang discussion. He was ambitious, a rival of Mercredi's and just a few years away from beginning a long tenure as national chief himself. As Mercredi tried to negotiate a truce between the gangs, Fontaine began meeting with a former leader of the Manitoba Warriors named Brian Contois. In an effort to tackle the gang problem, they planned to buy an old Young Men's Hebrew Association building and convert it to a young people's centre that could provide a positive environment for Winnipeg's aboriginal youth. Fontaine hired Contois as an adviser on a three-month contract, a move that raised eyebrows at police headquarters, particularly after Contois said he wasn't prepared to renounce the gang life until he had a solid, long-term job offer. Fontaine even arranged a meeting that brought together a skeptical police chief (David Cassels), Contois, and another Manitoba Warrior gang member. Later it became clear that the meeting was in itself a violation of Contois's parole conditions, because he was forbidden to be in contact with known gang members.

Fontaine pitched his proposal as a nonjudgmental approach to a thorny issue: "We see this as therapeutic for our community. We're not legitimizing gangs, but the fact of the matter is that they exist. And they exist for two main reasons – poverty and discrimination," Fontaine told the *Free Press*. "All we're trying to do is to give people a real apparatus and a choice for themselves to deal with the problem. I don't know how people can be critical of that."

A short time after that meeting, Cassels publicly indicated a level of cautious optimism about the prospects of working with Fontaine and known gang members. He was quickly warned by vice squad officers that Contois had been recently overheard on wiretaps arranging a drug deal. The police chief toned down his public enthusiasm but he couldn't warn Fontaine without compromising the investigation. A few weeks after Contois was hired by Fontaine, police moved in on Contois and charged him with drug trafficking.

Fontaine's initiative was in tatters.

David Cassels's tenure as police chief lasted from 1996 to 1999. He was brought to Winnipeg from Edmonton, shortly after the Richard Wolfe trial, the shooting of thirteen-year-old Beeper Spence, and the Headingley riot, a trio of events that ramped up the attention paid to street gangs. He was hired to implement a neighbourhood policing strategy that sought to improve safety by getting police officers out of their cars and closer to the people they were policing. After the shooting of J.J. Harper in 1988, the city felt the force needed a new approach to restore public confidence, particularly among the rapidly growing First Nations population. Cassels said that from his first meeting with the city's mayor, Susan Thomson, and the city commissioners, he could sense that "gang activity and a fear of gangs were a major preoccupation."

"The fear of crime in Winnipeg was growing. There was a tremendous amount of coverage in the media," he said.

He had a problem. Politicians thought that the gangs were primarily a police issue and that police could drive the gangs out of business fairly quickly – it was just a question of selecting the right strategy.

Nothing could be further from the truth, Cassels said. Usually, once gangs have taken hold in a city, it's too late. The issues that give rise to youth gangs – poverty, discrimination, family dysfunction, abuse – have typically been festering for years and cannot be solved quickly or easily; nor do they have much to do with policing. "The police are left with the destruction and asked to clean up the pieces," Cassels said.

"I remember the mayor expressed very serious concerns about the state of relations with the aboriginal community. My objective was to bring the police closer to the aboriginal community and to the city administration," Cassels said. "The police as an institution were not highly regarded."

Cassels's philosophy was based on close contact between police and civilians. He wanted his officers working with local citizens to solve problems, instead of following their traditional enforcement-first approach. The shift in emphasis was greeted with skepticism in the rank and file, many of whose members thought the new ideas were foolish.

"The mentality in policing is terrible," Cassels said. "Enforce the law and feed the failing criminal justice system. . . . [Policing] is not just about arresting people. That's not how relationships work. You have to do something meaningful for the people you serve. A police officer's role in a democracy is to help people, not just put them in jail."

Cassels arrived in Winnipeg to face what he called "a unique situation." More and more First Nations families were leaving the reserves to live in Winnipeg, but far too many couldn't find work in the city. They fell into a cycle of poverty and substance abuse – one often closely linked to domestic violence, the removal of children into state care, and the subsequent repercussive waves that ripple down the generations. Contrary to Cassels's description, the situation wasn't unique. The migration of First Nations people to the cities accelerated across Canada in the 1980s and 1990s; Winnipeg just felt its impact most acutely.

"I sensed right away that there was a lack of opportunity [for aboriginal people]. There was discrimination," Cassels said. "Among businesses there was very strong reluctance to hire these young people."

What he was met with was shocking even to a veteran police officer. For example, a young man was beaten to death, his head stomped into a pulp, merely because he was spotted walking past the home of a rival gang at 4:00 a.m. Killings tended to be like that in the Winnipeg gang wars: up close, brutal, and vicious; knifings, beatings, point-blank shootings. There's no separating the act from the consequences when you kill in close quarters. Citizens were afraid and that fear became the chief's problem.

"The level of violence was horrific," he said. "Higher than anything I'd ever experienced."

He held six community consultations where he listened to public concerns. He tried to calm their fears with a reasoned statement about risk. The city might seem unsafe, given the horror stories, but as long as citizens avoided the drinking parties in the most dangerous part of town, the threat of actually being the victim of violence was relatively low, he told them. In 1997 police reported that one-third of the emergency calls they received came from a four-block stretch of the inner city, Young-Furby-Langside-Spence – the streets that were the cradle of the Indian Posse.

"If you are able to avoid the drinking parties on Langside Street and don't make an unfortunate choice of spouses, your chances of being murdered in Winnipeg are virtually none," Cassels told the local paper. "Still, people have the perception that violent crime is increasing."

In the *Winnipeg Free Press*, columnist Terry Moore offered an assessment that seemed to resonate with many in the city:

> Winnipeg is home to a growing class of native adolescents of little education and unstable family background for whom the city offers very little in the way of constructive activity. No employer will hire them. No government will take responsibility for them. Few agencies take an interest in them. The Indian Posse and the Manitoba Warriors offer them personal acceptance, excitement, status and better economic security than is available to them elsewhere. Is it any wonder that they take the easiest path and turn to crime?
>
> . . . the social phenomenon of rootless, hopeless native adolescents is growing in our midst. That is a part of what Winnipeggers mean when they tell David Cassels that crime is increasing. It is no answer to say that most Winnipeggers do not murder each other. The authorities refuse to discuss the matter but the people know it is true. The longer we go on ignoring it, the tougher it will be to deal with.

Month after month, Cassels said, the intelligence unit came to him with new reports of increased gang activity. The number of known gang members kept rising, from 1,000 to 1,200 to 1,500. This was not something a Canadian city had seen before. In Winnipeg, officials were desperate to put a stop to the growth of these gangs – but how? Cassels believed that the answer, as difficult as it would be, would come from the combined effort of government, business, and social agencies that would provide opportunities for young indigenous people. But in order to even begin that kind of work they needed to carve out safe space – community centres and schools and local streets that could be reclaimed from the gangs – because in too many parts of the city the gang members had become the role models, the most noticeable adult presence, and the most likely source of employment.

Cassels's signature project, launched in late 1996, aimed at reclaiming a neighbourhood that had fallen under the control of the Indian Posse. He commissioned a single officer, Constable Dan Atwell, to patrol the Lord Selkirk Park Housing Development and make it his own personal police district, the way a beat cop of another era would have done. This was the same area the Wolfe brothers had dubbed Little Chicago when they were younger, and dozens of Indian Posse members lived and worked in the area. Their attitude suggested they ran the district with impunity.

On day one there was fanfare. The public housing body held a ceremony of welcome for Constable Atwell; the local media descended and there were stories of celebration and hope. On day two Atwell was on his own. Still relatively young and definitely nervous, he started getting to know the area, the "concrete teepees," as some locals called it. He was just one man, with no squad car, in an area populated by dozens of pretty tough gang members.

"It was scary as hell," he admitted.

It was Atwell's job to win over the local population. The hope was that together they could make life so miserable for the Posse that the gang would pack up and leave. He started with the crack houses; just by observing the pattern of people's movements it was easy to figure out where the drugs were being sold, and he shut them down one at a time. But, like whack-a-moles, they kept popping up elsewhere, so he quickly learned to employ different techniques. Sometimes he sent the health inspector or the building inspector to the houses. Another time he set up a lawn chair in front of an IP crack house and sat there for an entire day and night, driving away customers with his presence. He got some threats, but no one ever acted on them.

The gang tried to learn his schedule so they could avoid him but Atwell countered by being unpredictable. He varied his hours and worked an odd pattern of days and nights. He talked and cajoled and just plain showed up to every event to build trust with community members. "It was a completely foreign model of policing," he said.

It wasn't long before the community started to warm to him. They had spent years feeling captive in their own neighbourhood and they wanted help cleaning it up.

"When people are in a desperate situation, they're looking for that safety, that person they can trust that's going to come in and protect them," Atwell said.

He became a fixture in the neighbourhood. Everyone knew him, and he knew them. He was like a local politician. He was asked to sit on the board of fourteen different community organizations. But there were obviously tensions with the Indian Posse. One day he was at a burger joint on Selkirk Avenue that had a problem with Indian Posse members who would intimidate customers. That day three Posse members arrived while Atwell was inside. The owner pointed them out as they approached the restaurant and Atwell headed them off in the doorway.

He told them they weren't coming in. The leader of the trio was not having it, but he backed away, which led Atwell to take a step outside toward him. All of a sudden it was clear this was heading toward a confrontation. The leader started signalling to the other two to start flanking the officer, hoping to encircle him. Atwell retreated so as to keep his back to the wall as the three of them advanced. He got nervous. He was outnumbered and they weren't backing down. He grabbed for his service revolver, a .38 calibre with a skinny barrel, lifted it to shoulder height, and tried to stick it in the leader's face to back him off, but the standoff continued. Then he jabbed the gun barrel into the leader's mouth, hitting him with enough force to chip his tooth, Atwell recalled. After that the trio retreated.

"There were times when the challenge was put in front of you to see if you're tough enough to be there," he said. "The older people and the children, they wanted me to succeed. They were very good to me. It was the sixteen- to thirty-year-olds, that was the demographic that was the danger."

The Indian Posse didn't seem particularly well organized to him. It was more like an assortment of loosely associated cells, all of them calling themselves IP but with uncertain relationships. And this was largely true of the Indian Posse much of the time. These cells could assist each other if necessary, but they could just as easily be rivals for drug sales or status within the larger organization.

"There were so many factions of the Indian Posse," he said. "There might have been 500 members, but in 250 groups. I'm exaggerating, but it was something like that . . . Because they carried the Indian Posse name they caused fear."

Of all the things he witnessed in his four years on the beat, Atwell was most distressed by the number of young girls selling sex on the street to fund the gang's operations. Whenever he became aware of another girl working the streets, Atwell opened a new file. He said it was typical to have files on fifty girls at any one time, and on a given day as many as thirty would be working. Most were addicted to drugs – they charged some of the lowest prices in the city, Atwell said. Some were also incredibly young. Those in the nine- to sixteen-year-old range were able to charge more, he said.

Soon after he arrived in the area he started hearing about an Indian Posse member in his twenties who was recruiting girls for sex work. The man's name was Robert, and he appeared to have a mid-level rank in the gang, which was fairly high in comparison to other Posse members in the area; he also seemed to be running local drug sales. Robert's recruiting pitch amounted to targeting girls who did not live with their mothers (the separation often due to circumstances that were themselves inherently destabilizing, such as family violence or a parent's addiction or incarceration). The girls he went after were often as young as thirteen or fourteen and were being raised by their grandmothers. Robert would walk into the apartment as if he owned the place and throw a stack of condoms on the table for dramatic effect. Then he'd tell the girls to "get their asses out on the street" – they'd be working for him now.

The final straw for Atwell was the case of a six-year-old girl he used to walk to school. He won't describe what happened to her; he said that someone hurt her, and then he was overcome by emotion. After a time the beat got to be too much for him and Atwell moved on to a new job in a new district. He hasn't set foot in the Lord Selkirk area since.

Atwell is not one to sympathize with the excuses or explanations that Indian Posse gang members offer for their actions. Residential schools, poverty, addiction, abuse – none of them is convincing in his view. He didn't hold out hope for the sixteen- to thirty-year-olds he was policing, but it was the little ones who deserved better, who might have been able to break the cycle, he said.

"The Roberts of the world, these are mean, mean people. That doesn't reform, in my view," he said. "The adults had already made their beds. I knew there was no fixing them. I think the place to break the cycle was with the children. Give them goals, give them dreams, let them see what their potential was. Their potential was not their uncle. It was to be Wayne Gretzky, to be a leader in their community. That's what I wanted to happen."

The community policing program instituted by David Cassels carried on for a time but gradually disappeared after his depature. Cassels retired early, after a dispute with the police union led to an illegal walkout by officers in 1999. The conflict became so ugly that there was a four-hour stretch when not a single police officer patrolled the streets of Winnipeg. He considers the neighbourhood policing project in Lord Selkirk his most notable achievement. But he is also remembered for Operation Northern Snow.

The court proceedings against the fifty accused from Northern Snow dragged on for years. Some chiefs accused the justice system of racism after most were denied bail, even though they faced mainly drug charges. A special high-security courthouse was built to accommodate the large number of accused, but it was controversial in itself, since the special location and unusual courtroom design might prejudice a jury.

In the end, nearly all the accused made plea deals with the Crown. The plea bargains and relatively short sentences were treated as a failure by the press, particularly with respect to the new anti-gang legislation. The Crown defended the arrangements by saying it faced a number of obstacles to getting convictions at trial. Ervin Chartrand received an eight-year sentence for cocaine trafficking, the longest sentence of any of the accused. The gang was just a way of life in his time, he said. Today he has reformed and works as a filmmaker.

He's not an anti-gang campaigner, he says, because he understands the conditions that lead young indigenous people to join gangs. Instead he tries to follow traditional teachings and counsels others to avoid the violent life he knew.

Through the mid 1990s, while incidents of organized crime were falling across the country, they rose in Winnipeg, according to a 2010 report prepared for Public Safety Canada. The public perception of whether crime was rising or falling started to improve after the Northern Snow arrests, and the number of organized crime incidents also declined. The report concludes that it's quite likely this is evidence of the operation's positive impact.

12

LOVE AND TRUST BEHIND BARS
1999–2001

The first jail term in a federal penitentiary is usually the most important. As one psychologist with more than twenty-five years' experience in the Canadian prison system put it, those who receive a second sentence almost inevitably reoffend, "but a number of people come to jail once and learn from the experience and never return."

Danny was back for a second tour in June of 1999. Prison evaluators ran the rule over him again. He was a borderline candidate for a maximum-security prison, but they decided to give him the benefit of the doubt and maintain his classification at medium. He was still young, just shy of his twenty-third birthday, and he was typically cooperative and good-natured with authorities. Though he was allowed to stay at Stony Mountain, the native elder noted on his file that the time for games was over: Danny would either grow up and reform or he would sink deeper into the morass of the gang.

Privately, there were signs that Danny was a changed man. Lisa's pregnancy brought out a new side to his personality: he was caring and thoughtful in his letters to her; he phoned her almost daily. He talked of wanting to change, to get an education and get away from the gang influences in the city and start a new life on the reserve.

In a letter to Lisa in April 1999, Danny begged her to give their relationship a chance. He was anxious that she'd leave him, now that he faced seven years behind bars. He gushed about the baby's impending arrival, sympathized about the heartache she felt for her older child, who was still in the care of family services, and described the home invasion that put him in jail as a mistake – a rare admission.

Lisa asked him whether his gang brothers, the ones he claimed he trusted and loved, would be there for either of them now that he was in jail. In essence she was asking what his devotion was worth; the gang demands a lot and provides very little for those who pay a price on its behalf.

"I thought about this for a long time and you're right," Danny wrote in reply. "But I also don't look at it that way. I mean, if I'm in trouble I know I have back up with me instead of being six feet under," he said. "You know who I am and what I'm about but that stuff has nothing to do with our relationship. It's something I can't change."

He promised that things would get better. "In the long run people get older and have kids and go back to school and get jobs and then maybe things will change . . . right now it's just the fast lane for everyone. For myself I know I'm going to have to change because [of] that little monkey in your belly. I want to be there for you and him that's all I ever think about now."

A few weeks later he asked Lisa whether her feelings for him were genuine and used double question marks to emphasize his doubt. He seemed to think she might be more attracted to his money and his status in the gang than to him personally.

"Do you really like me besides the way I treat you?? Or do you like me more than that?? And do you like the kinda person I am?? Besides me being down with [the Indian Posse]. And am I the kinda guy you would want to stay with?? Or live with? . . . Why don't you tell me some things that I should do to keep you happy. Or should I just be me? I'm [not] saying I want to be someone else . . . I just want to stand on common ground with you. And make sure things work out."

It's understandable that someone starting a long prison sentence would want reassurance, but the level of openness and caring he showed is remarkable. This is the same Danny Wolfe who had demonstrated an enormous capacity for violent, uncaring behaviour – at least fourteen wanton drive-by shootings, by his brother's count – and who had twice threatened to kill someone while holding a loaded gun. The exchanges with Lisa hinted at the contradictory forces in Danny's character.

Their baby boy arrived in midsummer. Danny was overjoyed. Lisa brought their son to Stony Mountain a couple of weeks after he was born and Danny couldn't stop talking about how much the child looked like him. The photos taken that day show them together as a family for the first time behind prison walls. Danny is dressed in a white prison-issue T-shirt with WOLFE, D written on the chest pocket. His long hair is tied back under a white-and-green bandana and he's smiling slightly. The child rests in his mother's lap while Danny extends a protective hand around the baby. Lisa is wearing a football jersey in Indian Posse colours. She squints in the summer sun. Her smile seems hesitant, full of doubt. Later, Danny chided her for looking so unhappy in the pictures.

Lisa was nineteen years old, unemployed, and still trying to finish high school. When a parole officer dropped by to assess her for family visits to the prison, Lisa said she didn't know much of Danny's criminal history. What she did know didn't concern her, she said: "Everyone has problems." In her view Danny was a really nice guy, cautious and timid rather than a thrill-seeker. He had never been abusive. Most of their conversations were about their son, their goals for him, and how they wanted to raise him. The parole officer concluded that Lisa was a young woman with a lot of hope and a great many problems to overcome.

Six days after Danny entered general population at Stony Mountain, prison intelligence officials got word from an informant that he was already playing an instrumental role in smuggling drugs into the jail. The note on his file indicates that the officials suspected the drugs were coming in via visitors.

A former Indian Posse member who worked closely with Danny explained how the prison drug market operated. Since currency was scarce in jail, there had to be a trusted medium of exchange to make a deal, which meant someone on the outside had to act as Danny's banker. The buyers in jail called someone on the outside, persuaded them to get money to Danny's banker, and then, once the banker had the cash, Danny would release the drugs. It sounds like a slow process, but if Danny trusted the buyer it could be sped up. More importantly, it eliminated the need to rely on barter or inferior currencies such as cigarettes and made it possible to push prices higher, often ten times higher than street value. Cocaine, heroin, steroids, amphetamines, marijuana, hash – they were all big sellers. And the Indian Posse was well supplied in those days.

According to intelligence gathered by authorities inside the prison, it wasn't long before Danny was personally running the show. In late August someone the authorities described as a reliable source – possibly an informant either inside or close to the gang – identified Danny as a member of the five-person Indian Posse council, its leadership body in jail. Two weeks later another "reliable source" said Danny was one of the two highest-ranking members at Stony Mountain. At a meeting on September 12, the source said, Danny and the other members of council authorized a hit on a fellow prisoner, and shortly thereafter that prisoner was the victim of a vicious attack that put him in hospital with serious injuries. A few days later, guards had an Indian Posse member under escort, headed to a segregation cell. As he was taken away the prisoner called out to Danny to "take care of it." Danny just nodded. In a matter of hours, another prisoner approached the guards and begged to be placed in protective custody. He said Danny had called him a rat and informed him he would be murdered that night in the exercise yard. Danny as good as promised it.

Even though Danny was small, no one ever doubted his capacity for violence. The gang took hundreds of group photos at various prisons over the years and Danny always stands out as one of the shortest and skinniest. Many of the guys weigh more than 250 pounds, while Danny looks as though he could be knocked over by the breeze. But his friend Angus says that Danny was always respected, even feared.

"He looks like the kind of guy who would be pushed around, but when he has to do something, look out, because he really puts on his beat-down. It doesn't matter the size of him, he'll knock you out. He's pretty quick. I remember in Stony we were playing floor hockey and one guy hit him the wrong way or said something to him. Danny just turned around and gave it to this guy on the spot. The fight was over in ten seconds. He was out cold."

Although there was never enough evidence to charge Danny with any of the crimes he was committing in prison, the pattern was clear: he was heavily involved in violence, drug smuggling, and leading the prison's largest gang. He was a problem that had grown unmanageable, the authorities decided.

Two weeks later the prison recommended that Danny be transferred from Stony Mountain to a maximum-security jail, either in Edmonton or Prince Albert, the two options in the Prairie region. A large number of Indian Posse members were now being held at Edmonton Max, partly because they were wreaking havoc in the prison system: they had proved impossible to manage in lower-security facilities and were responsible for a number of killings and assaults.

When Danny told Lisa that a move to Edmonton was a possibility, she objected, concerned that he would get involved in more violence and pick up more charges. Danny told her not to worry, and suggested he could handle himself without her input. With his star rising in the gang, he would be increasingly able to order hits rather than have to perform them. Going to Edmonton, where many senior members were locked up, might also advance his gang career. The tension between Lisa and Danny over the move was not unlike that of a couple that has one partner up for a transfer at work.

Prisoners call segregation "the hole," a place that bends your sense of time and tests your sanity, like a deep darkness from which you might or might not emerge intact. There's little contact with the outside world. You might be without the familiar possessions of your cell. There's next to no sense of normalcy. Exercise is limited to one hour per day in the bullpen, an enclosed structure that affords not much more than a glimpse of the sky. It's the hardest way to do time in the Canadian prison system and Danny waited for months in segregation to learn where he would be transferred. The psychological impacts of extended time in solitary confinement can be devastating. In some prisons, as many as half the inmates in solitary display mental health problems, and nearly half the suicides in the Canadian prison system take place in these segregation units. Danny tried to be philosophical. "I did the crime I can do my time. As long as I got my tunes and t.v. I'm ok," he told his brother.

With twenty-three lonely hours to kill every day, Danny spent a lot of time writing letters, often to his mother, brother, or Lisa. He also maintained a network of correspondents to keep tabs on the goings-on within the gang. What he was hearing increasingly disturbed him, and for the first time he betrayed doubts about his fellow gang members and questioned how the Indian Posse leadership was handling its affairs.

"There's a lot of shit happening, all over bullshit stuff," he wrote to Richard. "I just keep my ass out of it and keep strong for myself. Too many fucked up people recruiting fucked up people."

Danny wanted to see some consequences for those who brought bad apples into the fold. Or, he suggested, maybe it was time to send a stronger, albeit cutthroat, message: An internal cleansing. "Just take out some of our bros so everyone knows we mean business," he said.

It's clear from Danny's letters that there was a lot of intrigue percolating inside the gang. Plotting, killing, informing to the police – the general pattern is evident even if the specifics are hard to discern. What's also clear is that discord was common and it contributed to a growing sense of fear and mistrust. Danny's faith was shaken. If Richard's stabbing hadn't opened his eyes to the gang's capricious nature, then the latest trouble did the trick. "You don't know who to trust," he wrote.

In the same letter Danny made a quick reference, for the first time, to the killing of his closest friend, Sam-Boo. It's odd, because although Danny was devastated by his death, he mentioned it only in the last lines of a long letter, as if it just popped up in passing.

"Did you hear about Sam-Boo, he pass[ed] away. That's too bad man. I pray for the guy."

The context is what really tells the story. Danny had said he didn't know who to trust. His brother had been stabbed and was on the outs with gang leadership, and now his best friend had been killed. Reading between the lines, he must have been wondering *What next?*

Sam-Boo had been his friend since they were teenagers. Danny kept several photos of him in his cell, often of Sam-Boo wearing a big smile and a Pittsburgh Pirates jersey. His death was obviously painful for Danny, as he wrote about him in letters for years to come, but he was unable to talk much about it, at least openly. In his next letter to

Richard in February, Danny again waited until the very last paragraph to broach the subject of Sam-Boo's slaying.

"We know who did that to Sam-Boo and the same thing is going to happen to them, fuck. No matter how long it takes. [Their] time is coming," Danny said. "That was a good bro, man."

Over the next several years Danny often reminisced about his old friend. He talked about getting a photo of him blown up and framed so that he could keep him close. But he never again delved into how and why Sam-Boo died. Other Posse members denied in interviews that it was an internal killing; they attributed it to a rival gang in Alberta. The police never charged anyone, and the truth of what happened is murky. Yet in a letter to Danny three years later, an old girlfriend asked what really happened to Sam-Boo. We don't have Danny's reply to clarify the record.

On February 16, 2000, after three and a half months in segregation, Danny was finally transferred to the Saskatchewan Penitentiary, a federal prison in Prince Albert, Saskatchewan. Prince Albert, unlike Edmonton, would put him closer to his mother. "Wolfe would benefit from further developing a relationship with his mother," a parole officer wrote. "It is the lack of close familial bonding during his young years that likely contributed to the subject and his brother having founded the Indian Posse street gang."

The Sask Pen had two distinct parts: the large medium-security wing and, within the same outer walls, an older, maximum-security wing, where Danny joined at least six other Indian Posse members, some of them friends from as far back as the gang's origins in 1988. The prison was unpleasant and rundown. Danny hated it.

The Indian Posse was in charge here, too, he told Richard, but the order of prison life wasn't as well established as at Stony Mountain, and a lack of order bred more opportunities for violence. Freed from the "hole," he immediately embarked on an intense exercise program. He lifted weights five days a week and bought a vat of weight-gain powder in an attempt to add bulk. Getting big was the only thing to do if he wanted to keep out of trouble, he said. The new prison depressed him, put him on edge.

"It's cold in these cells, like someone died in them," he wrote to Lisa. "The House of Misery is what we call this place. There's always someone getting [stabbed or beaten] here. Can't even shower without the pigs [guards] watching. They have gun towers all over the place. But people still get [stabbed and beaten]. Can't go anywhere without getting a pat down. Did you ever watch that [TV show] called Oz? Well if you did then that's how it looks over here. It's pretty fucked up."

Sleep was hard to come by. At night he was tormented by mice. "I think they crawl all over me when I sleep," Danny wrote. "I got one. It was about 2:30 in the morning and the pigs were doing their walk. Fuck they must've [been] wondering what the fuck was I doing jumping around in my underwear."

The upheaval brought about by Danny's transfer and the death of Sam-Boo coincided with increasing questioning of his direction in life. He told Lisa that he wanted to show her he could be a good man and a good father.

> We have our ups and downs but there's always a way to deal with them. I feel lonely sometimes but I know there's always somebody to talk to and I know that you're there for me so that makes me happy . . . But there's some things that I have to change in my life. So while I'm here I can work on that! So don't think I'm going to be the same man when I get out.
>
> I'm going to give [our son] something that I never had when I was small. [A] dad. I know [how] it is without a dad and it wasn't good. Just my mom was there for me and my

bros so that's why I have to change and I will. It just takes time. And time is all I got.

Danny, who was twenty-four now and perhaps gaining some perspective on his own childhood, talked of how he wished he had been there to see his son born. He had been looking for his own father in the prison system for years but had never found him. Danny encouraged Lisa to go back to school and get her high school diploma. He was keen, too, to encourage her to raise their son according to native spiritual beliefs.

"That's one thing we have to follow. Because without it there's no way to healing our selves and I know how it is without it. I felt lost, like there was nothing there for me," Danny wrote. "Now I know what's out there for me. And [I know] that I ain't alone."

He wanted her to let the boy's hair grow long so he would look, in Danny's words, like "a real Indian from the rez." Here and in other references Danny suggested that he believed kids raised on reserve were purer than those tarnished by the grind of city life.

Later that year, in a vulnerable moment, he asked Lisa a question. He was looking for her approval. It's obvious that he wasn't sure whether his bad-boy status would be enough to maintain her interest and keep their family together. Lisa was already accusing him of talking to other women, gang groupies that she referred to as "hood rats." Danny offered a preposterous false choice to gauge her commitment.

Let me ask you, who would you pick. Some guy with a job and does well for himself but gets treated like a bitch? Or some guy who will do whatever it takes to keep you and stands up for himself? Well you know what I'm trying to ask. I don't know, but do you like bad guys or good guys?

They say girls like bad guys more than good guys but I can say I'm the bad guy . . . You never knew what you were getting into when you met me, hey? I know you know most of the bros and I know you had an idea . . . [but] you never pictured us having a kid. So I have to protect you both with my life and that's what I plan on doing.

Unfortunately, the relationship was steadily sliding to an unhappy end. There was anger and jealousy and neither Danny nor Lisa seemed to make the other happy. Within a year Lisa was writing letters saying the future of the relationship was "up to him." Finally Danny blew up, accusing her of making all kinds of "allegations" about his relationships with other women. "Maybe next time you write you can say something without blaming me for some bullshit," he wrote. He signed off that letter not with *Love*, but as *Yours Truly*, the first time he'd ever done so.

A few months later he was bragging to his brother Richard that he had two girls on the side: "I just hope my son's mom doesn't find out."

13

POLITICAL AWAKENING
2000–2001

From the outset the Indian Posse had embraced a political rhetoric of native pride and anti-Canadian defiance. As Danny's faith in the gang's direction wavered, he began to reveal signs of his own political awakening. In a letter to Richard he wrote that being in prison had opened his eyes to the fact that indigenous people are disproportionately over-represented in jail.

"There's too much of our people, Indians, in jail and we are still here struggling," he wrote. "Look [at] the all jails man, mostly aboriginals. That's fucked up. I like to rap about that and write about it."

Danny was a big fan of African-American hip hop star Tupac Shakur, whose CDs were among Danny's few possessions in prison. Shakur was the son of Black Panther party members and his music often contained a political message. Danny wrote at night in his cell on a yellow legal pad, and the results were at times arresting. This piece, written in 2000, contains a reference to Jeff Giles, who was killed trying to stop an Indian Posse armed robbery in Winnipeg.

How did I come up
Chin up
A young Indian with snot on my nose
Dirty rag clothes
What could I do but be a menace
Too young to put me away
Now on a journey
From the physical abuse
Survive on the streets
Young punks causin' trouble
What the fuck are you going to do
When we rip you off.
. . .
So here we go with the circle that's been going on for too long
Blame it on who, when, where, how.
Drugs. Alcohol.
On my way to my fantasy
I want big cars, nice clothes, gold.
Fuck that, steal my meal for the day.
Hey where's the party
with a bunch of lost Injuns
Conflict breaks out
Pop pop there goes
. . .
Never looked up to me now they looked down at me
Tell me I'm no good
Because I'm Indian
Never knew
The meaning of what they say
You just better hear me.
Fear me.

Because I cause destruction
To your society
With no sympathy
Fuck your public heroes
Giles who
pump on his chest
As I sit here and laugh with mad joy
He never knew the meaning of an A.R.
Proceed
Face down
Nobody move
Nobody gets hurt

And this piece is a bleak take on urban life for aboriginal people.

Enough hiding the shit we want
To know all we want is you to stop taking
Stop taking our rights
Stop taking our land
Stop taking our humanity
Stop taking our lives
Civilization is isolation
Disciplined with poverty
No tradition in urban cities
We trying to make it work
Hurt is all we feel and see
Pain is all we have
Help us grandfather and grandmother
For we have nowhere to go
Lost in this place of hate

Hate was a strong theme in Danny's writing. He hated white people, he said. When sending a letter he always placed the stamp up side down to express his contempt for the Queen and the government of Canada. The practice was widespread among inmates – Richard and other members of the Indian Posse adopted it, too, for example – but Danny wanted to make a public show of his anger and defiance, even if his dealings with authorities were usually fairly cordial. Danny explained his motivation in a letter to his brother:

"I always put my stamp upside down. It's like, Canada Who? Canada Where? Fuck Canada. We were here first. Fuck their society. I say fuck the white people."

Danny justified his own violence and thievery as retribution for the evils of Canada's colonial policies toward native people.

"I just been doing what they been doing to us for the past 100 years and more. Fucking them! Haha. We have our own society, the red society. That's all we need."

He ended one letter to his brother with this: "My clan is the Wolfe clan. Fuck Canada, this land is our people." Canada was crossed out and written upside down and backwards. He also habitually signed off with phrases such as "P.S. Fuck Canada." Richard, in a similar vein, used to hang a Canadian flag upside down in his cell. He also got a maple leaf tattooed upside down on his middle finger. But their political activities never went much beyond sloganeering.

A few months after arriving in Prince Albert, Danny took over the chairmanship of the Native Brotherhood Organization, an important political role as well as a key leadership position for communicating within the gang. He told Susan, "Now I know what it's like to be a chief on the rez," as his grandfather had been. In that same letter he asked her to pass on a message to an elder she knew about rampant injustice in the justice system. By Danny's count, nearly 90 per cent of inmates in the high-security wing of the penitentiary were aboriginal, and the white inmates were moved to medium-security prisons much more quickly.

"The pigs here think they can play these games with the Indians well I don't think so. That's why I want to bring the heat on this place in any way I can," he said.

Danny was always perceived as a sharp student by his prison tutors and he dreamed of being able to pursue education more seriously. He told Richard that he'd come to realize that completing his schooling was more important and more challenging than being feared. He knew other gang members would mock him, he said, but he was prepared to face the taunts. Gaining knowledge was a sign of strength, not weakness, no matter what they said.

"I'm going to finish school so that I can get a job on the rez," Danny wrote. "It's so easy to fuck someone up man. We been doing that for too long. I want to do something hard now! And that's school man. Fuck what the bros say! I'm going to get my [diploma]. And that's a mission man."

When he read, Danny read only "Indian books," as he called them, and the only course that interested him in prison was native studies.

"I would rather learn about [our] people than take their fucken programs," Danny wrote. "It goes in one ear and out the other. And they call it punishment. Yah right. Give me a white boy and I'll show you punishment! Fucken red necks! They have no idea how notorious we are."

Danny's talk of personal reform proved short-lived. The more he adapted to life in Prince Albert, the more his outlook hardened. The chairmanship of the Native Brotherhood helped him carve out a more prominent leadership role in the gang. In June 2000, he told Richard he had learned some lessons about how to handle gang business and was now running gang operations in Saskatchewan. It was wiser to let others handle the dangerous, dirty work at the street level, he now realized, even if they couldn't always be counted on. He still planned to pursue education, but only for the purpose of making himself a better criminal.

"I want to finish school get a job and do all the other shit on the side," Danny said. "And see if they can catch me then! Fuck the jackings, let the strikers do all that shit." Four months later his ambitions continued to grow. He wanted to build a "big fucking army," he told his brother. "I know we can do it," he said. "Look what we started."

The Native Syndicate, another major aboriginal gang on the prairies, was founded in the prison system, according to the RCMP, and along with the Redd Alert out of Alberta, it was one of a number of new street gangs, comprising mainly young, indigenous men, that grew in the late 1990s and early 2000s. A year earlier, the Indian Posse had negotiated a truce with the Native Syndicate. It is not clear what role Danny played in that truce, but he seemed to support it. He might have hoped he could eventually amalgamate the NS and IP – he was sufficiently enthusiastic about it to draw a new logo combining the NS symbol with the IP and send it to Richard. But peace didn't last. It's hard to tell when or why the truce broke down, but Danny was still having his photo taken with NS members in the late fall of 2000, and not afterward.

Violence was still commonplace in Danny's world in Prince Albert. In May 2000, a Manitoba Warrior was stabbed. Danny was right there when it happened, and he either ordered it or did it himself, but as usual he got away with it.

One of his cousins who lived in rural Saskatchewan induced a spasm of frustration in Danny by joining the Warriors rather than the Indian Posse. This is how Danny broke the news of their cousin's decision to Richard: "[He] went with the Warriors, so fuck him. Treat him like a bitch now."

Later, that cousin's snub provoked a rare moment of reflection about gang life. In a letter to his mother, Danny confessed he could no longer protect his cousin. He also raised deeper questions, such as why he led a gang that through its violence, drug dealing, and support for prostitution did significant harm to his own people.

> I know you think about that, not just about [my cousin]
> but the big picture. Why we do this to our own people?
> I sometimes think about it too, but it's too late to do
> anything. That's just the way it is now! I wish I could
> change things back . . . more and more younger brothers
> are coming to the pen. They want that sense of power and
> control. But for some of them it doesn't work out like that.
> Because they don't take it serious enough.

For Danny it must have been comforting to think that as long as he took gang life seriously enough he could have power without suffering. It's hard to believe he was that naive, though, and perhaps he just wanted to reassure his mother. Less than a year had passed since his letters showed he was having serious doubts about the gang and the trustworthiness of the people around him. He remained mostly oblivious to the pain that he had caused – to his victims, to his mother, to his son and girlfriend – while the damage Danny and the Indian Posse were doing to indigenous people and the communities where they lived was a question he left unanswered. As he put it, it was too late to do anything.

14

THE LONG ROAD OUT
2001–2005

The guards arrived at Danny's cell shortly after sunrise on March 15, 2001. The plan was to extract him as early as possible, while the other inmates were still half asleep. At that time of day anger was at a low ebb and inmates were less likely to mobilize. The guards feared Danny's removal might spark a riot.

Stony Mountain wanted Danny Wolfe gone. He had returned to the Mountain from Prince Albert two months earlier, and two months of Danny Wolfe had been enough to convince the warden at Stony Mountain to ship him out again.

Gang tension had been brewing for weeks. In early March guards noticed a surge in the number of weapons seized in the prison. On March 3, Danny welcomed a female visitor, his records showed, and a scan found traces of cocaine on her body, which made authorities suspect she was smuggling drugs.

Five days later, on March 8, a group of about thirty Indian Posse members faced off against the Manitoba Warriors in the prison's recreation hall. The Posse lined up along one side of the gym, the Warriors on the other, like a scene from a music video, with the two gangs making a choreographed show of aggression. Then one member from each gang walked to the centre of the room, primed to fight. The two paced back and forth, taking each other's measure. Then, rather than brawl in full view of the guards, the pair took the fight to the washroom. The guards found the loser cleaning himself at the sink. When guards searched the area after they dispersed the two groups, they discovered seven homemade shanks, some of the knives as long as two feet. Danny, of course, had organized the fight.

In a report to his superiors, a prison intelligence officer said that the growing tension between the Warriors and the Posse had ramped up the level of violence between inmates. But tension within the Posse leadership seemed to be growing, too, because he reported "a fissure was occurring within the Indian Posse at this time." The warden ordered a lockdown. More searches turned up more weapons, and Danny and other gang leaders were placed in the hole to prevent an uprising.

Danny, they said, was shrewd enough to keep himself insulated "from actual hands on involvement in any illegal activity." They also knew, from monitoring his phone calls, that Danny was in touch with gang members on the street. He took regular briefings from lower-ranked Posse members and gave orders "regarding actions that must be carried out," usually using three-way calling to skirt efforts to block him from speaking to gang members. Danny would call someone, usually a girl, and she would either physically connect him on the phone with someone from the gang or act as a messenger on his behalf.

On March 14, the night before the guards were sent into his cell, Danny was overheard on the phone making arrangements to have more drugs smuggled into the prison. The warden convened a conference call with the assistant deputy commissioner of corrections and the warden of the Saskatchewan Penitentiary in Prince Albert to discuss what to do with Danny Wolfe. If he was reclassified to maximum security, Prince Albert would have to accept him again. The wardens decided to invoke a clause allowing for an emergency transfer with no advance notice to the inmate. The element of surprise was necessary, they agreed, because news of his removal could spark a riot among the population.

The guards entered Danny's cell at 7:15 a.m. and handed him an official notice from the warden:

> Your continued presence in population represents a serious and persistent threat to the good order, safety and security of the institution. Under section 23 of CD 576 we are transferring you to a maximum security institution to reduce your negative influence on the safety, security and effective management of the institution.

As he was led outside Danny yelled to the guards, and whoever else might be listening, "You can't stop the IP. We rule forever!" He was taken to a waiting bus where he was shackled and kept separate from other prisoners. A transfer meant no more visits with his infant son. He was angry.

After Danny was removed from Stony Mountain, his academic records were updated by his teacher. The report card portrayed Danny as a polite, hard-working, bright student who was respectful and positive and showed an open mind. And yet, other prison officials regarded him as violent, manipulative, and dangerous. Danny belonged to a group of offenders, one evaluator wrote, who had established "a fair degree of comfort with a criminal lifestyle" and was very likely beyond reform. "Unlike offenders in other groups, members of this group often view being a successful criminal as a major goal in their lives, in preference to achieving success in a more conventional manner. Their crimes appear to be motivated by a need to [prove] their ability to manipulate people and 'beat the system.'"

As he returned to the max unit of the Sask Pen in Prince Albert, Danny was still spitting mad about his transfer and wrote Richard to tell him the news. He blamed the Warriors, saying they had betrayed him by ratting him out to the guards (either for arranging fights or smuggling drugs). But, he said, being exiled to Prince Albert wouldn't hurt him at all. Besides, he had a new interest to divert himself: *The Sopranos*, HBO's Mafia drama.

Richard was still considered a high-profile prisoner, due to his once-prominent role in the Indian Posse. He had been out of the gang for more than two years, and his transfer to a prison in Ontario had made it easier for him to leave that world behind. But he barely knew anyone in these Eastern prisons and he was lonely, constantly bugging Danny for the names and addresses of girls who might be willing to write to him. Danny was usually accommodating.

"So what's up on that side of so-called Canada?" Danny asked, curious about the racial mix of Eastern prisons, having grown accustomed to native-dominated jails in the West. "Are there a lot of honkeys over that way or a lot of n–gers? Do they at least have a [Native Brotherhood]? And do you get to go to sweats? Do they even have that?"

The sweat lodge is a cleansing, spiritual ceremony that's usually offered to inmates in prairie prisons. Danny said he knew how uncomfortable prison could be without a spiritual outlet like the sweat. He was looking forward to taking part in a fast that coming summer. But he was wary of the risk that could pose, since the fast would leave him in a weakened state.

"I won't change the mentality I have for now, not while I'm in this cage. I ain't going to get caught slipping," he wrote.

Danny also told Richard about his plans for a new tattoo: "I'm going to get this tat and it's going to say Street Soldier because that's where we were and [I] still have that mentality. That will never leave. Because we lived it. Street survivors, Indian-style."

Although he struggled to articulate it, this vision of the street soldier was central to the brothers' understanding of themselves. They believed they had fought for survival as kids, raising themselves against long odds in an indifferent world. The gang was what they had built to defend themselves and to carve out a way to put food on the table and a roof over their heads. Danny offered a word of sympathy for those born into similar circumstances.

"It still happens today and there's nothing we can do about it," Danny wrote. "You know how shit is bro. It ain't changed. We just got older."

In a letter to his mother, Danny claimed that his emergency transfer out of Stony Mountain was cooked up, that someone had put "some bullshit" on him. He did boast, however, that it had been all over the news in Winnipeg. Even if he wasn't named personally on TV, he liked the thought of having the spotlight on the Indian Posse. His mother, heavily involved in her own spirituality at that point, had told him of receiving an Indian name and a special rock from the elders. Danny congratulated her and wondered why he hadn't received something similar: "I never got a rock. Maybe I'm not ready for something like that. Maybe in the future some time."

He was hoping to learn to speak Cree and was attending sweats and sharing circles regularly, he told her. As he often did, he asked about his younger brother, Preston. Danny was always keen to make sure Preston was behaving well and staying out of trouble.

"I just don't want him to experience what I went through! Unfortunately that's the path I took," Danny wrote.

Danny also told his mother how he had made sense of his own path in life, and how it had led him to the penitentiary.

"It was like I wanted to see how much I [could] handle in the most hardest way. Now I know what frustration, confusion, loneliness and hatred means. . . . Too bad it has to be like this, or in a place like this."

To get through the pain he drew inspiration from the historic struggles of native people, he said. But he still knew only a little history, and was hungry to further his education. His cell was filled with printouts taken from the Internet, with short biographies of figures such as Crazy Horse, Big Bear, and Sitting Bull, and the story of Custer's Last Stand featured among them.

"I try and focus on [our] people, what we went through and how we handled it. It's very interesting to learn," he wrote.

The tone of Danny's letters grew sharper the longer he was at Prince Albert. He said an elder, someone brought in by the jail to counsel the indigenous inmates, was caught getting oral sex from a male inmate in the medium-security jail. It was an Indian Posse member that caught them, Danny told Richard.

"That's a serious issue, fuck. They're supposed to be helping us not [getting] us to suck them off," he said.

Sexual abuse is a significant issue for many gang members. Danny always told prison officials, from intake officers to psychologists and psychiatrists, that he had never suffered sexual abuse, only physical abuse. He told Lisa the same. But in one of his poems he wrote:

All I ask for is help
But no one is there
For I have been abused
In all kinds of ways
I cry and hide my emotions
From everyone and everywhere
They beat me, raped me
Burned me
That is only some of the things
They did to torture me

. . .

Danny's time in group homes and prisons as a teenager, not to mention his transient childhood, could have exposed him to sexual abuse. But he never mentioned it elsewhere, nor do his prison records suggest it, so it's not clear whether he was a victim of sexual abuse.

In the pictures that Danny kept from his time in Prince Albert it's possible to glimpse a little bit of the life he led. He and his friends hung out in various cells decorated with pin-up photos of girls in bikinis. Danny and company are often playing video games or watching TV, smoking cigarettes and posing with stern faces. They stand with shirts off to display their muscles, staring blankly into the camera, and they make Indian Posse gang signs by forming the letters I and P with their fingers. The rooms look institutional and the peeling paint on the walls lends an air of decay. It's a bleak environment.

In July, the Indian Posse made a move against a native prisoner, someone Danny and Richard knew from Manitoba. This man was a convicted killer serving a nine-year sentence for beating his uncle to death, and clearly he made the mistake of crossing either Danny or another high-ranking member. He suffered a brutal beating that resulted in dozens of stab wounds. The prison was locked down for days and Danny got sent to the hole. Two and a half months later he was still there.

"I don't keep track of the time," he wrote to Richard. "I just do it. Day by day."

They didn't charge anyone for the stabbing, which Danny took as confirmation that he could get away with anything in this prison. He was also suspected of plotting to take a guard hostage, according to his prison files, yet he was never charged.

As yet more trouble piled up on Danny's doorstep, his jailers threatened to ship him to the Atlantic Institution in Renous, New Brunswick, a maximum-security jail far away from any concentration of Indian Posse members. That prospect made him nervous.

An emerging Corrections strategy against the gangs seemed to be to send the leaders and high-profile members to far-flung locations in Eastern Canada to separate them from the pack. Danny and Richard increasingly had to update one another on who was being sent where.

"There's four bros coming here from Stony and four going East but I don't know what joint yet," Danny wrote. "They're shipping everyone everywhere now. Good. Now we can rip shit up all over."

Some IP members were going to a super-maximum facility called "the SHU," the Special Handling Unit in Ste-Anne-des-Plaines, Quebec, the highest security jail in Canada. That brought with it some stature for the Indian Posse, a sense that the gang had finally arrived, and Danny wondered if that's where he would be heading eventually. Having seen the terrible riot at Headingley, corrections officials were vigilant about not allowing the Indian Posse to grow so large that it could overwhelm a given institution. By now, in the early 2000s, the Indian Posse was vying to be the largest recognized gang in the prison system. It had a significant presence in nearly all the Western jails, but the East was run by bikers – the Hells Angels and Rock Machine – who had been waging war in Quebec.

The cross-country transfers gave the Indian Posse a presence in places it had never been before. In the same way that entrepreneurs benefit from being exposed to the ideas of people of diverse nationalities and backgrounds, so the Posse hoped to benefit from making new connections with people from other criminal networks. They also hoped to recruit new members from different parts of the country and to extend their reach to Southern Ontario, Quebec, and Atlantic Canada.

Danny, though, was not much interested in being a pioneer at this point, given the significant danger associated with arriving in a new prison where he would have little backup. He tried to block his proposed transfer to New Brunswick by refusing to sign the document that would authorize it and even hired a lawyer to fight on his behalf. Diana Goldie, an Alberta defence lawyer, wrote at least two letters opposing his transfer that eviscerated the correctional system for its treatment of Danny. She wrote that although corrections officers suspected Danny of being involved in stabbings and beatings, and had placed him in segregation for months for that reason, they could prove nothing against him. "We are not yet in a society where CSC [Correctional Services Canada] can dispense with the concept of proof," she wrote. Belonging to the Indian Posse was not a criminal offence and not grounds for transfer, she added.

"There is nothing anywhere in Canada outside of the Prairie Region to motivate Mr. Wolfe in a positive fashion. As CSC must surely now realize, transferring young aboriginal males away from their communities forces them to strengthen the same negative associations that CSC deplores, i.e., the gangs. While CSC may not like the realities of aboriginal gangs, it is indisputable that they have grown and flourished under CSC's misguided efforts to stamp them out by transferring inmates from the Prairies, such as Mr. Wolfe, to places like the Atlantic region."

The prison, in its written decision, cited Danny's history of involvement in gang activity and the plan to take a guard hostage as sufficient reason to justify his transfer. Danny tried to play down his fears about being separated from the rest of the gang, but his anxiety was plain. Being alone and isolated would be very dangerous for him. Life would not be anywhere near as pleasant without the comforts – in the form of drugs, extra food, and deference from other inmates – that come to the most powerful gang members in an institution.

Shortly after he was told the transfer to Renous had been approved, Danny tried to escape. It was an improbable and doomed attempt but bold nonetheless. He was outside, in the exercise yard dedicated to the max-unit prisoners, probably alone or in a small group since he was in segregation, during his daily hour of yard time.

A guard spotted Danny standing by the fence and grew suspicious – it looked like he was up to something. The guard ordered everyone, including Danny, to clear the yard. When he walked closer to the fence and inspected it, he found a hole about a foot and a half wide, large enough for a person to fit through. How Danny cut the hole is unclear. He was never prosecuted because they couldn't prove when the hole had been made, or even if he had done it.

How close did he get to escape? A prison security official explained in an email to his colleagues that it would still have been difficult to get out, even if Danny hadn't been spotted.

"He was still within the walls of Sask Pen, so he still had a fair bit of work ahead of him before he was outside the confines of prison," the official said. "Basically he would have to get outside of the D exercise yard, cross two more fences that are [motion sensor] monitored and then get over the wall of the penitentiary."

It would not be the last time that Danny, facing an unpleasant future, would draw up a plan to escape.

Danny's departure was supposed to calm the atmosphere in Prince Albert, but he plotted to destabilize the prison right up until he left. In a letter to his brother he described how he tried to orchestrate a riot in his final days there. He told Richard that, as he was writing, the other inmates were starting fires and smashing up the common room. Guards had swarmed the area trying to establish calm. His own cell was filling up with smoke at that very moment, he wrote, and "the fucken pigs are all over." He broke away from the letter, only to return with the news that the prison had been locked down. The riot fizzled because other inmates didn't back the Indian Posse, he told Richard.

Corrections officials flew Danny and two other Indian Posse members under guard to Renous, New Brunswick, in October 2001.

The Atlantic Institution is a modern, maximum-security prison, built in 1987 and located about ninety minutes north of Fredericton by car. Shortly after they arrived, Danny's fears came true. The Indian Posse trio were admitted to the general population, where there were no other Posse members waiting to offer them protection or backup. The prison already held a number of Warriors, and they wasted no time clarifying the gang pecking order for Danny and company. Danny was assaulted "the moment he set foot in general population," according to CSC.

An inmate who was much bigger than Danny jumped him near his cell and quickly got the better of him. One description said he smashed Danny's head into the cement repeatedly until guards fired warning shots that forced him to back off. Danny sustained injuries so severe he had to be transported, in restraints and under guard, to an emergency care facility outside the jail for treatment. He was lucky to survive.

"It seems that the mixture of native gangs in Renous was not in their favour," a CSC official noted dryly in an email.

When Danny returned from a week spent recuperating in hospital, the warden decided that, for his own safety, Danny had to be placed in segregation. For the next several months he was stuck in a kind of limbo, isolated, unable to take any programs or do much of anything, while officials decided what they would do with him. What little can be gleaned from that time comes mainly from the notes of the psychologists, who were required to ensure he wasn't driven crazy by solitude.

After four months in segregation, during a mandatory review, a psychologist wrote that Danny "was very cooperative" and that he appeared "well adapted" to long-term segregation. Danny requested four books from the library, all related to First Nations topics, including *The Lance and the Shield: The Life and Times of Sitting Bull*, a biography of the iconic Hunkpapa Lakota chief who defeated General Custer at the Battle of Little Bighorn.

As he sat in segregation, Danny continued to write letters, though he didn't include any news of the beating or the extent of his injuries. He did his best to sound unconcerned about where he might be heading next, assuming he would be transferred from Renous. It wasn't unreasonable to expect the next move would be to another hostile prison. He was already fairly certain that he wouldn't be allowed to return to the relative safety of a Western jail.

"Might as well stay out east for a while and do shit up out this way! I ain't [scared]," he boasted. "I'll do what I do best, hurt people!"

By April 2002, Danny had spent six consecutive months in segregation. Over the last four years, he had spent nearly one in four days in isolation. The impact this had on him is not clear. He only sometimes agreed to speak to the psychologists sent to check on him every thirty days, and the notes they entered in his file are brief. In recent years, experts have expressed growing concern about the long-term effects of lengthy isolation, which can lead to increased anxiety, depression, and aggression. At the time, officials thought the best way to deal with Danny was to keep him locked up and alone.

After half a year in segregation, Danny was finally transferred to another maximum-security jail, Donnacona Institution, in central Quebec. A few Indian Posse members were already there and Danny soon fell into a comfortable routine. Records show that guards spotted him drinking homebrew and smoking drugs, signs that he was enjoying some of the comforts of a friendly prison again.

Danny quickly bonded with Mark, an old friend and fellow Indian Posse member from Winnipeg.

"We watch each other's backs," Danny told his brother. "We're always pulling rubbys [drinking – a reference to drinking rubbing alcohol]. Talking about the old days and keep[ing] it real."

Danny included a letter from Mark in his package for Richard. Mark and Richard hadn't corresponded in years and Mark was eager to let Richard know that he supported him, despite the gang's decision to turn on him. The letter is important because it shows the extent of unhappiness with gang leadership from other senior members. It's quite likely that schisms were occurring within the gang all the time – but now the rumblings were getting louder.

The move against Richard remained a sore point. Obviously it was the first thing Mark wanted to mention when getting back in touch, and Danny brought it up again with his brother in another letter sent around the same time. Now that other Posse members had actually tried to kill his brother, Danny took back what he had said six years earlier: There was no way he could hurt his real family for the sake of the gang.

> I won't let the street family hurt our family. Fuck that
> man! I know how to play the game bro! And that fucker
> who said shit about you is going to get it sooner or later
> man! You know who I'm talking about hey? I like to keep
> my [enemies] closer you know! I got a lot of bros who will
> back me too! So it's good to keep that liability and I know
> there's lots that still have respect for you too bro. And they
> know that's all bullshit what happened to you! So let's
> keep it real and make them turn on that sucker man!

It's not clear who Danny meant, but it's evident that he had a serious grudge against someone high up in the gang, a person who might have played a role in either the decision to stab Richard or commit some later act of disrespect. Danny also felt that there were others who saw things the same way.

Danny was keeping up with events on the outside much more closely than before, he told Richard in July that year. He was dismayed by what he was hearing, about how the gang was doing business and about how hard it was becoming to make money, thanks to police crackdowns.

There wasn't much opportunity for intra-gang conflict at Donnacona because there were so few Posse members. A laid-back joint, Danny called it. What information the Posse members could glean came via the telephone and the mail, making Danny more peripheral than he had ever been. Danny was amused one day when the prisoners, most of them French-speaking, were gathered around the television and a news item about the Indian Posse appeared. The reporter said the Posse was at war with a rival gang. Danny's status received a boost, since to that point his fellow prisoners weren't much impressed by the Indian Posse.

"It was funny because all the French guys here were like 'You guys at war!' We told them no it's the pigs doing all that shit. But to hear us on the news got them. I think they think we're just a small crew!"

Danny busied himself with the Native Brotherhood and got a job in the tailor shop. He was optimistic that he could earn some money on the outside with the skills he was learning. A supervisor later called him a respectful and polite worker whose ability and attitude improved every day. He was good enough to become a quality control supervisor, a role given to reliable inmates.

Danny continued recruiting for the gang and tried to outsource some work to Richard, telling his brother to pass him the contact information for any native inmates who might want to join the gang. More important, Danny said that a revolt was brewing against the current leadership, and that he was on the side of the opposition.

Like I said bro there's going to be some changes to the crew! Fuck those other so-called leaders. We have enough bros who want to plot and step up! You know who I'm talking about too, there's three of them! So what do you think about that?? And what are you going to do? Since there's brothers who still have respect for you! They always tell me to say hi to you and send [their] respect! Well I'm sick of them making up [their] own rules and shit! Anyways get back to me on that!

It's very difficult to know specifically who or what Danny was discussing here. It might have been that the transfer of so many IP leaders out of Western Canada had created an opportunity for new-comers to seize power in their absence. Whatever caused the rift, it's clear that Danny was becoming increasingly disillusioned. He was actively plotting to remove some of the leadership. But, he was also less well connected than he had been: "I have to write to Stony and see what's up there now. See what kind of battlefield it is there. Who's trying to kill who," he wrote. "I got a little of what's going on. But I want the update."

After a period of good behaviour, Danny's security level was dropped to medium, which meant he could apply to move to a less restrictive jail. He was wary at first. He had less than two years to go until he reached the mandatory release date at two-thirds of his sentence, so he considered just staying at Donnacona. The thought of a transfer made him tense. He didn't know what to expect in a new jail and he would always be a high-status target for someone looking to make a name for himself. Donnacona, even with armed guards in towers monitoring his movements, did have its comforts.

"I don't want to go to some other joint and end up [having to kill someone] just because of who I am," Danny said. "You know how the game is. Well at least I can eat good here and watch porn! Fuck it's better than a medium!"

Eventually, he changed his mind. He complained that too many informants were being snuck into the general population at the jail;

plus, the prison had effectively cracked down on drugs and alcohol. Danny was twice caught smoking weed and his still of moonshine was seized. After a few months "roughing it," in his words, he applied for a transfer to Western Canada. He was turned down by every single prison – they wanted nothing to do with him. The Indian Posse was hard enough to contain without bringing one of their leading figures back into the mix. Here is what Stony Mountain had to say:

> SMI is currently experiencing significant difficulties with the Indian Posse and we are actively working to develop population management strategies to address these difficulties. Receiving Wolfe into our population at this time will cause a further destabilization of our population resulting in further institutional violence . . .

The Saskatchewan Penitentiary said much the same thing, as did every other medium-security prison on the Prairies. Eventually Danny was accepted at the Cowansville Institution in Quebec.

At Cowansville, Danny received a letter from a woman he hadn't heard from in years. She had been in a relationship with an IP member that had since ended and she had moved on with her life. But the impressions she had of the gang's current state served to reinforce Danny's view that it had become something he and his brother never intended:

> I must admit I am proud and very thankful that I was part of the crew (you know who) back then, back in the day. Because the way these girls get treated now from this new set of members is pretty disgusting! They get talked down to, treated only like a piece of meat, and totally disre-spected! . . . You guys were great. These new guys are jerks.

These guys are big time power tripping, maybe 'cause
things are intense right now these new guys don't know
how to handle it and they take it out on these poor girls.
See that's the difference you guys knew how to handle
things and you kept everything and everyone under
control. Nothing was taken out on us girls. There is not
enough respect and pride like there used to be, that's for
sure. The seniors need to step in, show these new young
guys the proper way of things!

Danny took her concerns seriously. He passed them on to a
friend, one of the gang's senior members, and within weeks the tensions roiling within the Posse exploded in public.

On September 26, 2003, an Indian Posse member named
Gene Malcolm was shot in the back outside a house in Winnipeg's
North End, the first salvo in a battle over drug profits that would split
the gang. Clarence "Shrimpy" Williams led a small, breakaway group
out of the Indian Posse, according to police. He and his brothers were
very close to Danny and Richard. As a teenager, Danny had often
taken the name of one of the Williams brothers as his alias when he
was trying to deceive police.

Danny had spoken to members of the faction on the phone just
a few months before the battle erupted, and he had mentioned the
conversation in a letter to Richard back in June. He said they had told
him they were making a lot of money selling drugs. Apparently, jealousy over Shrimpy's success and a desire to share in his profits led to
bloodshed between different Posse factions.

A week after Gene Malcolm was shot, Danny got a letter from
another long-time Indian Posse associate, who was serving a life sentence for murder in another Canadian prison. The letter said Malcolm
had miraculously survived the shooting: "The grandfathers wouldn't

have yet another young brother taken out like that. Blessed him with the strength to fight to live. I last phoned to hear he came off life support."

Two Posse members were arrested, the letter said, and the word on the street was that they were high on crack at the time. Crack smoking was a strict no-no in the gang. There was no discipline, no one was following the rules, and the gang was splintering, Danny was told.

Danny was torn up by the internecine strife; he told Richard: "Since I heard all of that I haven't phoned 'cause whatever the fuck is going on I don't care to hear anymore of everyone turning on everyone. It's too much. Guess the good old days are just that."

According to Danny's friend Angus, who used to run cocaine into remote communities for the Indian Posse, the breakaway crew had set up a very lucrative drug operation, more successful than any enterprise in the gang's history. It ran on the pizza delivery model: buyers would dial a number and get drugs delivered to them. The most valuable piece of the business was the phone number. The issue was that the rest of the gang was jealous and wanted a larger cut of the proceeds. The rebel group resisted – and then people started getting shot.

On October 4, a team of Posse members from Edmonton arrived in Winnipeg. They met four Winnipeg-based gang members at a local hotel to hatch a plan, according to police. The objective: Get Shrimpy. At the hotel they sawed off the barrels of two shotguns. Then they went to Teasers, a local strip club, to finalize the details. It was there that police, who had been listening to the gang's conversations via wiretaps, swarmed the plotters as they tried to leave the club. They arrested six men and charged each with two counts of conspiracy to commit murder.

The story provided by the police was that Shrimpy had set up a rival gang known as the Cash Money Brothers. One insider said that Shrimpy did eventually break away from the IP but that the creation of the rival gang was a by-product of even more conflict within the Indian

Posse: "It was all about money. [Shrimpy] was making the most money, and whoever was making the most money at that time had to give their 10 per cent, give back to the kitty, give back to the bank."

But, this insider said, one of the gang's fast-rising leaders, Brad Maytwayashing, played it differently. According to the insider, Brad – a tall, square-jawed criminal – and his acolytes were becoming greedy. Brad saw the breakaway crew making as much as $50,000 a week and demanded a substantial cut – more than they were willing to give.

Danny was clearly pained by the conflict. He aimed to regain control of the Indian Posse and rebuild the solidarity of the old days, which was not going to happen easily. He would have to bide his time. Over the next year, Danny's behaviour inside the prison improved dramatically. He became nearly a model prisoner. From late 2003 through July 2004, he had no major disciplinary incidents, and he convinced prison officials he had successfully distanced himself from the gang. In a report written in the spring of 2004, as Danny was nearing his release date that summer, his parole officer raved about how he had demonstrated that he could follow the rules and avoid violence. It was "a wholly different picture" of Danny, and he seemed to be following his brother Richard's lead in withdrawing from the gang, the officer wrote: "Staff witnessed significant change in Daniel's behavior for approximately two years from April 2002 to date," the officer wrote. "He does not want to be a gang member and plans on avoiding such associates."

During this stint in Quebec, Danny came in contact with notorious Quebec gangster Gerry Matticks, the alleged boss of a Montreal crime syndicate. Danny said Matticks used to come to him with letters in hand, asking if he would read them to him. Matticks admitted he had never learned to read or write. Danny was astonished; Matticks was the sharpest criminal he had ever met. "Running the fucking shit," as Danny put it, and yet, he "couldn't read or write." It might have been Matticks's influence that pushed Danny to take a calmer approach to doing time in prison. Danny aspired to move away from the rough-and-tumble world of the street and to insulate himself from risk, maybe even to get a legitimate job while running drugs on the side. Matticks used to tell stories about how the crime group, which had its in roots in Irish working-class Montreal, managed to hold off the Mafia when they tried to move in on the ports. They ended up cutting a deal to share the profits, Danny later recounted, full of admiration.

Danny was also close to the bikers while he was in Quebec, a group he had long eyed with suspicion. In the late 1990s, as the Hells Angels vied to extend their criminal network across the country, they had come to Winnipeg looking for allies. Danny, in a conversation that was captured on a prison wiretap, described how the Indian Posse had met with the Hells Angels. The Hells had proposed making the IP a puppet club, like a minor league branch of a major league team: the IP would continue what they were doing, mainly the risky street-level drug dealing, armed robbery, and prostitution work, while the Hells would act as their drug suppliers and help with organization and logistics. Danny said the IP was willing to consider the alliance; however, the Hells wanted to be in control, while Danny wanted the IP to be equal partners.

"We just told them, 'Hey man, we won't fucking stand in front of you, we don't stand behind you. We stay side by side if we're gonna do this,'" Danny said. The Hells turned them down. They wanted to call the shots, Danny said: "They wanted control. We just said 'No.' And ever since then we've [had to] back off them."

Danny was a proud man and it bothered him that the Indian Posse was still fighting to be recognized in the criminal world, dismissed as small-time by these biker gangs. He had also clashed with a gang called the Apollos in Regina over drug turf and the armed robbery of a drug dealer when he was getting the Indian Posse established in Saskatchewan. Later, the Bandidos offered the Indian Posse a similar partnership opportunity, but Danny didn't like it. "They want us to be them," said Danny. "My heart knew already." The Posse turned down the offer. Danny wanted the gang to grow on its own terms.

"Danny always hated the bikers," his brother Richard said. But he might have been learning from them at Cowansville. He had matured, done his reading, and clarified his sense of independence and ambition.

As his mandatory release date neared, prison authorities spoke glowingly of the support network in place for Danny and, amazingly, rated his reintegration potential as "high." It was quite a turnaround: a year earlier he had been considered so threatening that no prison in Western Canada would accept him on a transfer. But now he was being actively courted to mentor others in a program to divert young indigenous people from gangs.

On July 14, 2004, at 5:30 a.m., Danny departed the Cowansville jail on a bus destined for the Montreal airport and a flight back to Regina. He had spent nearly six years behind bars.

The shock of being out in the world again can be overwhelming for inmates. Richard remembers what it was like for him when he arrived at the airport following his own release. Seeing so many people in an open space was disconcerting, he said. People moved around as they wanted, approaching quickly and standing close behind in line or on the escalator. In jail, that behaviour would have been interpreted as threatening; here, it was just a matter of course. The noise, the sights, the way the world has changed: inmates drink it all in at once. Simple things like speaking to a stranger in the store, or choosing which cold drink to buy of the thirty varieties available, can be intimidating. Everything seems to move so fast. Richard said the day he was released he was exhausted by the range of emotions. The most prominent of them? Fear.

Danny had $209 in his pocket when he arrived in Regina. It wasn't exactly the typical bulging billfold of the gang kingpin, and he was expecting to sign on for welfare right away. He had no ID whatsoever: no driver's licence (he had never passed a test), no health card, no Indian status card. He did have a letter of reference from Corcan Industries, the prison employer, which stated that he had worked on several different machines during his 962 hours of work in the tailor shop. The personal touch in the recommendation was so minimal – one sentence – that it's hard to believe it would persuade any employer to hire him: "We had been satsifact [sic] of his work and behavior during this time." As Danny re-entered the world, the odds were stacked against him.

He did manage to get a part-time job, briefly, at Silverado Demolition, but he had to quit when his shift times clashed with a course he had to take as a condition of his parole. Danny told corrections officials that he didn't really want to be in Regina. He saw the city as a high-risk environment, since all the temptations that had led him to trouble – drugs, alcohol, other gang members – would be readily available. He'd much prefer to be left on his own on the reserve, which he saw as almost a zone of purity. He told them there would be fewer opportunities for trouble.

At Oskana, the halfway house where he was required to live for a few weeks, he met an instructor named James Squire, who was leading a seminar to help ex-cons avoid going back to jail. They saw each other twice a week for three hours, and over the course of that summer Squire developed a great deal of insight into Danny, certainly as much as anyone who had worked with him in the prison system. Danny had a long way to go if he was going to avoid reoffending, Squire concluded. He might have been a model prisoner for the last year, but surviving in the real world, making a living without resorting to drug deals or armed robbery, was going to present a serious challenge.

"Daniel's overall attitude to the criminal justice system and conventional institutions was adversarial to say the least," Squire wrote. "He openly admits to having had an 'Us versus Them' attitude towards the police and other such authority figures and generally saw society as being dominated by white systems governed by white rules that made the white richer and the Indian suffer."

That thinking was, in essence, the founding ethos of the Indian Posse. Their initial aim was to make enough money to live and stay out of the state system of foster parents and group homes. Once they got locked up, it was to assert themselves and gain power.

"Daniel readily admits to feeling that he had no legitimate ways of making a living, so crime became a full time job as a means to attain food, clothing and a place to stay," Squire said.

Danny had ways to justify the pain he inflicted as a result of his crimes, he told Squire one day. He committed crimes as a kid because he needed to survive, he said. When he was robbing homes and businesses, he told himself that insurance would probably cover the losses. As long as no one was hurt, it was a victimless crime; or that's how he saw it.

Squire said that Danny had found healing in prison by turning to a traditional way of life. Learning "the old ways" had helped Danny change his way of thinking, Squire said. He used to think he was alone; that no one cared whether he lived or died; that those who claimed to care had made him a criminal. Now he had replaced those destructive thoughts with spiritualism. Danny had always had great respect for his culture, Squire said, but he didn't know how to practise it until he was introduced to ceremonies inside the prisons. The instructor seemed to believe that Danny's transformation was real, up to a point. If Danny started hanging around with his old friends again, he would likely go back to a life outside the law, Squire predicted.

In September, after several weeks in Regina, Danny left the Oskana halfway house and moved in with his mother at the Okanese

First Nation. He got a part-time job working in the reserve's ranching business, taking care of the cattle and buffalo, and got a contract to provide firewood for cultural ceremonies. The parole officer's reports on Danny are glowing, describing his positive attitude, commitment to change, and high degree of motivation. A week before Christmas he was granted a pass to travel to Winnipeg. He stayed with Lisa for one night and then brought their son, now five years old, back to Saskatchewan, to experience life on the reserve for a few days.

Lisa and Danny had drifted apart over the years. They talked about reconciling, but Danny didn't want to move back to Winnipeg and Lisa didn't want to move away from her family. Still, Danny was overjoyed to be able to spend time with his son. Much of his focus in recent years, at least as it was reflected in his letters, had been on becoming a good father. A week with his boy was not enough time, but he was glad to have it.

Shortly after the New Year in 2005, he ran into trouble. His mother began to suspect he was getting high. She let it slide for a couple of weeks, but then he spent two nights in Regina without a pass and without telling his mother. He seemed distracted, she said, and he wasn't as motivated as he had been when he arrived. She called Danny's parole officer, concerned, and on January 25, 2005, they staged a mini-intervention in Susan's home. Danny's parole officer, Sandra Lavalley, drove up from Regina. They settled in for a chat at the kitchen table. Susan asked Danny why he wasn't talking to her, why he thought it was okay to travel without a permit and without telling her where he was going. She worried about him, she said, and had no idea whether he was okay or not. Lavalley asked Danny if he'd been drinking.

Danny started to rage. He said he was tired of having to prove to everyone that he had changed. He felt pressure from everyone all the time, as though they watched his every move. He was exhausted by their expectations. Susan tried to calm him. She said she was proud of what he had accomplished, and that she recognized it wasn't easy. Eventually Danny admitted that he had been smoking marijuana. When his mother told him that was not the traditional way, that marijuana had no place in a traditional indigenous lifestyle, he agreed that it was probably a bad thing, but said it helped him calm down. Still, he promised to quit. Susan said she would arrange a special Shaking Tent ceremony to help him keep his promise. The intervention worked. Danny avoided being sent back to jail.

Danny's relationship with his mother was complicated. The last time he had been free, they had really only been starting to get to know one another. Susan had never attended a court appearance and had visited him only a few times in jail. She hadn't even known when he was first sentenced to the penitentiary. By her own description, she had been mostly absent from his life between the ages of seven and twenty-four. Their relationship was still loving and full of laughter, but Susan had changed her life. She was no longer the absent parent ruled by her addiction, and she wanted her son to learn from his mistakes and to change. To that end, she was keeping a close eye on him and taking her responsibility to his parole officer seriously. Danny might have assumed that the old rules still applied, or that his mother would seek to protect him. If so, he was wrong.

On June 9, 2005, Danny was called to an emergency meeting with his parole officer. Lavalley told him point-blank that the understanding she had extended to him in January no longer applied: She had reliable information that he was using drugs. She also knew that Danny, at this point a twenty-nine-year-old man, was dating a fifteen-year-old girl. He was going back to jail, Lavalley told him.

Danny denied the charges. He knew his own mother had informed on him and he told his parole officer he had no idea why she would make these wild and false allegations. Lavalley asked him to explain his relationship with the fifteen-year-old. He had no answer except to deny it. In her report, the parole officer wrote that Danny's mother brought forward a lot of information about him during the months that he spent in her home, but most of it was trivial. In this case, Lavalley followed up with her own investigation and confirmed that Danny's girlfriend was just fifteen. The state had to intervene. Lavalley informed Danny that warrants of suspension would be issued and he would have to report to police to turn himself in.

Danny was furious with Susan, the only person he thought he could trust, and he told Lavalley that he couldn't go back to prison. He would be destined for the provincial remand facility, Regina Correctional Centre, where other gangs, particularly the rival Native Syndicate, held more power than the Indian Posse. It was too dangerous, and he was afraid he would be a target, he told Lavalley.

"He was very fearful of turning himself in," she wrote in her report.

Danny told her he needed to go home to get his possessions before heading to the police station. Then he hatched a plan to escape. The next morning Lavalley spotted Danny at the bus station in Regina. She confronted him and he confessed he felt he had no choice but to run. Lavalley called the police, but by the time they got there Danny had vanished.

As police issued a nationwide warrant for his arrest, Danny went underground, back to the reserve at Okanese to lie low. He spent two and a half weeks staying with friends and managed to avoid getting caught; then, once he felt it was safe to travel, he made his way to Winnipeg. After a year on the outside, living sufficiently above-board to avoid any police notice, he was back on the run. His girlfriend, a beautiful teenager named Shenoa, was three months' pregnant.

15

MURDER IN THE PENITENTIARY
2005–2006

Danny was back where it all began, on the streets of Winnipeg, living on the front lines of the gang world. But this wasn't the plan. His goal, outlined to Richard during his long sentence years earlier, had been to distance himself from the dangers of the street. He had dreamed of upgrading his education, finding a real job, and moving drugs on the side. He had enjoyed the quiet life on the reserve, to a point. As a counsellor who saw Danny in those years put it, when he told everyone of his intention to turn his life around, he was very convincing.

Winnipeg looked like a different place now, six years since he had last been there. The city was poorer, Danny thought. The North End was in bad shape, and the West End, where he and Richard had grown up, the area north of Portage Avenue near the University of Winnipeg, was much rougher than he remembered. He saw prostitutes, many of them teenagers, working openly on the streets where he had played as a kid. He later wrote about it to Richard, who was at a prison in Ontario in the tenth year of his sentence for attempted murder. "It's all different over there Bro. It looks more ruff on the north side. The

West side, nothing but hookers bro, all over the place! It's the crack [that has] taken over. It's crazy," Danny said.

His comment is intriguing. Danny failed to mention that it was their own criminal organization that sold the drugs, that enslaved the prostitutes, and that was responsible for the violence that plagued the primarily indigenous neighbourhoods where he had grown up. It's not clear whether Danny accepted any responsibility for the gang's contribution to this despair. The Indian Posse was not alone, after all. As he said in his letter, there were always new crews popping up: "Lots of names bro, they come and go." But none had lasted like the Indian Posse.

Danny returned to his place in the city's criminal class. Many of the specific details of his criminal activities in this period remain secret, since those who know are afraid to talk about unprosecuted crimes. In his letters Danny said he set himself up selling drugs with a long-time friend in the IP. What impact the tensions inside the gang had on him isn't clear. His pregnant girlfriend, Shenoa, stayed behind in Saskatchewan when Danny ran to Winnipeg, leaving him to concentrate on making money and surviving on the run. Over his time in prison Danny had claimed to have come up with insights on how to better run a criminal operation, although he kept those ideas to himself. Whether they worked or not isn't clear either, but he did manage to avoid getting caught for a few months. Unfortunately for him, his business partner was not as disciplined as he was. When Danny got pinched for jumping parole, the big-money business quickly went under.

"We had our shit going on but I got put back in and he pulled a drunk and lost everything," Danny said in a letter. "Left me with nothing. Oh well, what can you do when you're not there to hold [their] hand. But he's still a good brother . . ."

Following his arrest, Danny's parole was revoked and he was sent back to Stony Mountain in September 2005, forced to complete the last year or so of his seven-year home invasion sentence.

Life at the Mountain was, on the surface, better than in other jails. The Indian Posse had their own massive range and their own weight room, to cut down on the risks they posed to the rest of the population. Drugs were frequently available because the gang had well-established smuggling systems, and they were all close to friends and family for visits. But internally the gang continued to boil.

The tension that had erupted in the Get Shrimpy plot was still near the surface. A year earlier, in April 2004, the gang's senior members had executed a coup to overthrow one of the leaders. Brad Maytwayashing was ruthless and unpredictable and had been an unwelcome wild card for years. He disciplined members over minor transgressions, which was very unpopular. As dissent grew, the old hands whispered about whether to take him out. At the time, Danny had been on his own out east, but he agreed with the others: Brad had to go.

On April 13, 2004, Brad was being held with several other Indian Posse members at the Remand Centre in downtown Winnipeg. Brad was being led through an Indian Posse range when he was violently attacked. He didn't see it coming. Raymond Armstrong, a senior member, reached out to shake Brad's hand – and in the next instant threw a punch that landed square in Brad's face. The beating was on. The rest of the gang jumped in and pummelled Brad, spearing him with broom handles and swinging improvised clubs. The blows rained down on him for several excruciating minutes. Finally, guards steamrolled in to break it up. Brad was rushed to hospital in critical condition.

Officers charged ten Indian Posse members for the vicious gang assault. Armstrong ended up with an additional two years in jail for his role in the attack and was there to welcome Danny back to the IP's dedicated range at Stony Mountain when he returned in September 2005. The change at the top hadn't solved the discord, though. One of the leading plotters in Brad's overthrow was a cruel, wiry criminal named Sheldon McKay. Like Brad, Sheldon had joined the gang a few years after its founding, during the period when it was swallowing up rivals.

With Brad gone, McKay began to consolidate his power. McKay was a mean character serving a life sentence who proudly wore a tattoo on his arm that said *Fuck You*. When he was just sixteen years old, he slashed the throat of his girlfriend's mother and left her to die. In 2000, after he finished serving that sentence, he killed again. A group of Indian Posse members ran into three members of the rival Nine-Os gang while they were buying beer in the North End. The fight escalated and one of the Nine-Os tripped and fell as he ran. His brother turned back to help him, but the mob caught them and set upon them in a parking lot near McPhillips Street. The Nine-Os were beaten, stabbed, and stomped on until they lost consciousness. Adrian Bruyere, only nineteen years old, later died. After the killing, the IP group went to a party, where McKay committed to memory the face of every person in the house, letting them know he was taking inventory of those he would kill if anyone talked to police. The threat didn't stop an informant from calling police to say that McKay was bragging about killing someone. The cop who arrested McKay, Detective James Jewell, described McKay as the personification of evil.

Like Danny, McKay was small, about five foot six and 160 pounds. He rose to the top of the gang through cunning, pitting the other high-ranking members at Stony Mountain against one another to augment his power. After Maytwayashing was deposed, McKay organized a nine-person council. Danny was part of the inner circle, but he was uneasy about his place. McKay would ask for meetings several times a day, summoning senior members to his cell one at a time, rather than as a group. The meetings unsettled the other council members, creating an impression of plotting going on behind the scenes. According to a Posse member who testified in a murder trial,

McKay ordered a hit on a senior Indian Posse member who was serving time in Prince Albert. He put a hit on another senior member too, and wanted to issue a disciplinary beating against Tyson Roulette, who at the time was allegedly raking in the lion's share of gang profits from dealing drugs on the street. McKay wanted more control.

"There was a lot of tension about the calls McKay was making," said Jeffrey Bruyere. "You get paranoid."

Bruyere, an emerging leader (and not related to McKay's murder victim Adrian Bruyere), had been closer to McKay than most. But something changed as McKay grew more powerful, and their relationship disintegrated. McKay made capricious demands, at one point insisting that a high-earning gang member on the street drop everything to fetch some milk for his girlfriend who was at home with their kids. He also authorized a hit against one of Bruyere's strikers, but Bruyere caught wind of it and stopped it. McKay was making enemies.

Travis Personius, an Indian Posse member from The Pas, Manitoba, was also on the IP range at Stony Mountain at this time. He said McKay used to hit the young strikers for no reason, knowing they didn't dare hit him back. McKay liked to humiliate people, he said. He wasn't strong or tough, in Personius's estimation, but he was feared. "He was an asshole," Personius later said of McKay, in court.

At Stony Mountain, Personius was McKay's personal bodyguard. When they were walking around inside the prison or the exercise yard, McKay insisted he stay close to him, in case he was attacked. Personius had the risky task of carrying the weapons for McKay, usually a blade in his waistband or pants pockets during the day. When McKay felt things were under control he'd wave Personius away.

Kim is an indigenous woman who was hired to work with the IP inmates as a counsellor. She remembers walking on to the IP range for the first time wondering what on earth she had signed up for. At the time the inmates were locked up in their cells twenty-three hours a day, because there had been so much violence in the prison. Every time they moved through the institution, out to the exercise yard or for a traditional ceremony, the rest of the penitentiary had to be locked down to prevent anyone from coming into contact with them. No other unit would even agree to play floor hockey against them, so fearsome was their reputation. The range was set up with twelve steel-doored cells on the bottom tier and twelve on top – twenty-four inmates in all. The first time Kim met the Indian Posse members, they all walked up with their chests puffed out, strutting to demonstrate their toughness.

Danny was a relative breath of fresh air; in her eyes, a friendly, easygoing guy who liked to laugh and was willing to confide. Once, he offered to make her a cup of coffee and, realizing that they didn't have a coffee pot, she went to check on him and found him wringing out a white sock that he'd used as a filter. "It's fine," Danny said. "It's brand new." Sitting down over coffee was one of the best ways to connect with the men, Kim found. She used to bring them flavoured Coffee Mate, a treat that the guys appreciated for the way it broke up the monotony of their prison routine. When she sat down to chat with Danny, she listened as he described how much he missed his son, and how he dreamed of leading a normal life, with a house and a family and maybe his own business. He also talked about his love for his mother and how he still sometimes struggled to get over the anger he felt toward her for the way he was brought up. Kim asked Danny to consider how his mother was raised, to ask himself how her history might have led her to act the way she did. A week later Danny said he'd thought about what she said and written his mother a letter.

Danny grew protective of Kim. One day she introduced herself to a new guy on the range and he just ignored her and walked away. Danny saw what happened and chased him down and spoke to him privately. Five minutes later the new guy meekly returned to apologize for his rudeness. Another time, an inmate grew frustrated with a project she had assigned them and he violently smashed it. Danny jumped up and shouted, "You don't do that in front of her!" When Kim's daughter died tragically, Danny was among the first to offer her a hug.

"He was a very compassionate guy," she said. "A lot of them that do time don't want to feel. They just sort of put that away, they suppress it. They become a totally different person, they don't want to feel. A lot of these guys, since they were in their teens, they've become their own little robots to survive."

For his part, Danny was unhappy. At twenty-nine, he felt he was getting too old for the hyperactive thrill seeking of a jail full of youngsters eager to prove themselves, and he just wanted to do his time in peace. He didn't see eye to eye with McKay and didn't approve of the way he operated, but he wasn't keen to start another conflict, nor was he sure he had the support of the rest of the council. Kim said the two of them pretended to get along; it was a facade.

One day in late April 2006, the situation finally came to a head when a young gang member smuggled a large package of drugs into the prison. It had been a long time since the IP had any drugs and many of the guys were anxious to use them. McKay, sensing an opportunity to flex his power, took control of the package and placed the drugs with another gang member, instructing him that no one was to have any pills. Danny took the pills anyway, an act of open defiance.

McKay was furious, and he confronted Danny on the range. Bruyere, who had also taken some of the pills, was there when McKay stormed up to them.

"He was pissed off," Bruyere recalled. "He said, 'What the fuck? We could've used those to kill someone or something.'"

McKay's anger was so intense that it frightened Bruyere: this was sure to end in bloodshed. Danny hurried to see his old friend Raymond Armstrong to discuss the situation. He knew that he was in the hot seat, and that if he didn't move on McKay, McKay, feeling he had no choice, was sure to move on him, because Danny had clearly disrespected him and too many people knew about it. Danny had already heard that McKay was ready to order his killing. McKay, too, knew this confrontation was coming. Barely a month before, he spoke to Kim and asked her how she would feel if she woke up one morning and heard that he, McKay, had been killed.

Armstrong had been one of Danny's closest friends since they were twelve years old, and Danny knew he could count on him for support. They quickly needed to rally more people to their side, including the rest of the council, whose approval they sought to kill McKay. This was Danny's other side: cold, calculating, and capable of murder. One person who did time with Danny said later he was shocked by the way Danny could turn so cold, so quickly. "Even though he's the nicest guy, he's fucking sinister," this gang member said. "Even if you're his best friend he'll kill you."

Danny and Armstong went to see Bruyere. He had been so shaken by the earlier encounter with McKay that he was working on his shank when they arrived at his cell. He was relieved to see them. They needed only a few words to seal the pact.

While the plotters got together, McKay was outside in the yard, running laps. When he finished, he went inside and the rest of the gang council, including Danny, Armstrong, Bruyere, Adrian Young, and Raymond Chartrand, followed. When they got to his cell, McKay was already lying on his bed, watching TV. They surrounded him in a half circle, and Danny went to shake his hand. "What's up? So you think you're the man?" Danny said.

McKay stood up. "No," he replied.

"No," Danny agreed.

Danny threw the first punch, but McKay was ready to fight for his life. Chartrand got in behind McKay and wrapped his massive arms around his throat. As blows flew in from all angles Chartrand squeezed until McKay stopped struggling and slipped to the floor, unconscious. But the blows continued, and several people stomped on his chest and back. In the moment, the council members seemed to be uncertain as to whether they should beat McKay, but spare his life, as they had done with Brad, or whether McKay had to die. The others looked to Danny for a decision: "This guy's not leaving this cell," he said.

Danny was holding a piece of white fabric, either a towel or a long-sleeved white T-shirt. He slipped the cloth around McKay's neck and started pulling on both ends, cutting off the oxygen to his brain.

Danny said everyone present had to take a turn, so they would all be equally culpable. He paused and handed the white cloth to two others, each of whom took an end and pulled for a few minutes before handing off to another pair. When they were sure McKay was dead, they flipped him over on his bed and covered him with the sheet.

Travis Personius, the man whose job was to protect McKay, was standing a few metres away at the pay phone and watched as everyone entered the cell and closed the door. Moments earlier Ray Chartrand had asked him to keep watch for guards, but none was around. Personius could see only a blur of motion behind the tiny window, but he knew something was going on. He could hear the squeaking of sneakers sliding on the floor, like a basketball game, he said. He could also hear the rustling, pounding sound of a struggle. A few minutes later every senior member of the IP filed out of McKay's cell, but not McKay. They looked pumped up, energized, Personius said. Danny walked out holding the murder weapon, the piece of white fabric, at arm's length, one hand on each end, his elbows locked, as though he was trying to keep it as far away from himself as possible.

The group quickly dispersed. Danny went straight to the laundry room, Chartrand went to the showers, others began cutting up all the clothing they had been wearing – jeans, shirts, shoes, all of it. Danny mopped a line from Sheldon's cell back to the kitchen, removing any trace of footprints leading to and from the murder scene. Then he went back to his cell and removed his shoes and clothes.

That night most of the range worked to dispose of evidence. As they tried to flush fragments of shoes and jeans down the toilets, the toilets jammed and overflowed. The correctional officers, attributing the overflow to a rainstorm that was raging outside, saw the inmates furiously trying to mop up the water before lights out and gave them an extra thirty minutes to try to clean up the mess. Almost all the cells on the lower part of the range had to be checked for flooding. Guards who went to McKay's cell assumed he was sleeping.

It wasn't until the following afternoon, when McKay's girlfriend arrived for a visit, that guards noticed he wasn't answering their calls. A guard walked out onto the range looking for him. "McKay, visit," he called impatiently from the doorway to his cell. "What the fuck, you dead or something?"

A pungent smell wafted out as he opened the door wider. He kicked the bed frame and there was no response. McKay was lying face down, his head turned away from the door. His fingers were purple. The guard pulled back the blanket and saw a footprint-shaped bruise on his back. He stepped back outside, ordered the inmates to their cells, and triggered an emergency call. Within minutes, officers were swarming all over the range.

The prison was locked down for weeks. The RCMP interviewed every prisoner, one by one, careful to ensure that each inmate was interviewed for exactly the same length of time. If anyone was interviewed for a longer period it might have put that inmate's life at risk, since it would suggest they were cooperating. But the Indian Posse held together. Nobody spoke, nobody caved to police pressure, and nobody was charged; at least, not immediately.

On the night of the murder, once they were back in their cells, Chartrand, whose cell was next to Personius's, couldn't stop himself from talking about what had happened. They stayed up until three in the morning, Personius said, each sitting close to a vent that allowed them to communicate.

"Fucking guy was whacked," Chartrand told Personius. "Choked him out, sleep rolled him. Bros held his hands. Fucking guy was plotting on everybody," he said.

The story was that in addition to his conflicts with Danny and Bruyere, McKay was also plotting hits on high-ranking members on the street, particularly Tyson Roulette and Darrell Lavallee. At that time the pair were the highest-earning members of the gang. They were threatening to leave if McKay wasn't taken out. Something had to give.

An informant later said that after the killing Danny was careful not to discuss what had happened. He had sworn the others to secrecy and was not going to break the oath himself. But another informant said that Danny, at some point in the year after the murder, told him that "the fucker deserved it." The power had gone to McKay's head; he was "plotting against brothers, doing greasy things behind other people's backs and spending money from the kitty," the informant quoted Danny as saying.

It was a big decision to take out a boss. Once he was backed into a corner, however, Danny seems to have arrived at it fairly quickly. There were many good reasons to take out Sheldon McKay: he was unnecessarily violent toward the gang's younger members; he made arbitrary decisions that irked other senior leaders, and made everyone tense and unhappy. But just a week before McKay was killed, Danny made a surprising revelation in a letter to his brother. He mentioned that the Indian Posse was in heavy recruiting mode. They needed more people to keep up with the other gangs. Their principal rivals on the prairies were still the Manitoba Warriors and the Native Syndicate, but there were new players all the time, including the Mad Cowz and the African Mafia, two Winnipeg gangs led primarily by children whose parents were refugees from Africa's civil strife. Danny attributed the gangs' growth to the demand for crack cocaine, a volume-sales business that demands an army of suppliers and muscle.

"The door is open for the family," Danny wrote. "People are coming in like crazy. The numbers [are] going up now. It's the rock that changes the game bro."

Danny said that as the other gangs grew, the Indian Posse, traditionally one of the largest gangs, had been the last to follow suit and expand its membership. "Every other family's numbers [are] up except ours so we had to swallow some of our pride and open the door," he said.

What was truly remarkable, though, was that the Posse was going to allow recruits from all ethnic and cultural backgrounds. There had been a handful of non-native members in the past: Ron Taylor, who was black, was notable for being the first, but the gang's rhetoric was actively hostile to other ethnic groups. Danny was clearly ambivalent, if not outright opposed. He had always been outspoken in his opposition to white authority, which he tended to see as synonymous with white people in general.

"Now we got white, black, might as well say all nations," Danny wrote to Richard. He emphasized, though, that the gang could only be led by indigenous people. Any outsider could never rise to the highest ranks of the inner circle.

"We will run the circle, *neechis* [the Cree word for friend or brother] always," he said. "We will never forget who we are."

He was likely looking for Richard's approval. It was a contentious decision and one that his brother, when he was leading the gang a decade earlier, would not have allowed. Although he had been pushed aside in the intervening years, Richard's opinion still influenced

Danny's thinking and Danny wanted to put the best spin on a major change. It sounded like enough of the council approved that Danny had little choice but to go with it. He asked Richard to send him any potential recruits who might qualify under the new rules.

"Bro, I never thought this would happen," Danny said. "But people are for it and it's all good for now."

It's possible that the decision to open up membership irked Danny sufficiently that he decided to take on McKay, but there's no evidence that it was any more than a small factor.

Once McKay was out of the picture, Danny was free to do as he pleased. When the lockdown ended in July 2006, two and a half months after the killing, Danny had less than six months remaining on his sentence. He was on easy street. It was time to start planning for the future. He was going to run the gang's Saskatchewan operations. He needed to recruit some new soldiers – and he needed to stay off police radar.

16

IN COLD BLOOD
2007

James was the living embodiment of how the Indian Posse became Canada's largest street gang. He was fifteen years old and his world was collapsing when he was taken in by Danny Wolfe in August 2007.

James woke up alone one morning after a long night of drinking. He had been at the pow-wow on Saskatchewan's Standing Buffalo First Nation reserve, having driven about seven hours with friends from his home in The Pas, Manitoba, to get there. He had just discovered that his travelling companions had returned home without him, leaving him stranded.

Danny assured James that he would look after him. James was welcome to stay as long as he wanted, he said, even suggesting that the teen should enroll in the local school for the coming year. After all, James had run into some problems back home. Maybe a fresh start would be a good thing.

Danny knew what he was doing. He had a young man he could use and he was determined to bring him under his control, using all the tools of manipulation he had learned in prison and as a recruiter.

James, already an Indian Posse member, was nearly a generation younger than Danny but had grown up in similar circumstances. His mother had a serious addiction to alcohol. His parents fought and his father spent time in jail before they separated. To this day James reacts physically to the sound of something breaking because it makes him recall the thrown plates and glasses that usually accompanied their battles. He explained that his parents didn't know any better, because that's the way they were raised.

In school he had trouble paying attention and completing tasks. He was impulsive, uncooperative, and overactive. He was held back in early grades, and when he was eight he was stabbed by a classmate. At eleven, he brought a knife to school. Although his intellectual and emotional capacities were rated as average or above average, he found himself most at ease with a criminal element.

If there is one major shift that reflects the different eras in which Danny and James grew up, it's the influence of gangs. When Danny was eleven, there were a couple of relatively small street gangs concentrated in the big cities. In James's life, they were all around. He had older relatives on his mother's side involved with the Indian Posse, and some who belonged to the Native Syndicate. On his father's side some relatives were with the Manitoba Warriors. For an indigenous teenaged boy, particularly one prone to act out and searching for a sense of belonging, gangs were difficult to ignore. This was the world the Wolfe brothers had made.

One day eleven-year-old James was hanging around The Pas, a roughneck lumber town of five thousand people on the banks of the Saskatchewan River. He was already a bit of an outsider. He struck up a conversation with an older man just out of the penitentiary, who happened to be an Indian Posse member and, as it turned out, knew some of James's relatives. A psychologist would later note that James had a poor sense of boundaries and often spoke to people he shouldn't have been talking to. After a few days the man got in touch again, offering James a task. His assignment, a kind of initiation test, was to steal some marijuana. He was in.

The Indian Posse will sometimes use kids under twelve to move drugs and weapons because they don't look like the usual suspects and if they get caught they're too young to be charged with a crime under Canada's youth justice laws. So James started as a drug mule. He would take drugs to customers or move them from one location to another. Soon he moved up to drug rip-offs, where he would invade a rival dealer's home and take his stash. Sometimes he flashed an IP hand signal to threaten his victims to keep quiet; sometimes he used violence.

James liked being in the gang. It was better than being picked on. His close friends joined too, and girls paid more attention to him. He and his friends had money and they looked cool, he thought. Eventually James went to Winnipeg where his gang missions involved ferrying guns around. At the age of fourteen he was formally inducted into the gang and got an Indian Posse tattoo. He eventually reached a stage where he was entrusted with a mission to kill someone, but for reasons that are unclear the plan didn't come together.

In the summer of 2007 James was still not much more than a boy. He was small and slight and wore a sleepy expression on his face. He was smoking marijuana six times a day and popping opioid pills. He had been suspended from school indefinitely for threatening to stab another student and, with nothing better to do, he devoted his energies to the gang.

Much of the Indian Posse's local business was done across the river from the town of The Pas on the neighbouring Opaskwayak Cree Nation reserve. OCN's population was about half that of the town, but it had a new casino and hotel and a wildly popular junior hockey team, making it one of the most prosperous reserves in the province. There was also a strong demand for drugs and a thriving Indian Posse chapter to cater to the local market. As the gang prospered, band leaders were increasingly concerned. After several band members had been threatened in their homes, the council passed a resolution to banish anyone from the First Nation if they were involved in gang activity, a first in the province.

The RCMP, which had its main station in the town of The Pas, had been asked by the band to build a station on the reserve to provide a more effective local presence. During the construction of the new police station the building was burnt to the ground, twice. Both times the IP was suspected; the second time, on August 17, 2007, James was arrested and charged. When he was being moved from his cell a short time after being charged, however, he launched an audacious escape. One RCMP officer said James punched his way out, fighting through his captors and making a dash for freedom. Incredibly, he managed to get away, running across the bridge to the reserve and then along its dirt roads to a house where he could hide. He sought out his girlfriend and said goodbye, then he found two friends with a car who were willing to help him get out of town. They headed for a pow-wow on the Standing Buffalo First Nation in Saskatchewan.

They met up with Danny Wolfe at Trapper's Bar in Fort Qu'Appelle. James had met Danny when Danny was in The Pas just a few months earlier, in May, on gang business. On that trip Danny managed to get charged with marijuana possession and impersonation for trying to pass off a fake ID. It wouldn't be surprising if James was eager to work with Danny. One younger gang member who did time with Danny said young people were always drawn to him. They tried to impress him and sought his approval. He said he once went so far as to offer to kill someone just because he thought it would please Danny, only for Danny to give him a withering look that made him feel foolish.

Danny had been living back at Okanese since his release from Stony Mountain in November 2006. He had arrived by bus, once again with just a couple hundred dollars in his pocket. He and his mother enjoyed a better relationship this time; he was able to see his girlfriend Shenoa and their infant daughter; and Danny was also reunited with his younger brother, Preston. By some accounts, Danny had as many as four hundred Indian Posse members under him in loosely organized cells across Saskatchewan, but he needed a more reliable local crew to sell drugs and act as muscle for debt collection if he was going to keep building his network.

Trapper's was a fairly typical prairie roadhouse, with a pool table, video lottery terminals, and an off-licence that sold beer. The clientele was a cross-section of the blue-collar, agricultural town and its surrounding First Nations communities. After drinking at Trapper's, James and his friends headed back to Danny's place. Danny was staying in the basement of his cousin's house on the reserve. They smoked some weed and eventually James passed out. When he woke up, his friends were gone.

"You're under me now," Danny told James.

He made it clear that he was calling the shots now in James's life. James would not be turning himself in to face the arson and escape charges, Danny said. "If you last five years [the cops] will forget about you," he promised.

Danny also told James that he would find him a girlfriend to make up for any regret he might feel about leaving Manitoba. The gang might even send James to Europe, Danny said vaguely, because they had friends there in the Triads, the Asian crime syndicates.

Over the next few weeks Danny kept James supplied with pills and alcohol. James enrolled at the local school under a false name, claiming he was from Manitoba and staying with an aunt. He told the school he didn't want to fall behind due to unfortunate family circumstances, and they let him in. James later said he did as he was told because he was scared of Danny, who was trying to get him to commit crimes. But James was well acquainted with the criminal lifestyle. The decision to enroll him in school is curious, and it reflects the high hopes Danny had for James. He wanted to ensure he got his education, which could keep doors open down the road. Having a presence in the local school could also help build a pipeline for Indian Posse recruiting.

Danny's younger brother, Preston, was now twenty years old. In his letters from prison Danny had been preoccupied with making sure Preston didn't follow his older brothers into a life of crime, constantly urging Preston to stay in school and behave himself. But, by his late teens, Preston was proving to be as tough as Danny and Richard and similarly drawn to the thrill of gang life. Despite his family connections, though, Preston was afforded no special status in the Indian Posse. He was working his way up as muscle, collecting debts and dispensing violence.

In February 2007, a few months after Danny's return, Preston was arrested for the murder of a young steel worker named Vincent Morisseau-Poorman in the town of Fort Qu'Appelle. Preston and the victim had been part of a group that left a bar together after a long day and night of drinking. Something went wrong, and Morisseau-Poorman was shot dead. Witnesses implicated Preston, and one alleged that Preston later admitted to the killing.

Danny was upset by Preston's arrest. He hadn't had much contact with his younger brother but he was loyal to him and he wanted to see him achieve things in life. Although Danny was proud of the gang he and Richard had helped build, he knew that it was a hard, vicious existence that he didn't want his brother to experience. Preston also had advantages that Danny hadn't had growing up: his mother provided a more stable home life through his teenaged years after she gave up drinking. Preston didn't need to fend for himself in the way that Danny had. He could go to the same school for two consecutive years and not have to worry about where he would sleep on a given night or how he might pay for his next meal. But there were still many challenges for Preston to overcome.

As with Richard Sr., Susan had a difficult relationship with Preston's father, Clarence Buffalocalf. Clarence, too, had a drinking problem, and there was violence in the home. There were many nights when Preston was young that she doesn't remember at all. It was in this period that Richard was arrested, tried, and sent to jail for nearly twenty years without her knowing.

Shortly after Danny returned to Okanese, Preston was charged with a serious crime. The little boy whom Danny tried to shield from the gang world was being drawn into his older brother's life. When Preston was arrested, the Crown and the police never explained what they believed the motive had been for the killing. But the allegations were serious.

Danny, in February 2007, was leading what appeared to be a fledgling Indian Posse chapter in the Fort Qu'Appelle area. He had only a handful of followers, who were mainly young and inexperienced. He was also trying to find work as an anti-gang counsellor. He pitched himself as someone who, for a fee, could talk to youth groups and scare them straight. He had done a few such speaking jobs, which were centred on this basic, point-form essay that he wrote in late 2006:

My name is Daniel Wolfe. I am Cree native born in Sask, Regina. Raised in Central Winnipeg by my mother not knowing my father. During my childhood I looked up to my older friends who were in and out of institutions which I looked up to as my role models (father image). Environment filled with family violence, poverty, alcohol, drug abuse. Not having stable parents or relatives to raise me. I began to associate with older first nations who had the same background as myself. Who never knew their cultural traditional ways. Which led into a life of crime, alcohol and drug abuse, lack of schooling and respect for myself and society. During my teen years I helped found an aboriginal street gang which involved me in drug dealing, crime. . . . While incarcerated I found myself more and more with the traditional teachings (pipe ceremonies, sweats, sharing circles). I would like to share my [knowledge of] a life of poverty, addictions with the younger and older people in today's society. Educate them with the realities of street life, recognizing indications of youth getting into gangs, and recognizing how gang life can tear a family apart.

He hoped his occasional speaking gigs could be turned into something more permanent. It was not an idle dream; gang prevention work was a growing field, and his motives might not have been entirely pure. At the same time in Manitoba, some former members of the Manitoba Warriors had set themselves up in an anti-gang program in Winnipeg, called Paa Pii Wak. They were receiving hundreds of thousands of dollars in government funding and were using it to run what was allegedly a gang clubhouse, police said. Warriors members were being released by the authorities into the custody of their own gang higher-ups. They were also using "scared straight" sessions to recruit, rather than to dissuade young people from joining up. The enterprise was eventually broken up by a police raid and several arrests. It was a massive black eye for the governments involved. It was also cited by police as evidence of how wary one should be of gangsters who claim to have reformed.

Danny was still doing a convincing job of presenting himself as someone who wanted to change his life. He was living in a room in the basement of his cousin Tatiana's house on the reserve. If he had money, if he was making a living selling drugs, he wasn't flashy about it, his mother said. He seemed to have about as much, or as little, as anyone else. He had a closet full of clothes, a few new baseball hats. There were two handmade dream catchers, as well as a poster of rappers Dr. Dre, 50 Cent, and Eminem, on his wall. Pride of place in his room was given to a huge photo collage of fellow Indian Posse members. The photos were arranged so that they covered a piece of cardboard about two and a half feet tall cut in the shape of an Indian Posse logo. It looked like the kind of thing you might find in a junior high yearbook alongside photos of the debate club or the homecoming dance. Instead, these were posed portraits of some of the country's most notorious drug pushers, thieves, and killers.

Danny was at Tatiana's house on the reserve one night in mid-September. It was well after midnight and he was still awake. It was an unusually hot week, with temperatures that hit 30 degrees Celsius. Maybe he was bored, maybe he had been drinking, maybe he needed to let off steam. Danny took his .22 calibre rifle upstairs and stood on the deck, aiming the weapon into the trees. He squeezed the trigger and opened fire. He let his clip empty in automatic mode, the shells going off in rapid succession, the projectiles sailing into the dark and interrupting the silence of the prairie night.

Not far away in a neighbouring house, Ernest Tuckanow was sleeping in his bedroom. He had brought his infant child into bed with him because of the unusually warm weather and fallen asleep with the window open that night. Around 5:00 a.m. Tuckanow woke to the sound of the shots. He got up and looked out the window. He saw Danny and someone else on the deck. Danny was holding a .22 with a large ammunition clip. Tuckanow had a flash of anger. What if a bullet went astray? What if one hit his house, or his sleeping child?

"I got pissed off," Tuckanow said later. "Don't need that shit around here."

He phoned the police. The Okanese reserve is policed by the File Hills police service, a small aboriginal policing outfit with limited resources. A File Hills police officer drove out to the area, looked around, and left without speaking to anyone. The whole event seemed innocuous, but Danny had made a huge mistake and it was the first step in a great unravelling.

A few nights later, Danny sat at the bar in Trapper's drinking a bottle of Bud. He was wearing a New York Yankees hat and a tank top that left his heavily tattooed arms and torso exposed. Just before leaving the penitentiary he had added three or four new tats that another IP member etched into his skin using a razor blade, baby oil, and soot. There was a silhouetted image of Stony Mountain Penitentiary on the back of his neck and a wolf paw on his calf; and then there were the older ones: *Indian Posse* in red script across the back of his shoulders, a face covered with a bandana on his back, *Pride* down the back of his left arm, and *Red til Dead* at the top of his chest.

Danny wasn't looking for trouble. He had been drinking with James earlier in the day and was now sipping his beer, waiting for a couple of friends. It was just before eight o'clock. Another group came into the bar. They were boisterous, laughing, jumping around and pounding back drinks. The biggest man in the group was Percy Pascal (his real name was Bernard, but everyone called him Pudge). He looked like a football lineman, with huge, meaty hands and chubby cheeks that seemed to swallow up his eyes when he smiled. He was normally warm and shy, but on his cheek, just below his left eye, was a very noticeable tattoo – the logo of the Native Syndicate gang.

Pascal was twenty-three years old and in a mood to celebrate. He had been out of prison for about two weeks and the day had started well. It was September 20, family allowance cheque day, and his family drove in to Fort Qu'Appelle from their home on the Pasqua First Nation for breakfast. His mother gave him five bucks to play the VLTs and he cashed out with $870. He had planned to do something constructive with the money, like getting a photo ID; instead he fell into an old habit and walked into the liquor store, emerging with a twenty-six-ounce bottle of liquor that he immediately started drinking. It wasn't even noon yet, but it was a gorgeous day. He bumped into someone he hadn't seen in ten years, Michael Itittakoose. Mikey had been a great friend when they were kids. Since then, though, Pascal's life had been filled with dramatic twists that included running away from home, living on the streets, stealing hundreds of cars, escaping from prison, and generally making a name for himself as one of the most fearsome young members of the Native Syndicate gang.

"I learned how to survive on my own. I learned how to make some money by stealing and I used to feed myself. I'd pretty much eat one meal a day and drink lots of water," Pudge said. "I'd steal from stores. Clothes, meats, whatever."

In many ways, Pudge Pascal resembled a young Danny Wolfe. He was described as friendly, funny, bold – an exciting person to hang around with. Pascal, though, was living in a world already transformed by the arrival of gangs like the Indian Posse. The Native Syndicate was the third of the big-three aboriginal gangs on the prairies, after the Posse and the Warriors. It was formed in the prison system by inmates who didn't want to be subject to either of the two existing gangs. Its members were almost entirely indigenous and its iconography and symbols were borrowed from First Nations traditions. As the gang grew, it spread to the streets of cities and reserves across the Prairies, becoming a major rival in recruiting and drug dealing. By the early 2000s, it had become the dominant gang in Regina, which earned it the nickname "Syn City."

The organization had had its eye on Pudge Pascal for some time, and the attraction was obvious. He was a big, tough kid in the prison system. Pudge said he resisted the pressure to join for months, but he eventually relented, was given an initiation beating, and got his Native Syndicate tattoo. When he bumped into his old friend Mikey in Fort Qu'Appelle that September day, Pudge was proud to show off his gang tattoos. The gang had become an important part of his identity, but seeing an old friend brought him back to his childhood. They laughed together, reminisced, and drank glass after glass.

"I was drinking heavily," Pudge said. "I started out with a twenty-six ounce, a forty ounce and then a sixty-six ounce [bottle] of Silent Sam. Hard vodka. That's what I drank all day and night. I was mixing my vodka with wine coolers. I was tanked."

As evening fell they headed to Trapper's Bar with some friends in Cordell Keepness's blue pickup truck. They were joking around when they entered and the mood was light. It's hard to know what happened to change it, but at some point Pudge caught sight of Danny and the tattooed script that ran in a half circle around Danny's collar: *Red til Dead*. He didn't know Danny, but he knew that tattoo meant Indian Posse. Fort Qu'Appelle had for years been a mainly Native Syndicate town, so it was strange to see such an open display of colours from the Indian Posse. Maybe that was the point. Still, if Pudge heard alarm bells, he didn't heed them.

Pudge was there with a lot of friends, while Danny was, at that moment, alone. Pudge was much bigger than Danny, and a decade younger. He asked Danny if he knew their gangs were at war. They went back and forth briefly with insults on both sides, but no one can remember what was said. Suddenly a pool cue flew through the air like a javelin, although it's not clear who threw it. Danny retreated behind the pool table and slipped off his socks. Then he plucked a ball from the table and dropped into his sock, giving himself a weapon he could whip like a club. Pudge and his friends decided to leave and headed for the door. Danny chased after them, calling them out in the parking lot, challenging Pudge and his companions to fight. They simply drove away.

What ran through Danny's head in the minutes that followed will forever remain a mystery, but one thing was clear: He had been disrespected in public. Several people had seen and heard it. What's more, he was not in a position to brush it off. He was a high-status member of his own gang, which comes with its own set of expectations, but he was also struggling to maintain that position in a gang world that was shifting. It was easy to be a top dog in the controlled world of prison. There, his contributions were valued; he could be fun and charismatic, and get along with people, settle disputes, make strategic decisions, smuggle drugs and weapons. But staying on top on the outside was proving more difficult. He was getting older, and perhaps felt his status slipping. On the street there was always someone younger and crazier willing to step up and do what he wouldn't. There were fewer people around who remembered what he'd done years earlier. At times he seemed to admit these doubts in his writing. Would he have the same status in the IP in the years to come? Not if he allowed people to treat him like a nobody in public.

Danny also had yet to issue the ultimate order for a street boss: a murder. Now he had an opportunity. Years later his friends would say Danny had no choice, that if he didn't move on Pudge and the others, it would have been a sign of weakness and they would have moved on him. Danny picked up his phone and started making calls.

Joseph Crowe, who was selling beer in the bar's off-licence, overheard a snippet of what Danny said into his phone: "They don't know what's coming for them."

Gerrard Granbois was at home on the Okanese reserve that night when Danny called him. Gerrard was dating Danny's cousin Tiffany, and Danny saw Gerrard as someone he could count on. Tiffany's boyfriend was young and fairly naive, but in Danny's mind, he was going to have a role in his fledgling crew. Danny was amped up on the phone. He said there were some guys at the bar giving him trouble and he wanted Gerrard to borrow a van from Danny's cousin Tatiana and bring the gun. Tatiana wouldn't lend her vehicle to Gerrard, which frustrated Danny. He couldn't go after these guys without a vehicle and some backup. But he was undeterred, and somehow made it all the way back to the house on the reserve, a distance of fifteen kilometres. He convinced Tatiana to let him take her blue GMC Safari. The van had picked up a brown hue from the dust of the dirt roads around the reserve. It was filthy inside too. Before he left, Danny got his gun, a .22 calibre rifle with a banana clip that held twenty-five rounds of ammunition, wrapped it in a sheet, and carried it to the van. He and Gerrard drove to a friend's house where James was drinking. James climbed into the back seat.

After getting some gas they drove into Fort Qu'Appelle. Danny took the wheel because Gerrard had trouble seeing at night. The talking had stopped. The three of them were tense, perhaps even frightened, and they were focused on finding Pudge and the blue pickup he and his friends were driving when they left Trapper's. Danny patrolled up and down the roads of the quiet town. Finally they spotted the truck sitting outside a modest, white clapboard bungalow at 302 Pasqua Avenue. The lights were on inside the home and the muffled sounds of a party could be heard. Danny parked the van a little ways away, down an alley and out of sight. The three of them got out. Danny tied a red bandana around his face, leaving only his eyes exposed, just like the image he had tattooed on his back. James did the same. Danny grabbed James by his shirt to snap him to attention, then handed him the rifle and prodded him in the direction of the house. Gerrard, the getaway driver who couldn't see in the dark, waited by the van. He watched them run up to the house.

Danny had killed before. He had choked someone to death, stabbed people, committed more than a dozen drive-by and walk-by shootings. But he had never done anything this brazen. He had never simply entered a house and opened fire before, and didn't know what to expect on the other side of the door. Was this a Native Syndicate house? Would they be walking into a roomful of guns?

James carried the rifle, trying to avoid crunching the dried leaves that had fallen on the rickety wooden stairs. He had twenty-five bullets to dispense; all he had to do was hold down the trigger. They stood before the closed door. Danny raised his leg and unleashed a powerful kick, smashing it open. They stepped a few inches inside and immediately started shooting.

Jesse Obey was sitting on a couch that jutted out from the living room and placed him directly in front of the doorway, just a few feet from where Danny and James stood. He had been playing pool in the bar a few hours earlier when Pudge Pascal started the argument with Danny.

It's not clear whether it was James or Danny who held the rifle when the door swung open. James claims he froze in the moment and that Danny grabbed the rifle from him, which is possible. But this was partly Danny's test to see whether James was committed enough to shoot someone. If there was a moment's hesitation, it wasn't long enough for Jesse Obey to react to save himself. All he saw was the gun. He had time only to turn his head away from the flash of the barrel. The first shot pierced a hole in his cheek and smashed through his mouth, destroying half his teeth. He fell sideways and lost consciousness immediately.

A few feet beyond Obey, but still in direct sight of the front door, was the main bedroom, which belonged to Marvin Arnault and his sixty-three-year-old wife Christina Cook, known to all in town as Granny. Granny was a woman who liked to have people hanging around her place. She always welcomed young people and allowed them to drink and socialize in her home. Granny's view was that it was better to have the kids nearby than looking for trouble someplace else.

That day she and her husband had been to Regina to see a doctor, and when they got home, her daughter told her that she had kicked some kids out for being too noisy. But a short while later the group returned, led by Mikey Itittakoose, a friend of her grandson, and Percy Pascal, whom she called Pudgie.

Mikey came in and gave Granny a hug. He asked about her medical tests and they sat on her bed and chatted for a while. There were four or five people sitting around talking in the bedroom, men and women of varied ages, including some of Granny's friends, and another eight or ten people milling around elsewhere in the house, in the living room or the kitchen or downstairs.

When the door swung open, Granny saw a silhouetted figure in the entrance. He was wearing a long, black leather coat and his face was covered with a bandana. She saw only his eyes and the burst of flame from the muzzle.

Everyone dove for cover, but there was no place to run, she said. She knew guns from her days growing up in the country and she could tell this was a .22 semi-automatic. As the shots popped one after another in rapid fire, she tried to count them. She looked over at Mikey. His white hoodie exploded with patches of red. She cast her eye over him and counted three wounds spilling blood.

Cordell Keepness was also in the bedroom. He saw everyone scrambling for safety but he couldn't process what was occurring quickly enough to respond. By the time he understood it was too late.

"I got shot in my right forearm and my left hand and my side. I just felt my arms getting hit. I just fell after that," he said. "I just fell on the bed and then rolled over and fell on the ground."

With people dropping around her, Granny stood up. She needed to act.

"I said, 'Girls, come on, help me,'" she said. "'Let's call the ambulance.' They didn't give me the phone. Of course, everybody is panicking."

One of her friends was cowering in the closet. She could hear her praying out loud as the bullets continued to fly. Granny shouted at her, "Oh for God's sake you're ready for your Creator. Help me look for the phone to call an ambulance."

She fumbled around on the floor until she found the phone. Just as she started dialling, Danny and James spotted her. They had avoided shooting any of the women to that point. But Granny posed a threat.

One of them yelled, "Shoot the old lady, she's calling the cops."

The shooter swivelled in her direction. At the same moment, Marvin Arnault, who had ducked for cover in the bedroom, made a snap decision. He had to save his wife. He dove across the room and threw himself on top of her just as the bullets flew. They landed on the floor between the two beds, Mr. Arnault lying on top of his wife. For a moment it was just the two of them, lying together in the midst of a bloodbath, listening to the shooting, listening to the screaming, listening to one another breathe. Granny was being crushed under her husband's three-hundred-pound weight. She tried to wriggle free.

"Are you hurt?" Marvin asked.

"No," she replied.

"You know I love you, eh, Chris?"

"Yeah," said Granny.

"Look after the boys."

Granny paused. "Are you hurt, Marvin?" she asked.

"I think so," he said.

Those were his last words. He died in her arms.

Granny looked over at Mike Itittakoose. He was on the floor between the beds, not moving, the red patches on his hoodie growing larger. She knew he was gone too.

Roughly two minutes had elapsed and Danny and James continued to shoot their way through the house. In the panic, people had scattered in all directions. Some headed for the basement, some tried to break through the wall to get to safety, some ran into the kitchen.

Danny was focused on Pudge, the guy who had publicly disrespected him. At first, Pudge wasn't sure what was happening. He thought someone was playing a joke. But the screaming and panic felt too real. Right up until that moment, Pudge, who had seen a lot of violence and dished out all kinds of beatings, had never been shot before. As he watched the shooting unfold he was sure he was going to be hit and was just waiting for the gun to find him. It was terrifying. The first bullet struck him in the shin and he grabbed at the pain. When he was shot a second time, he bent double. He wanted to throw up.

"It hurt. I remember those two. And then the third one, it hit me in the balls. That's when I dropped down. The people that were in there said he unloaded on me."

Danny, who had been spraying others in the room, kept the gun focused on Pudge. There was a pause as Danny and James removed an empty ammunition clip and replaced it with a fresh one. Then they resumed firing. As Pudge tried to curl up in a ball, they shot him repeatedly, the bullets slicing into his limbs and sides. He managed to find the strength to move and stumbled from the living room down the stairs to the basement, where others were hiding. They said he jerked around and was screaming incoherently. Then he came back up and stumbled around the kitchen. He was in shock. He was blacking out. The walls were smeared in blood; the floor was slippery with thick clots of red. He fell to the ground and passed out. Pudge had been shot nine times.

The shooting lasted a matter of moments, perhaps as long as two or three minutes, but for the people in the house it felt like it might never end. Danny and James hadn't even ventured more than a few feet inside the door. No one in the house knew who these two shooters were; all they knew was that they had been targeted by masked gunmen.

Having fired somewhere between twenty and thirty rounds, Danny lowered the weapon and turned to walk out the door. Granny was watching him. He tugged at the bandana covering his face and offered one parting phrase to make sure the survivors got the message.

"That'll teach 'em to mess with IP."

They descended the stairs and walked quickly back to the van. According to James, Danny was furious with him for freezing up at such a crucial moment. He shoved the gun back into James's arms. "Go," he said, directing him to the van. "Hurry up."

Danny had taken his revenge, but the plan to get James to commit the crime had backfired. "I should just bury you," Danny said.

The van sat waiting in a dark alley near an Esso gas station. Gerrard had watched nervously from afar while the whole thing went down. He'd heard the gunfire, heard the screams, and now he jumped into action, opening the van doors as he saw Danny and James coming back. The two shooters locked eyes with him quickly before jumping in. They wrapped the gun in the sheet and stowed it away. The engine came to life and they started to roll. Danny was tense as he drove the van away from Pasqua Avenue.

"We shot some people," he finally said to Gerrard, breaking the silence.

They drove to a store in nearby Lebret and bought some beer, an alibi if anyone asked where they had been driving that night, Danny said. He walked the others through their story: *We went to get beer, we came back to the rez and drank it, that's it.* If everyone kept quiet they'd get away with it, he promised. But they had to stick together. They were all in it now. If anyone found out, he and Gerrard would get life sentences, he told them. James might get less because of his age, but he'd still be locked up a long, long time.

Danny started to consider how he would dispose of the gun. They were going to drive to Murray Stonechild's house on the Okanese reserve. On the way Danny decided to drop Gerrard at Tiffany's house.

Danny told Gerrard to get him a new pair of pants and a shirt. His plan was to burn the ones he was wearing to eliminate evidence that might tie him to the scene. Sometime later he scrubbed his hands to remove the gunpowder residue. He had been wearing a hat and mask so he felt confident no one would identify him. He also was fairly sure he had left no DNA behind.

17

CATCHING THE KILLER
SEPTEMBER–DECEMBER 2007

The 911 call came in to Fort Qu'Appelle RCMP around 10:15 p.m. that night, just a few moments after Danny and the others drove off in the van. One of the survivors at 302 Pasqua Avenue had scrambled outside to a neighbour's house and called for help.

RCMP Constable Jan Lussier was one of four RCMP officers on duty and the first to respond. Stabbings and shootings are not uncommon in the area, but a home invasion shooting with multiple victims is an extreme for a small prairie town. Lussier didn't know what he was heading into. The shooters were at large and possibly still in the area. As is often the case in small-town Canada, Lussier would have to respond with minimal backup in conditions that urban police forces would only tackle with overwhelming numbers. Lussier, though, had the advantage of a partner he trusted completely: his wife, Constable Jill Lussier.

Before they could get to the house a second 911 call came in, this time from Granny Cook. "Tell them to hurry it up," she said. "There's two dead already."

When the officers drove up five minutes later, they found the house quiet, the front door closed, and no one around outside. They

Richard Wolfe, age 7, in a school photo. He taught his brother to survive on their own, stealing food from gardens and dumpsters. (1982)

Danny Wolfe, age seven, in a school photo. He was described as a quiet child with a livewire presence. (1982)

Danny in a school photo, age approximately 12, circa 1988, when the Indian Posse was founded.

Danny with his great aunt, Ann Callahan, a pioneering nurse. The critical care wing of Winnipeg's largest hospital is dedicated in her honor.

Danny with his mother, Susan Creeley. As a teenager, Danny talked of how he dreamed she would one day beat her addictions. Later, she did not hesitate to turn him in for breaking his parole conditions.

Richard Wolfe photographed in jail by the *Winnipeg Free Press*, circa 1994. His outspoken style led the gang to discipline him, and although he remained close to his brother Danny, he eventually drifted away from the Indian Posse.

PIMOTAT

ROSSIE

Newly enlisted soldier Leonard Creeley and Pimotat, an uncle and respected community leader from the File Hills, Saskatchewan. Leonard is Danny's great-grandfather, a man who lost his farm after returning from the war with permanent injuries.

OLD & YOUNG INDIANS   FILE HILLS AGENCY

The recruits from the File Hills school with William Morris Graham (centre), the local Indian Agent who controlled many aspects of his students' lives, and First Nations elders. Leonard Creeley is in the third row, second from left.

Danny Wolfe in prison,
believed to be in 2009.

Danny Wolfe displaying some new tattoos. He
once told an undercover officer the tattoos told
the story of his life.

Danny photographed inside a federal penitentiary. Despite weightlifting and even taking
steroids, he was always small and slight, but a fierce combatant.

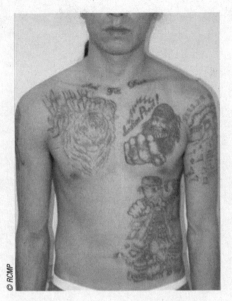

Danny's tattoos, documented by the RCMP, included the script "Red til Dead" around his collar.

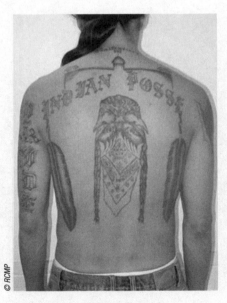

Danny's back, with the outline of Stony Mountain penitentiary tattooed above his Indian Posse back patch and a masked figure.

The blue van used on the night of the shootings in Fort Qu'Appelle.

The house at 40 Okanese where Danny was staying with his cousin.

WANTED
RECHERCHÉS

KEENATCH, Cody
1989-08-21

AGECOUTAY, Ryan
1982-09-26

PEWEAN, James
1983-01-19

WOLFE, Daniel
1976-06-24

BUFFALOCALF, Preston
BORN/NÉ: 1986-06-24

ESCAPED FROM REGINA CORRECTIONAL CENTRE

CAUTION/ATTENTION
ARMED AND DANGEROUS/VIOLENT
ARMÉS ET DANGEREUX/VIOLENTS

CANADA-WIDE WARRANT/ MANDAT PANCANADIEN

WANTED FOR **ESCAPE**

RECHERCHÉS POUR **ÉVASION**

ORIGINAL OFFENCES INCLUDE **A RANGE OF**

INFRACTIONS INITIALES INCLUENT ::

PROPERTY OFFENCES TO MURDER

CRIMES CONTRE LA PROPRIÉTE ET MEURTRE

ISSUED BY SASKATCHEWAN RCMP

DIFUSÉ PAR LA GRC DE SASKATCHEWAN

IF LOCATED, CONTACT/ SI LOCALISÉS, INFORMER

THE NEAREST RCMP DETACHMENT OR POLICE DEPARTMENT IN YOUR AREA

LE DÉTACHEMENT DE LA GRC LE PLUS PRÈS OU UN SERVICE DE POLICE LOCAL

OR

OU

CRIMESTOPPERS AT 1 800 222-TIPS

ÉCHEC AU CRIME À 1 800 222-TIPS

COURTESY OF THE RCMP WANTED PERSONS UNIT   *PUBLIÉ PAR LA GRC. DES PERSONNES RECHERCHÉS*

 Royal Canadian Gendarmerie royale
Mounted Police du Canada

Canada

Wanted: This notice was posted in locations across the prairies as police searched for Danny and company following their brazen escape from the Regina Correctional Centre in 2008.

Danny flashing an IP sign to the cameras as he leaves an RCMP van on his way to court in Regina in 2008. Security was tight during the trial.

Richard sent this photo to Danny when he was in prison. He's showing off a new tattoo – "outlaw" – written on his forearms.

climbed the steps and knocked. There was no answer. They were about to break down the door when finally it was opened from the inside. They glimpsed a scene that was far beyond any violence they'd come across before.

The house was in chaos. People immediately surrounded the officers, upset, incoherent, and crying. They were saying some were dead, but they also seemed confused, unable to explain what had happened and who was hurt, with no clue as to who was responsible. Constable Jan Lussier could see blood on the floor and on the walls. As he stepped inside he saw two women bending over bodies. He also saw Jesse Obey, whom he recognized from around town. Obey's cheek had been blown apart, but his eyes were open. Lussier looked him in the eye, searching for a sign of recognition. Obey returned the officer's gaze but his eyes seemed vacant. His cousin Gwen Obey was frantically attending to him, but she was unable to form any words. Then Lussier looked beyond them to the bedroom. He saw two figures slumped on the floor, facing away from the door, as if they had fallen over while trying to kneel; they were very still. Lussier had been a cop in Fort Qu'Appelle for several years. He knew Marvin Arnault by sight and knew this was his house. And he knew that he was probably dead.

The Lussiers tried to secure the area, get help to the wounded, and preserve possible evidence. Another officer arrived and stayed outside to help corral those who had run out once the shooting stopped.

"It was a pretty chaotic scene," Lussier said. "Our number one thing was the safety of everybody involved. We only had one officer outside maintaining a perimeter for us. Our goal was to get as many people out of the house and away from the house as quick as possible."

They found thirteen people inside. Two were dead; three were taken to hospital by ambulance with major gunshot wounds. The surviving witnesses were so thunderstruck it was difficult to make sense of what they were saying. Someone in a mask and a long black coat had walked up to a strange house, kicked down the door, and opened fire. It was the most shocking crime the local officers had ever encountered.

Robin Zentner, a corporal in the RCMP major crime unit in Regina, was on the case almost immediately after the first details of the shooting hit the radio. Major Crimes in Regina handles all the homicides in the southern portion of the province, and it was Zentner's job to quickly assemble a team that could get out to the crime scene and begin the investigation. This looked like a stone-cold whodunit, and the shooters were still on the loose. Time was of the essence.

The key to solving a murder often lies in understanding the backgrounds of the victims. Corporal Zentner had spent five years working out of the detachment at Fort Qu'Appelle, and as someone with local knowledge, he would help identify the people in the house to spare their families the trauma, and he could help piece together their various connections. He might also be able to provide insight into any feuds or rivalries that might have played a role.

After collecting an initial team of seven officers to gather evidence, Zentner arrived in Fort Qu'Appelle around 2:00 a.m. He was an experienced police officer but the scene at 302 Pasqua was unlike any he had seen before.

"You could see that it had been hysteria in the house," he said. The walls were painted with blood. There were spots where it had pooled on the floor, and it looked like some had tried to bleed over the sink or use pots and pans to collect the blood. "People obviously ran all different directions. There was trails, you could follow their footprints where they had run, and there was bullet holes in the wall and cartridge casings and bullet fragments on the ground."

Brass-coloured cartridge casings littered the area near the entrance. The two bodies were still more or less where they had fallen, despite paramedics' vain efforts to revive them. One lay near a blood-stained piece of paper that detailed how survivors of residential schools could apply for compensation for sexual and physical abuse. The witnesses who'd been in the house were badly shaken up. Many were taken to the RCMP detachment in town to provide statements. Within hours, the police had some understanding of what had taken place, but no suspects in mind.

"At the time we had no idea that Danny Wolfe was responsible," Corporal Zentner said. "All we knew is that masked men came into the house and started shooting. They made reference to the Indian Posse and ran out the door."

Fort Qu'Appelle was not known to have much of an Indian Posse presence; the largest gang in the area was the Native Syndicate. There were occasionally gang-related disputes on the surrounding reserves, but rarely in the town of Fort Qu'Appelle.

The first major break for investigators came when witnesses mentioned the brief skirmish in Trapper's Bar. The bar had surveillance video, which meant they might be able to get an image of their suspect. Constable Donna Zawislak drove over to the bar on the morning after the shooting and asked to see the surveillance footage. She watched it for hours. Danny Wolfe was by some distance the best-known gangster in the area, but he had kept a low profile since his release ten months earlier. The type of killing, too, seemed out of the ordinary, not something a high-ranking gang member would do. The skirmish was hard to spot on the video, and very brief. Even if the incident appeared inconsequential, the images confirmed for Zawislak that Danny was there and seemed to have been involved in some sort of confrontation with one of the victims of the shooting. From watching the video, it seemed likely to Constable Zawislak that the victims had never heard of Danny Wolfe and had no idea who they were dealing with, because they didn't tread very carefully. "People didn't know him by name but he wasn't shy about his tattoos. He was wearing a tank top at the bar that advertised that he was

Indian Posse. . . . The IP guy being new to town and the NS [Native Syndicate] guy, he was with people he knew. This was their town and they're going to approach someone who's not normally seen at the bar and Danny wasn't at the bar a lot prior to that," she said.

As the narrative took shape, investigators started to sharpen their focus on Danny. They had been told that the suspect in the bar had a tattoo on his neck that said *Red til Dead*, which matched what they knew of Danny's tattoos. They started making some inquiries about him and heard that he was recruiting in the area, so they quickly established he wasn't finished with gang life. They also discovered that he wasn't keeping appointments with his parole officer and hadn't completed the post-jail counselling that was a condition of his release. Then, via the File Hills First Nations police, they got a report of the shooting incident from five days earlier, when Ernest Tuckanow had been wakened by the sound of gunshots.

The RCMP now knew they were investigating a career criminal with a network of gang members at his disposal. It was going to be a difficult case to prove, but they had enough evidence to nail Danny for breaching the conditions of his parole. That would get him behind bars and perhaps make it easier for accomplices to turn on him. The major crimes team took over the gun investigation from the File Hills police and asked the courts for a warrant to search the house where Danny was staying, in the hope that they would find the murder weapon.

Corporal Zentner was on the surveillance team, and by this point they were all over Danny, with surveillance on his phone and officers watching nearly every move. They knew, probably from monitoring his phone, that he was planning to head into Regina. The drive in to the city presented the best opportunity to arrest him safely, they thought.

One morning, about a week after the shooting, Susan and Danny set out in her car to do some shopping in Regina. They had completed most of the hour-long drive to the city when Susan glanced in her rear-view mirror and saw an RCMP cruiser approaching at speed. It was closing the distance between them incredibly quickly, although without using sirens or lights. Susan knew they were going to be stopped. Then more police cruisers appeared in front of her and some came up from the side. Still others blocked any roads leading off the highway. They were boxed in and surrounded.

Danny swore. He was sitting quietly in the front passenger seat and his head swivelled around as he assessed the size of the arrest party. He started fumbling in his pockets as his mother slowed the car down and pulled to the side of the road. He pulled out two cell phones. He started taking out SIM cards but realized there wasn't time to destroy them. He had only seconds before the officers would be at the door.

"Here," he said to Susan. "Take these." The phones were filled with numbers and text messages that Danny wanted to conceal. There was a good chance they wouldn't seize anything his mother was carrying, he thought.

"What do you want me to do with them?" Susan asked, holding them gingerly at arm's length. The police officers were already approaching. Danny grabbed the phones back. "Forget it," he said angrily, and dropped them on the floor.

When they reached Susan's car the officers asked Danny for his identification and then pulled him outside and pushed him up against the car to search him. They told him he was under arrest.

"They made a big scene," Susan said. It was a bit dramatic for a parole violation. Susan was surprised; she didn't suspect that Danny had anything to do with the shooting in Fort Qu'Appelle.

With Danny safely behind bars, the police could get on with the more delicate aspects of their investigation, such as finding the murder weapon. With their warrant in hand, later that day they went to Tatiana Buffalocalf's home, where Danny had been staying. They looked through his room in the basement, carefully photographing his posters, dream catchers, and his photo montage of Indian Posse members. They noted and photographed the clothes in his closet, a collection of T-shirts carefully hung on hangers. Under the stairs they found packaging for a store-bought rifle but not the rifle itself. Danny might have already disposed of the gun, but the police did seize shell casings that had fallen near the deck, in the same place where Ernest Tuckanow had seen Danny shooting in the early morning just days before the murders. Lab tests later revealed that the hammer markings on those shell casings, a kind of firearm signature that varies from one gun to another, matched the casings gathered at the murder scene. That was the first domino to fall.

The police had also been keeping an eye on Gerrard Granbois. They knew that he was hanging around with Danny and suspected he might know something about the shooting. Granbois didn't have a criminal record and was not an experienced criminal, but he had been drawn into Danny's world, mainly through his relationship with Danny's cousin Tiffany. Granbois was also a witness to the shooting death that had placed Danny's brother Preston behind bars. The police needed Granbois and thought he had strong incentives to talk. With Danny behind bars, there was a chance he'd feel he could speak to police without getting killed. They picked him up in late November and brought him in for questioning.

Granbois at first held firm when the RCMP spoke to him. His relationship with Danny's cousin gave him a reason to stay quiet, and he was involved up to his eyeballs in the crime. He was in the van that night, and the police couldn't be sure he wasn't a shooter, too, since James wasn't yet on their radar. As Danny had warned, Granbois was looking at life in prison. But after a few conversations with the RCMP, he started to come around to the idea of turning on Danny. What sealed it was the offer of an immunity deal, plus a lot of money to move himself and other members of his family out of the province. If he was going to testify against a founder of one of the country's most violent street gangs, he needed some assurance that he would be protected. So Granbois became a paid Crown witness, at the same time agreeing to testify against Preston in his murder case. The police were willing to let him walk free in order to take down the two brothers.

The RCMP had pulled off a major coup. Up until that point they had no murder weapon and no witnesses who could convincingly place Danny at the scene of the crime. Another major break was the discovery of the vehicle. The police knew the shooters probably had a vehicle to facilitate their escape, and they also knew that Tatiana Creeley's van was missing. They sent up a plane to conduct an aerial search of the entire region and finally spotted it abandoned on a small, rural road about an hour away from Fort Qu'Appelle. They got a warrant to search the vehicle, which turned up two shell casings whose markings matched those from the crime scene and those found near the deck where Danny fired into the woods. That was a big piece of evidence.

But even with those pieces and Granbois's testimony, the RCMP needed more. Granbois would be tainted by the money and immunity he'd received. The officers had to keep building their case. They monitored the phone calls Danny was making from the Regina Provincial Correctional Centre after his arrest. It's not clear whether he was using a cell phone or the jail phone under someone else's personal identification number, but clearly Danny thought he would be able to speak without being monitored. It was from these conversations that police first caught wind of James and deduced that he must have had some role in the crimes.

In one call recorded by police, a high-ranking Indian Posse member ripped into Danny about the killings. He'd seen the stories in the newspapers, many of which mentioned the fact that the killer had explicitly identified himself as Indian Posse. "Is this you I'm reading about? What the fuck bro man? I don't approve of this shit," the caller said.

Danny was worried about James, who had left the area shortly after the shootings. Since James was still legally a child, he'd face a relatively short sentence, even for murder. But could he be expected to stay silent? Danny didn't think so. He was young, after all, and Danny had serious doubts about his reliability.

Danny started calling his friends in the gang for help. He needed to be sure that the witnesses would be silent. If necessary, they could be silenced permanently.

18

REGINA CORRECTIONAL CENTRE
NOVEMBER 2007–JANUARY 2008

Danny was feeling distinctly old when he sat down to write to his brother Richard in November 2007. For the first time in his life he was the oldest inmate in his section of the jail. When he looked in the mirror he no longer saw a swaggering young gangster; he saw himself as a thirty-one-year-old father of two about to be locked away for decades.

The arrest had surprised him. He didn't think the police would be able to gather sufficient evidence, but he hadn't counted on the relatively easier route of nabbing him on a parole violation first. He tried to play it cool in his letter to Richard, saying the charges were bunk and that he was sure to be let free. Of course, Danny knew that the police could read his letters so he wasn't about to confess in writing. A year earlier he wrote that he suspected "the man" was intercepting his mail to get better intelligence on the gang, since the cops didn't seem to know as much about the inner workings of the Indian Posse as they did about other gangs.

The guards placed Danny on a range with his little brother Preston, who was awaiting trial for the murder of Vincent Morisseau-Poorman. Danny was trying to teach Preston the ways of jail, "schooling him in," as he put it. He had a life's worth of lessons on how to do time. Danny also talked again of making a change in his life. He wanted to go straight, he told Richard. "We're not getting any younger bro. We have to make that change now! I told mom to show me the way on that road now so I have to chill on all that other shit. We have kids to think about."

Those few sentences are the closest Danny ever came to expressing remorse for the destruction he caused, but it was clear that something was troubling him. He knew that he would be lucky to get away with the killings in Fort Qu'Appelle; that he would have to hope the others stayed silent. But he was also reflecting on what he'd done with his life. People who knew Danny said that since he had returned to Okanese and for much of 2007 he had seemed sincere in his attempts to change. He was serious about spending more time with his daughter, who was a little over a year old and living with Shenoa in Regina. His son was further away, in Manitoba, but he wanted to bring him to Saskatchewan to teach him about the ceremonies and a traditional way of life. The positive changes in Danny's life only made his murderous shooting spree in Fort Qu'Appelle harder to understand.

It hadn't been as simple as a flash of anger. Nearly three hours had elapsed between the encounter in the bar and the home invasion. He had stalked his victims, methodically searching every street of the town until he found the blue pickup truck. Once inside the house on Pasqua Avenue he fired carefully and with intent. He shot only men in a house where half the occupants were women, though he did take aim at Granny Cook.

Why did he do it? Why involve himself when he could have ordered someone else to do it? Why not just ignore the insult and walk away entirely? It's not easy to explain. Part of the answer lies in understanding what Danny saw as valuable. He was vain and proud, prizing his reputation above all else. Gangsters need to be feared. To be known as someone who will kill or maim is as important to the job as a credible resumé is to a professional. If a gangster isn't feared, debtors don't pay and rivals make incursions. As Lawrence, Danny's longtime friend put it, a little violence at the right time can prevent more blood-shed down the road.

"That's why sometimes you have to get caught, so everyone knows what you're prepared to do. Once it's in black and white [i.e., on a criminal record] everyone can see it. It's legitimate. That's the point," Lawrence said.

Danny couldn't allow himself to be disrespected in public; he had to respond with overwhelming force: that's what was expected of him. He had spent most of his adult life obsessed with reputation and status, and his world revolved around ego and pride. He had other options, of course; he could have walked away or he could have issued a beating. He chose the worst path.

But in the aftermath Danny was starting to see the hollowness of his purpose. What was it all worth? His reputation had grown even bigger, but would he ever get to enjoy it? Was this all his life would ever be?

"Sitting over here with a bunch of young guys. I'm the oldest on the range! Fuck that sucks and I ain't even that old. Sure don't feel like it. I can still rock n roll like a young guy! Haha. Still pick up the honeys like crazy. Oh well, what else can I do?" he wrote.

He started to ponder these questions as he waited in his cell. Week after week nothing happened. The police made no move to lay a murder charge. Danny ushered in the New Year, 2008, with Preston at his side. His court date was just a few days away and he allowed himself to be optimistic. He thought he would likely be released once the minor firearms charge was resolved.

Danny knew Granbois had been picked up by the police but he was confident that he had coached him well enough to deflect RCMP questioning. They went to Lebret to buy beer: that's all Granbois had to say, Danny told himself. How hard could that be? The kid, James, was more of a concern. Danny knew he had been shaken up by the shooting, so he put the word out to people he trusted to make sure that the kid didn't waver.

The Posse eventually caught up with James and beat him until he was ready to break, to make it clear that he had to stay silent. When he grabbed a rope and tried to hang himself, his gang brothers stopped him. They just wanted to be sure he could be trusted, they told him. "I'm solid," he pleaded. "Kill me!" One took a knife and stabbed him in the back of the neck. The knife pierced the skin on one side of his neck and came out the other. The gang scared James, but they spared his life and let him go. Soon, however, his name came to the attention of police investigating the homicide; the detectives say they got the information "through the grapevine," but it was very likely through an informant or by wiretaps, either of Danny's calls or of calls made by other members of the gang.

James could have tried to take the rap by saying he acted alone, thereby sparing Danny, but he wouldn't or couldn't. The gang still expected him to "hold strong" and say nothing. He told a psychologist later that his lawyer advised him not to be a rat. But perhaps he thought he could get a lighter sentence if he could convince a judge he was coerced.

On January 11, three and a half months after Danny's arrest and three days before the court date he expected would set him free, the RCMP notified his lawyer, Estes Fonkalsrud, that they were going to charge Danny with two counts of first-degree murder in connection with the shooting in Fort Qu'Appelle. Fonkalsrud called his client at the Regina Correctional Centre to deliver the news. Danny was crestfallen. He was so close to freedom, and now he might never walk free again.

When he got the news Danny called his mother. He couldn't hold it together any longer.

"Mum?"

"Yeah."

Danny was silent for a moment as he tried to get the words out.
"Mum," he said again.

He started to choke on his tears.

"What? What," she asked.

Silence. Then Danny handed the phone to Preston.

"What's up with Danny?" Susan asked.

"Well, they charged him," Preston said.

"What for?"

"That thing that happened down there," Preston said. He didn't need to elaborate. The Fort Qu'Appelle shooting was the biggest story in the province. Susan took a moment to digest it.

"Really eh?" She didn't quite believe it. "That's what they said? Oh my."

Danny took the phone back, having slightly regained his composure. He told Susan to call his cousin Tatiana and Gerrard Granbois, to be sure they had their story straight. He knew that police had visited his friend Murray Stonechild and shown him a still image from a security camera of the two of them buying beer in Fort Qu'Appelle that night. That meant police were all over the case.

"Yeah, okay," his mother said. Her tone of voice suggested she would think about it.

"So that's what it is now?"

Susan could still hear Danny's sniffles through the phone. She spoke sternly to him.

"Pick yourself up and ask [the prison elder] to go see you," she said. "You tell him what's happening. And pray with him when he's smudging you. See what's happening now? Now you've got to live right."

At 2:50 p.m. that day, RCMP officers arrived at the Regina jail. They formally laid the charges and read Danny his rights.

"Daniel Richard Wolfe, you are under arrest for the first-degree murders of Marvin Arnault and Michael Itittakoose and the attempted murders of Percy Pascal, Jesse Obey, and Cordell Keepness on September 20, 2007. Do you understand?" the officer said, according to his notes.

"Yup," said Danny.

"You have the right to retain counsel without delay. Do you understand?"

"Yup."

"Do you want to call a lawyer?

"Yup," he said again.

Danny was then told he'd be taken by car to RCMP divisional headquarters to be held in a cell . He protested and asked the officer why that was necessary when he was already in jail. He could just as easily stay put until he had to make his first court appearance; why take him all the way across town to a smaller facility? The officer replied that the RCMP could better guarantee his privacy in their own facility, where they had a sealed room for prisoners to communicate with counsel. The answer defied logic, since prisoners at the jail spoke to their lawyers every day without concern.

If Danny sensed that something was up, his instincts were right. He was about to walk into a carefully constructed trap.

Danny was placed in the cells at the RCMP station overnight. It was cold and uncomfortable, with no blankets to sleep under and the lights kept on all night for safety. He was offered only an old copy of *Reader's Digest* to pass the time. The next morning he got a breakfast of limp, floppy waffles in his cell. Meanwhile, the top officers of the RCMP's major crimes squad were putting the final touches on their plan to ensnare Danny.

Staff Sergeant Maureen Wilkie was running the operation. That morning, before nine, she met with a veteran undercover operative named Don Perron. He had been chosen for this assignment for his ability to play the role of a biker connected to a criminal group such as the Hells Angels. Right up until this point, Staff Sergeant Wilkie did not believe they had enough evidence to convict Danny. He was a highly experienced criminal and he would not fold in an interrogation; he would probably intimidate all those involved with him and he would have taken care to destroy as much evidence as possible. From the moment she started working on the case three and a half months earlier, Staff Sergeant Wilkie thought it would be a tough one to crack. To prove Danny's guilt beyond a reasonable doubt, the RCMP needed a special operation. They had arrested James a week earlier and he wasn't talking. And since he was a young offender, the police could not legally use an undercover operator against him. It had to be Danny. The hope was that the Indian Posse leader would unwittingly convict himself.

Cover stories, if they're going to work, need to be short and simple and convincing. Staff Sergeant Wilkie gave Sergeant Perron the basics of the scenario, replete with criminal lingo: He had been arrested that morning on the Trans-Canada highway heading toward Moose Jaw. He had spent the previous night in Regina, a stopover on his westward trip from Montreal. He was carrying some chunks (guns) in his truck for a bro somewhere out west. The cops found the chunks and arrested him. He wasn't speeding, so why was he stopped and searched? Someone must have dropped a dime (snitched) on him. He also had a Canada-wide warrant for aggravated assault, the result of a beating he delivered for an unpaid debt. He should've made sure the fucker couldn't talk. He's the kind of guy who does some odd jobs for his bros. He doesn't have much of a criminal record, some old shit, but he's careful what he does.

Perron was dressed in blue jeans and a long-sleeved grey T-shirt, his head shaved and wearing a full moustache. He knew this was a homicide case and that the target was a high-ranking member of the Indian Posse, but in order to keep his mind clear and his curiosity genuine he was not told anything more about Danny. After his briefing, Perron was taken outside, where he slipped on a pair of handcuffs and sat down in the back seat of an RCMP cruiser, to make it look as though he was in custody. Then they waited for the scenario to unfold.

At 10:15 a.m. a fire alarm, faked for the purposes of the sting, sounded inside the RCMP division offices. Danny was still in his cell and, naturally, during a fire, getting people out of cells is a complicated but important part of the evacuation. An officer unlocked his cell door and led him outside, where he was placed in a locked police car for the duration of the fire alarm. Moments later, an officer placed Gerrard Granbois in the same car. It was a surprise to both of them. They just looked at each other for a moment. Then Danny broke the silence: "Fuck." If the police had Granbois in custody, things were bad, Danny realized.

The cruiser was driven out of the docking bay so they could wait at a distance until the building was evacuated. The car was wired to capture an audio recording of Danny and Gerrard's conversation. Staff Sergeant Wilkie was hoping that Danny would say something to incriminate himself.

"Stick to the same story," he told Granbois. "We were just in town to pick up beer and then went back to the reserve." Danny knew, given the photo that the RCMP had shown Murray Stonechild, that they could already prove he was in town and at the bar that night. A flat denial was implausible. He kept it simple for Granbois, who, in Danny's mind, seemed a little too soft for this.

"Where did they arrest you?" Danny asked.

"At home," Granbois said.

Danny noticed, though, that Granbois was wearing his paint-splattered work pants. A question flickered through his mind and was quickly gone. "Just stick to your fucking story, that's all you've to do, man," he said.

Meanwhile, as the RCMP officers watched from a distance and tried to listen, panic set in as they realized the recording equipment wasn't working. Later they would learn that they had set the machine to record at a very high quality, which meant much less recording capacity. The machine had simply filled up by the time Danny started talking. They had blown that aspect of the operation, but there was still an opportunity to get Danny.

As Danny and Granbois sat in their vehicle, the patrol car carrying Perron pulled up just ahead of them in the parking lot. Danny would have been able to see inside to catch a glimpse of Perron. The uniformed officer stepped out and walked around back to open the trunk. Then he called to another officer standing nearby, gesturing for him to come over. As the officers stood leaning over the trunk, one pulled out a very impressive looking AK-47 and started showing it off. Then he pulled out an Uzi, followed by a sawed-off 12-gauge shotgun. It was quite a display of firepower. The officers marvelled at the guns, holding them up in the light to get a better look. They even high-fived each other in celebration. Danny took it all in from his seat at the window.

The fire alarm lasted about ten minutes and, once it was over, they brought Danny back into the docking bay. They made him wait in the receiving area while they booked Perron but kept him close enough to see what was taking place. They wanted to be sure that Danny got a good look at the supposed biker. The whole process was crucial to establishing the undercover officer's credibility.

19

INTERROGATION
JANUARY 2008

Once Danny had been booked he was taken to an interrogation room, where he sat alone fidgeting for about fifteen minutes. Then the door opened and RCMP interrogation specialist Chuck LeRat introduced himself.

LeRat, a twenty-three-year-veteran, was known as the polygraph guy, an expert who travelled all across the province getting accused criminals to come clean. He had been preparing for this interview for more than a month, ever since the target became clear, studying Danny's parole files, his criminal past, his family, anything that could help him understand where Danny was coming from. LeRat knew about the simultaneous undercover operation, but all that would be superfluous if he could get a confession.

Danny, his hair tied in a long ponytail, was seated in a chair with his back to the wall and an open laptop computer facing him on a long desk. He was wearing a prison-issue grey sweatsuit that looked too big on his slender frame.

LeRat, squarely built and barrel-chested, sat down a few feet from Danny, on the same side of the desk.

"How are you?" LeRat asked.

"I'm alright," said Danny, cautiously.

LeRat extended his hand for Danny to shake, but Danny turned his head away, rejecting the offer. LeRat let his hand drop and continued, undeterred. "Know why you're here?"

"I've been charged already," said Danny, curtly. He crossed his arms and lowered his head and sat staring directly at the floor. Everything in his body language suggested LeRat was wasting his time. He wasn't going to talk.

LeRat gave Danny some time to call a lawyer, and then walked in and out of the room a few times in quick succession. The interview was being recorded on video, he told Danny, and he wanted to make sure everything was functioning properly. Danny, left alone, eyed the laptop on the desk next to him. He got up and walked to the door and peered through the narrow window to gauge how far away LeRat had gone. Then he crouched in LeRat's chair and ducked in front of the computer, trying to read the icons on the screen.

He furrowed his brow, leaning forward on the seat. But he soon heard footsteps approaching and jumped back into his own chair just as the door opened and LeRat re-entered. Danny played it cool, looking around the room absently as if nothing had happened.

LeRat left the room again. Danny leapt back in front of the computer, scanning the file names and trying to figure out what he might be able to see. He manoeuvred the mouse with his right hand and clicked into a file, opening a video that he watched with intense interest. Just then LeRat came back in. Unbeknownst to Danny, LeRat and several other officers had been watching on camera from another room. This time Danny was too slow to click out and get back to his chair and he looked stricken as LeRat confronted him.

"Curious?" LeRat asked. "What are you in right now? Who's that?"

"It's Gerrard," said Danny.

"It is," LeRat said, sounding slightly amused. It was a piece of theatre that had gone according to plan.

The hope was that Danny would be unsettled by making the discovery on his own. Now it was time for the next stage of the operation.

LeRat gave Danny a detailed description of the evidence against him. They had video of his altercation with the victims at the bar; they knew he matched the description of the person who did the shooting; and they had spoken to the two people who were with him that night, Granbois and James.

He then offered to show Danny the video he had tried to click on. LeRat sat back as the video sprung to life and Danny leaned in to watch Granbois, who was speaking on camera. The video cut to the spot where they parked the van before the shooting, followed by images of the route they took from Fort Qu'Appelle to Lebret and then back to the reserve.

"They just kicked open the door and then I heard shots. Boom boom boom," Granbois could be heard saying on the tape. "They were only in the house about five minutes. They said, 'Don't say anything or the same fucking thing is going to happen to you,'" Granbois recounted.

"What else was said in the van afterwards?" asked a voice on the tape, presumably an RCMP officer.

"[James] said he shot a guy five times, or two people, and Danny said he shot a guy in the face," Granbois said.

LeRat clicked off the video. "I wanted to show you that, Danny," he said. "It's not a bluff."

Danny calmly put his head down on the desk, his face inscrutable. He had not yet said a word.

"What are you thinking, Danny?" There was a long pause as Danny stayed quiet, trying to avoid eye contact.

"I guess you're thinking Gerrard ratted you out . . . It's what

happens. When the ship starts sinking people jump off. It's self pres-
ervation," Le Rat said.

LeRat was employing an interrogation strategy known as the
Reid technique, or a version modified to comply with Canadian laws,
he later explained. It was developed in Chicago, Illinois, in 1946 by a
man named John E. Reid, and its aim is to elicit truth "without threats
or promises" by using sound reasoning. The first phase is known as
positive confrontation. The suspect is told that there is no doubt that
he is responsible for the crime. After that, the interviewer develops
themes and potential explanations. These explanations often provide
some kind of moral justification for the suspect to lean on. The goal is
to convince the subject that his fate is sealed and then persuade him
to explain his actions and reasoning to the questioner. In so doing,
he'll reveal his methods and admit his guilt.

That was all LeRat needed from Danny. The RCMP had no
DNA evidence linking Danny to the crime scene and they had no mur
der weapon. The evidence of motive – the exchange in the bar – was not
very strong. Even if Granbois and James turned against him, a good
defence lawyer could argue they were only trying to save themselves and
raise enough doubt to get an acquittal. A lot was riding on this operation.

LeRat told Danny about his trip to Manitoba to meet with
James, who had turned himself in. He said James seemed like a nice
kid who had gone down the wrong path over the last year, but that his
father was supporting him. Then LeRat played the audio of Danny's
phone call to his mother the day before, when he broke down in tears
and Preston had to tell Susan that Danny was charged with murder.
All his calls had been intercepted, LeRat explained. Danny seemed
surprised. He listened as the conversation with his mother played over
the computer's speakers.

"You got to do right now," LeRat said to Danny afterward, echo-
ing the words Susan had used at the end of the call. He let the phrase

hang in the air for a moment to allow the tension to build. "That was yesterday. Those telephone calls were intercepted from the jail. There was a lot of conversation on those lines prior to that, with you being in the correctional facility," LeRat said.

He pulled out a sheaf of papers, picked one, and laid it before Danny. It was a series of roughly a dozen mugshots. Many were high-ranking members of the Indian Posse.

"I want to show you these photographs," he said. "They've identified these individuals being on the telephone lines."

LeRat paused to let the information sink in. He wanted Danny's mind to race through the criminal conspiracies that had been discussed, the errors he had made, and how they might affect others.

"There's a lot of things they've disclosed," LeRat said. "Intimidation of witnesses, drug trafficking, you name it. You know who those people are. You spoke to them."

The interrogator needed more to get Danny talking. He played a new video, taken less than an hour earlier, after the fire drill, when Granbois had told police what Danny had said to him while they were in the squad car: "Just stick to the story. We went into town to pick up some booze."

Danny watched intently. He started rubbing his right arm vigorously, wringing it like a wet towel.

"What's he talking about?" LeRat asked. Danny said nothing. Granbois continued to speak in the background: "He said the gun is gone. That's all he said. He didn't tell me where it went."

It was all adding up to a lot of evidence in the hands of police. LeRat moved to the most important part, the part he couldn't explain. "The only thing we didn't have was why. You had no ties to these people," he said. "The only thing left to figure out is what the hell your intent was when you went in there.

"Was it to settle a score or make a statement? Then for Chrissakes say it. But if it was to kill as many people as you could, then I've gone off the straight and narrow and I've misjudged you, Danny."

LeRat was moving into a new phase of the interview. He needed to build the plausible explanation that Danny could accept. This would take some work.

"What you had going against you that night, Danny, is that you're impulsive," he said. Impulsive but still honourable, he was quick to point out. Danny hadn't injured any of the women in the house. He hadn't told anyone that there was going to be killing, at least according to Granbois's account, and maybe Danny hadn't intended it, LeRat suggested.

Danny and LeRat talked for a while about prison, trading stories about the incompetence of the correctional service and of prisoners being murdered in jail. They agreed that some of the deaths were due in part to errors made by the guards. This was something Danny cared about. He was interested, listened carefully, and looked him in the eye. LeRat was finally starting to build some rapport. LeRat asked how long Danny had been associated with the Indian Posse. Danny said he'd been with the gang since he was nine or ten (he was twelve in 1988 when the gang was founded).

"Are you the longest-standing member?" LeRat asked.

"There's three of us left," Danny said.

"Your brother Richard has got to be one of them," LeRat said.

Danny shook his head.

"He left a long time ago when he got his [sentence]. He took his time and left. He's on the straight and narrow now . . . He's been doing okay for himself. He's gonna get out right away. He'll probably do good."

"Good for him," LeRat said.

"He just wants to get out and do his own thing, the family thing and work and stuff," Danny said.

"What about you?" LeRat asked.

"I'll probably die inside," Danny said.

"Why?"

"Because that's just the way it is, man," Danny said.

"You ever think about getting out?" LeRat asked.

"Yeah," said Danny.

"What's the biggest factor in you not doing that? Be upfront. I'm just curious," LeRat said.

Danny curled up in the corner of his chair.

"Probably drugs and alcohol," he said. "Drugs and alcohol are my downfall."

"You have an addiction?" LeRat asked.

Danny shrugged. It was mostly drinking and smoking weed, he said.

"If I was to roll the dice, Danny, I would say that anything you've fucked up on in the past you've probably been doing when you were doing drugs and alcohol. When it comes to policing, if there were no drugs and alcohol there'd be far less policing – 90 per cent of the time that's what we're dealing with is people abusing substances . . . Politicians talk a big talk about substance abuse and how they're going to crack down on it and how they're going to build centres for substance abuse and addiction. A lot of talk but at the end of the day there's not a whole lot done . . . But for the most part that's why I have a job, unfortunately. I call a spade a spade. Drugs and alcohol, that's what forces people to do it."

LeRat asked how old Danny was when he first tried drugs. Nine or ten, he replied. He asked Danny what it was like growing up in Winnipeg. "It's not a bad city," Danny said with a shrug. How far had he got in school? Just grade nine, Danny said. "But I read and write," Danny hastened to add. "I just don't have the grades to pass."

"I'm not the sharpest knife in the drawer. I don't have a postsec-ondary education," LeRat said. "I have grade 12, the minimum to get on the force . . . But I got street sense, and that goes a whole lot further.

"Street sense is more valuable than any education . . . University can't teach you that. You either have it or you don't. . . . You've spent some time on the streets. You've dealt with a lot of people in a lot of different circumstances. I guarantee you, you're probably sharper in that ability to assess people than 70 per cent of the police officers out there."

Danny seemed engaged. LeRat was flattering him, but in a way that matched Danny's image of himself, as someone without much book learning, but who was wise in the ways of the world.

"Yeah, I can read people quick," Danny said, his pride evident. LeRat continued in this vein for a while. Danny listened, nodding his head and stroking his chin. After a few minutes LeRat sensed it was time to get where he wanted to go.

"You've been with the gang a long time and you've experienced a lot, seen a lot of things," he said. "Has anyone ever told you that one charac-teristic you possess is being impulsive? Ever hear that terminology?"

"I think I heard it before," Danny said.

"A lot of people are like that. It's a tough one – it's something you've got to work with. It's like, if I put a ball on that table right now, those who have that part up here that causes them to be impul-sive, they'll pick the ball up, start feeling it and throwing it up in the air. The others will think about it, but they have the ability to sit back and focus. They'd like to pick the ball up because they're curious, but they don't have to. . . . When you're impulsive you tend to do things before you think."

Danny could see where all this was going now. He sat sideways at the table, his eyes on the grey fibres of the carpet, his hands fiddling with a bottle of water.

"The only thing that's left is your intent. I don't pass judgment," LeRat said. "If it was just a matter of you going in there to settle a score and not take anyone's life, then clarify that for Chrissakes. I'm not here to put words in your mouth, but you're the only one who knows."

LeRat kept pushing. He was nearing a crescendo, hoping the wave would sweep Danny up in its momentum. "Look at the mountain of evidence here, Danny. I've only shown you a portion of it," LeRat said. "You know how the system works. The [jury] is going to base their decision on the basis of facts that have been gathered."

Danny put his head down on one knee. His eyes were aimed straight at the floor. He stifled a yawn. He looked almost childlike.

LeRat leaned in close, sensing a breakthrough. During his weeks of preparation LeRat had concluded that the only person Danny really listened to was his mother. Now he reached for the emotional touchstone he hoped could put Danny over the edge.

"As your mum said, now you've got to start doing good. And you can do it. It's your decision," he said. "What remains to be determined is what your intent was when you went in there." Fifteen seconds passed in agonizing silence. Danny wouldn't answer, LeRat wanted to wait him out. Finally the officer spoke: "Danny, did you want to kill those people that night?"

Danny's eyes shot up. He briefly met LeRat's gaze, and just as quickly he looked away. He held his right knee with two hands, pulling it up close to his chest as though he were trying to protect himself.

"Was that your intention that night?" LeRat asked. "It's the only question that can't be answered. [James] can't say it. Gerrard can't say it. Your mum can't say it. You're the only one."

Danny didn't take the bait. Intention was dangerous ground; it was an admission to first-degree murder, even if LeRat was giving him an out. Danny could always say that he never intended to kill anyone, that faced with these people who attacked him he was hit with a flash of anger, and perhaps it would only be a manslaughter or second-degree murder case. But he wasn't going to do that either.

"What I know of you, Danny, I'm confident you do want to tell the truth and you're in a bit of a struggle right now to determine what you're going to do," LeRat said. "The truth has to come out . . . I listened to you cry. Not just to anyone, but to your mother. When I listened to you on that audio that told me a lot about you. You've got a hard shell out there, Danny, but there's a lot of good inside you." Years later LeRat would say of Danny, "He was bad, but he wasn't rotten to the core."

"When you left the bar that night was it your intention to kill?" LeRat asked.

Danny said nothing.

"At 7:44 in the evening, the verbal altercation. Two and a half hours later . . ." LeRat just trailed off, not bothering to mention what happened next. "See how impulsive that is? Danny, you know what the truth is. Just be upfront."

LeRat sensed that the momentum he'd built was slipping away. Danny had been wavering a few minutes earlier but he wasn't about to topple. LeRat slowed down again and tried a new tack. He asked Danny who he most admired. Danny didn't answer.

"Two people that I see, your mother and your brother Richard. Because from what you've told me they've been able to overcome some pretty big barriers in their lives," LeRat said.

He was about to spin a story about redemption, but before he could go any further, Danny interrupted.

"What time is it?" Danny asked.

It was after 4:00 p.m. They'd been at it for more than five hours. Danny had indicated from the beginning that he did not want to speak. He looked lethargic. He pinched the bridge of his nose.

LeRat offered to get him some water and then left the room. Danny studied the photos on the table of the people caught on wiretaps talking to him. His foot twitched quickly back and forth.

LeRat was gone for five minutes. When he came back, Danny was slumped in his chair, his chin in his hands. LeRat offered him one of the cupcakes wrapped in wax paper that he had scavenged out in the office. Danny was wary.

"It's not poison," LeRat said. "One of the guys' wives made some cupcakes," he added, biting into one with lip-smacking appreciation. He sat close to Danny, both of them on the same side of a table pushed up against the wall. Danny eyed his cupcake but didn't eat.

"I just want to show you something," LeRat said, picking up the computer mouse again.

LeRat played an audio file of a conversation Danny had with another high-ranking Indian Posse member.

"Is this you I'm reading about?" the IP member asked on the recording. "What the fuck bro man? I don't approve of this shit."

LeRat explained that he knew the gang had pursued James in the weeks after the killings and beat him up to test his loyalty. Danny listened and reached for the cupcake. He unwrapped it slowly and carefully, one fold of the wax paper at a time. At first he nibbled, dropping a few sprinkles into his mouth. Then he gobbled it up, eating half the cupcake in a single bite and licking his fingers clean.

"He got stabbed up. Kicked around. He's still alive as you see." LeRat paused for effect, showing Danny a screen grab on the laptop from James's videotaped statement, letting the fact that police had arrested James sink in.

"A lot of phone calls [were] intercepted up till yesterday, Danny. As you can see they're covering all the bases on you now."

Danny let out a loud, insolent burp, refusing to give LeRat the satisfaction of seeing him worry.

"People in the gang are probably pretty proud of what you did. I bet they're expecting you to step up to the plate," LeRat said. In this case, that would mean admitting his crime and taking the sentence that came with it. "I don't imagine you've backed down from much in your life in the past," he added.

Danny brought both his feet back up onto his chair, making himself look slight and compact. With one hand he picked at his hair, then he picked at his toes, still avoiding eye contact and saying nothing. He took a sip of water.

"I'm trying to show you what I've told you. I'm not bullshitting you," LeRat said. "All this is just a small portion of it. Look at everything there. Danny, it's all there, like I said. A person with just simple common sense, if they have the opportunity to review everything that's presented as evidence, and this is just a small portion of it, they're going to come to the determination that you were there."

Danny pulled his hair back and smoothed his ponytail, keeping his chin tucked tightly into his chest.

"I believe you went into that house because you were angry. You were pissed off because of the verbal altercation you had in the bar. And if you hadn't been drinking it wouldn't have happened in the first place. It's pretty simple math. If they hadn't pissed you off and there hadn't been a verbal altercation it wouldn't have happened in the first place.

"You say you're one of the three founding members left in the Indian Posse so of course it doesn't take a rocket scientist to figure out you've got some pretty good stature in the IP. I know there's a lot of people in the gang that respect you. A lot of people respect what you did, your actions and why you did it. . . . You're not a stupid man. You're a very intelligent individual. As you said before you may not have the education to show for it, but it's all there."

LeRat started building a new aspect to his argument. The police heard Danny giving a lot of orders in the phone calls they intercepted, he said. Not many of those orders were ever carried out by the gang. No one was listening to Danny.

"You've directed a lot of people to do a lot of things but nothing's gotten done. The respect you thought you had at one time is slowly diminished," LeRat said. "Danny, maybe it's time to retire."

Danny's leg was starting to pulse like a jackhammer. LeRat pushed further on this new tack, suggesting that Danny's days were numbered.

"There will always be someone bigger and stronger than you to push you out," LeRat said. Danny nodded, acknowledging the truth of the statement.

"It's quite evident that the network you had going here and all these people doing things for you is kind of falling through the floor. Based on what we've heard, nothing's happening. No one is doing anything any more for you, Danny. And there's going to be two, three, five people standing in line waiting for you to leave."

It was a harsh diagnosis, one that was embarrassing for a man with Danny's pedigree – but it was also true. LeRat again raised the subject of how Richard and Susan had changed the course of their lives, saying the ability to seek redemption must run in the family. LeRat had determined, correctly, that nothing mattered more to Danny than family. He also was hitting on some things that Danny had confided privately to others, that at times he was tired of gang life, tired of being the old veteran on the prison range, the dad who could never see his own children. LeRat kept pushing.

"You're smart enough to know the end of the line is coming . . . The frustration in your voice. Things are not happening, things are not getting done. That last one we listened to about James, someone's supposed to have tabs on him. Go find the little bugger. You listen to that now and it's like it's not a big concern.

"Now there are others moving into that [leadership] position. It's not just the IP that are like that. It could be a major oil company. Just like I mentioned, in the RCMP there are those willing to step over others to get to the top. You put a lot of time into it but like any other job you got to look at doing something else eventually."

Danny fiddled with the cap of his water bottle, flipping it over in his hands. He didn't say a word.

"Look at Richard. He was in the gang a long time and he decided to do something different. People respect that," LeRat said. "What's the oldest gang member you've ever heard of? I don't know any over forty."

Danny stayed silent.

"You said you'll die inside. You're only defeating yourself."

Danny finally spoke. "It's true," he said. He really did think he'd die in jail. Everything LeRat was saying would only have confirmed that for him.

LeRat decided to take a break to grab some food. When he left, Danny got up and started walking around. The room was cramped, barely three metres by four metres. His back hurt. He walked back and forth along the length of the room in a quick, pitter-pat manner. He could take five small steps and then had to turn and retrace his path. He did it over and over again, at least fifty times in his white socks. This was the exercise routine of someone who had spent enough time in solitary confinement to know how it's done. For seven minutes he continued, methodically taking five steps and turning back.

LeRat came back in and placed a bowl of chili in front of Danny. "We'll see how good this is," said LeRat, playing the cheerful skeptic.

"Why, what's wrong with it?" said Danny, suspicious.

LeRat talked about food for a while. He mentioned that he travelled a lot for work and that he'd learned there was nothing like a bowl of soup and a bun when you're eating on the road. Danny just grunted, still trying not to engage more than necessary.

"Did your mum make bannock?" LeRat asked. LeRat was manoeuvring the conversation to Danny's indigenous background.

"Yeah," said Danny, although his mum wasn't around much, he said. It was often an aunt who took care of him when he was running around the street.

"Where was your mum then?" LeRat asked.

"In Winnipeg," said Danny. "A lot of my family was in the residentials," he said. He assumed LeRat would immediately understand what he meant. Just mentioning the Indian residential schools has become code for all manner of pain, abuse, and subsequent social dysfunction.

"Which school?" LeRat asked.

"All over. Gordon's, Lebret. Three different schools. Same with my grandma and my [grandfather]. I'm kind of like the aftermath of that I guess," Danny said.

"Caused lots of problems, residential schools," LeRat said.

Danny nodded. He ate his chili quietly, apparently deep in thought. After a while he spoke. "I did all my [schooling] inside, trying to find out who I was, where I came from."

"How'd you make out?" LeRat asked.

"It just came down to my mother neglecting me, from our stories and everything else," Danny said. "Our stories" is a phrase that suggests something like a mix of history, culture, and identity.

"You ever talk to your mum about that?" LeRat said.

"Couple times but I really couldn't. We both know what we done. I couldn't point fingers at her, she couldn't point fingers at me. I can't blame her for anything. She did the best she could. It was just me running around the streets and stuff. I always hung around with guys that were older than me so I had to learn fast," Danny said.

LeRat recognized a pattern that he had seen many times. "I don't want to sound like a psychologist, but kids hanging around with people much older . . . it's not a natural progression," he said. "You can see how you're leapfrogging your childhood into something you shouldn't be in." He finished his chili, wiping the empty bowl with his bun. He mentioned that chili with beef wasn't really to his taste. "What I live on is wild meat. It's a lot leaner," LeRat said, establishing his credentials as a hunter and an indigenous person who followed some of the traditional ways.

Danny jumped in immediately.

"Yeah, that's what I do too," Danny said. LeRat could see he was growing in Danny's esteem, so he quickly built on it, establishing his credibility, trying to give Danny a good feeling about him.

"I still trap beaver and muskrats and I've done that since I was twelve years old," LeRat said. For the first time he had Danny's full attention.

"As a kid I used to do that as my spending money. Now I do that because it's who I am, it's part of me."

Danny said that he'd never trapped, but he had been hunting. They talked about this for about twenty-five minutes. LeRat went on about how fur prices had taken a dive, thanks to tree huggers, Greenpeace, and the Europeans. Danny nodded his agreement.

Finally the conversation dried up. Danny turned his chair around. "That chair hurts my back. Oh, fucker," he said.

Having made some personal inroads, LeRat got serious again. He started asking why Danny had used such inexperienced people on this job. James was just fifteen and Granbois was in way over his head, he said. "When you use people like that, Danny, you got to realize they're going to crumble, and everything else crumbles too," LeRat said. "They barely knew what the hell they were doing . . .

"You're done, Danny. You're done. You're finished. You've got to realize that."

Danny pursed his lips and nodded. He seemed to agree. LeRat cited Susan's words again. "Like she said, you got to do good now," LeRat said. He knew he was getting somewhere.

"I don't think you wanted to kill anyone that night. We all know you had the capability to do that. But you would've covered your tracks. You would've used credible people."

Now he was appealing to Danny's vanity. LeRat paused for a moment to reflect on the foolishness of bringing James that night. "Maybe for that one night there [it] seemed like there was lots of guts and glory involved and after that he kind of fell off the plate," LeRat said. "I know he went to turn in his colours. That's when he got some loving. I know that. I seen his stab wound. He got one right in the back of the neck and along the back of the head and I think they broke his nose . . . He's got a gaping wound in the back there but he never did get it stitched and it's not healing real well." Danny said nothing. He twirled his thumbs.

LeRat got back to building a case for Danny's capitulation. He mentioned that police had overheard Danny ordering other Indian Posse members to intimidate Ernest Tuckanow so he wouldn't testify to seeing Danny firing off his deck.

"You see, Danny, the gradual slide. No one ever did approach [Tuckanow]. That's why I say, Danny, you're finished," LeRat said. "No one wants to do anything anymore for you."

Danny got up from his chair. He was either in serious pain or just trying to find a way out of this interrogation. "Fuck I can't sit on that chair, man," Danny said. He then lay down on the floor, stretched out at LeRat's feet.

LeRat proceeded as if this happened all the time. "You can't even get someone to run around and make simple phone calls for you," LeRat said. "It's a dog eat dog world . . . No one seemed to want to give a shit [about finding James] . . . Not their problem."

"What am I gonna do?" Danny asked, still lying down, his arms in the air stretched out wide. It was as though he was reaching for help. He looked as though he wanted to say something and then thought better of it. "Ah, fuck," he said. And then he went quiet again.

"What you did was wrong," LeRat said. "But the personality traits I mention are admirable."

Danny agreed. "But like you say, I'm done, man. It don't matter what you say or do now," Danny said.

"How do you think you're done?" LeRat asked.

"I'm just done," Danny replied. He started to laugh. "Really, I am. I laugh because . . ." His voice trailed off before he could explain himself. He seemed ready to give up. "Can you give me a Tylenol? I need Tylenol. I'll talk to you still but I can't sit in this fucking chair," Danny said.

While LeRat went to look for Tylenol, Danny got up off the floor and started pacing again. He pulled his hair back and looked over the photos of his contacts from the wiretaps. "Holy shit," he said out loud.

He took the Tylenol that LeRat offered upon his return and sat back down on the floor. As they kept talking, Danny tried to claim that he wasn't in the gang anymore, but LeRat wasn't buying it. If he'd left the gang, why was he issuing orders to all these gang members? Danny had no answer.

"What would your brother Richard do in this situation?" LeRat asked.

"I don't know," said Danny.

"How well do you know him?"

"I grew up with him. We had all the same friends and then we got older . . . Now I don't know. He's smarter, he knows what's up now. He knows the mistakes he made."

Danny added that the world had changed in ways his brother was still unable to grasp, because he had been locked away so long. He mainly turned to his mother for spiritual advice these days. "My mum always tells me, don't be scared where you're going, be at peace with yourself. So, now all I got to do is make peace with myself, 'cause like you're saying, I'm done, man. I'm done. Life itself, my life, is not done, but I'm stuck in those walls. I know what goes on in those walls."

"Have you ever asked for forgiveness, Danny?" LeRat said.

They were both quiet for ten seconds. It was a long, heavy silence. Danny looked at LeRat and then looked away. LeRat was close to a breakthrough. He was trying to magnify the empathy he felt for Danny, so Danny would feel his understanding. Forgiveness was what he could offer. It was right there and Danny looked like he was ready to grasp for it.

But the seconds ticked away and Danny sat still and quiet. They kept talking for a little while longer and the moment of wavering passed. The breakthrough never came. It was after 8:00 p.m. when LeRat finally conceded he wasn't going to get any closer. At the end, they shook hands.

"We'll be in touch," said LeRat. "Have a good sleep there, Danny."

It would be anything but a restful night for Danny Wolfe.

20

THE UNDERCOVER OPERATION
JANUARY 2008

Danny recognized the man sitting across from him in the police cell where he was placed immediately after his interview with the interrogator. It was the same biker he'd seen that very morning, the one from whom the police had apparently seized the Uzi and the AK-47, among other weapons. Danny had taken careful note of him when they were processed at the desk. Of course, unbeknownst to the Indian Posse leader, this was not a biker at all, but a veteran RCMP undercover operative, Sergeant Don Perron, whose job was to get Danny to incriminate himself. Their cell was wired for sound.

Danny, tired and unhappy, listened as the biker complained that someone must have informed the police that he was going to be driving through Saskatchewan on his way out west. How else could they have known he'd be carrying guns, he wondered. He explained that he had a secret compartment in his truck for stashing weapons. To open it, you have to hit the brake and then flip a switch, a fairly complicated trigger that a regular cop on a traffic stop should not have been able to figure out, yet he had seized Perron's guns.

Danny was impressed, and he wanted to impress Perron as well. Motorcycle gangs are usually the top dogs in prison and the criminal world. Danny hated the way they treated the Indian Posse and hated the notion that he should defer to anyone. He mentioned, showing off his own bona fides, that he used to have a truck with a hidden compartment, too. "Until I ended up in fucking Edmonton, got jacked," Danny said. "They found it. I got away though." As they warmed up to one another Danny revealed more about his situation. Danny told Perron that the cops had been interrogating him for the last ten hours. He and Perron realized they might have something in common: someone had talked, and it was about to cost both of them in a big way.

"Fuck, I can't believe they know," Danny said, dropping his voice to a whisper. "This guy is so fucking stupid."

"The guy ahead of you?" Perron asked, referring to Gerrard Granbois, who had been brought in before Danny for processing after the fire alarm that morning.

"He talked," said Danny. "They showed me. And he wouldn't even fucking know anything about pen life, know what I mean? . . . I did eleven years, man."

"It's always easier to work alone, bro. Look at you and look at me," said Perron. "That's nice art," he added, nodding at Danny's tattoos.

"It's my life," said Danny. "Used to do drive-bys in the 'Peg . . . shot people . . . I'm one of the founding members of the IP."

"I like this here, it's cool," said Perron, pointing to the tattooed script that ran around Danny's collar.

"Yeah, 'Red til dead,' man. I'm red, what can I say."

"This other guy, he's not too fuckin' swift or what?" asked Perron.

"Weak," Danny said dismissively.

They talked some more. Perron just tried to keep Danny chatting, saying as little as possible and encouraging him with a receptive ear. Eventually Danny started letting out his frustration.

"They showed me a video of people around me telling them where I was, telling them fucking lies. They take it off and showed me a fucking video of him, this little guy [Granbois on video]. He gave it all up. Showed me, showed me the fucking video of him taking the fucking bad guys [RCMP] for a ride and then how we got there," said Danny.

"Holy fuck," said Perron.

"I ain't gonna come home, man. This is it," said Danny. He started recounting the highlights of the long, drawn-out interrogation he'd just been through. He talked about how Sergeant LeRat had told him he was caught, that it was just a matter of formalities now.

"He's like, 'Oh, you're done.' And I started laughing at him. 'No kidding,' I said. 'I am.'" He chuckled darkly again. "We all know what I'll be walking back into," Danny said. He could see his own death approaching, and it was going to be in jail.

"I'd rather let my own fucking bros take me out rather [than] let some fucking Native Syndicate or fucking lawyer or fucking any other crew take me out. I'd rather have my homies take me out rather than giving the other fucking people satisfaction to say, 'Hey I took out this fucking bad guy.'"

He talked about his legacy, building the largest street gang in Canada. "I helped fucking start the fucking shit. Now we're two thousand, close to three thousand bros, man. Across Canada now."

Danny told Perron that he'd seen the officers showing off the guns seized from his truck during a fire alarm that morning. Danny said he now realized that the fire alarm was faked for his benefit, but he thought the only purpose of the RCMP's ruse was to put him and Granbois together. He described what happened as they sat in the back of the RCMP vehicle.

"My bro jumped in, looked at me. I'm like, ah, fuck man," said Danny. Seeing Granbois in custody was very bad news; he just didn't realize how bad. "[I told him] just stick to your fucking story. That's all you gotta do, man, you know. As soon as we come in, he goes right back into the room and tells them [about the killing]."

Danny went on again about his interrogation with LeRat. "Guy's drilling me and drilling me," Danny said. "All day. Holy fuck."

"What's he expecting?" Perron asked.

"[He's] got me already. That's it, I don't know," Danny said. "Showed me pictures, showed me videos, showed me fucking wiretap."

"That's hardcore," said Perron.

Then Danny tested Perron with a quick verbal jab, eyeing his reaction carefully. "I thought you were a cop," Danny said.

Perron was in the cell alone with Danny. Keeping up the act when caught by surprise like that had to be nerve-wracking, and his response was not at all convincing. "Well, like I said, if I see you this morning and I see you now, man. You look pretty solid to me now, bro," Perron said. The answer made no sense, but Danny didn't dwell on it and gave no sign of alarm. Maybe he concluded the RCMP wasn't capable of tricking him twice in a single day.

Danny mentioned that he'd met some suspicious bikers in Fort Qu'Appelle. He said they'd approached him saying they knew some people in his family, but he thought they were cops so he kept pretty quiet with them. Perron responded by asking if Danny had ever met someone called Mario, or another guy who looked like a Wookie from *Star Wars*. These were not real people and Danny did not pretend to know them. He was trying to assess Perron, figure out who he was with and who he knew. The guns, if they were real, were the tools of a serious criminal. Danny said he knew a lot of bikers from his time in prison, guys from the Rock Machine, for example, and they had run dope into the prison together. But the trouble with bikers is that they just didn't understand the Indian Posse, Danny said. "Who we are, you know? We're a different kind of cultural community," Danny said. "I know all the bros involved in two-wheelers and I keep trying to tell them, the two-wheelers, whether they're Big Red [Hells Angels] or Bandidos or whatever. I told them, 'You learn, we're in Canada, man. This is fucking Indian country,'" he said. "This is who we are. We'll always be here . . . And this is what I'm trying to get across. Any time we go to them, they want to control. They want to take our shit, you know?"

"Yeah," said Perron.

"They want all our crazy motherfuckers. That's what they want," said Danny. Perron agreed. This was one of Danny's favourite topics, the exploitation of indigenous gangsters by white biker gangs. There was a pause as Danny thought for a moment. "I should've took a gun and shot myself," Danny said.

"Fuck that shit," said Perron.

"It's basically what I did," Danny replied. "I knew. One morning I woke up and out of nowhere, boom, it hit me. It's like, I fucked up and I know it's coming."

"That's a sick feeling," Perron said.

"It is. I think that everything I done in my life so far I think I fucking deserve. You know what? I had a dream about this," Danny said. "I had a dream my mother was taken away in a yellow car . . . And I remember waking up crying that day, saying 'no.'"

Danny had known then that it was over. He had been to a ceremony months before where the spirits had told him, speaking through the elders, that he had to change his life. The elder said that in his vision he could see a wolf approaching, growling. And a buffalo telling him to get a new life.

"That's big in your culture, eh?" said Perron. "The wolf growling, what did that mean?"

"It was mad," said Danny. He explained that during the ceremony while he was praying an elder came up and slapped him several times on his back. The elder said the *Mooshums* (the grandfathers or their spirits) were warning Danny to stay away, and that they were asking what was on his back.

"Really?" said Perron.

"And the wolf, too, said something about 'came with the wrong people this time,'" Danny added. "I should have listened. I should have gone with my mom and shit. Listened, you know. I'm spiritual, I fast four days, four nights without water . . . but I can't interpret shit the way [the elder] did for me."

The conversation meandered for a while and eventually they came back to Danny's predicament. Perron's goal was to extract some kind of admission of guilt from Danny, so at every opportunity he tried to steer the conversation back to Granbois. "So this guy ended up getting paper laid on him too?" Perron asked; by "paper" he meant a criminal charge.

"Yeah, he gave up what kind of fucking thing I used," Danny said, meaning what type of gun. That kind of specific information is valuable evidence.

"Ay-ay-yi," said Perron.

"I had a .22 with a twenty-five shot [clip] . . . I got rid of it, but still. They won't need it . . . They got this guy talking. That's it, man," said Danny. He had always suspected James, the fifteen-year-old, would be the weak link, not Granbois, he said. He mentioned that when they were together in the police car during the faked fire drill he could sense something had gone very wrong. "[His] eyes were looking watery, eh. And I just read him right there. Fuck," said Danny. "I knew, man."

He said he had gotten word to Granbois a few weeks earlier that the police were looking for him. Granbois had assured him he was solid. Danny kept after him, but then it got harder to track Granbois down. "Any time I thought about it I got that fucking knot. I knew," Danny said.

James would get seven years at most. But he and Granbois would get life sentences. "I'll probably just fuckin' get somebody to do me in," Danny said. "But until then I'm gonna keep being who I am. Keep me in remand, I'm gonna fucking terrorize the streets from inside too. I'll create monsters and send them out. That's what I'm gonna do. I created how many monsters already? Monsters. Send 'em out to kill people and come back with a life bit."

Then he made a major confession, on a case police had been unable to solve for more than a year: "I did one inside already," Danny said.

"Yeah?" said Perron. "Gotta take care of business."

"Took out one of our own. He was doing life too," Danny said, referring to Sheldon McKay, though he didn't mention his name. "He was just bossing around, bossing me around, bossing a couple of other guys who were right up there – highest you can go in our fucking crew . . . All of a sudden he comes in [acting like he's] the fucking top dog. All of a sudden he tries to fuckin get me and another fucking guy," said Danny. "Our bros who're supposed to do it come to me and told me."

"Come running to tell you?" asked Perron.

"Yeah. So I just fucking said, 'That's it, man. Enough is enough,'" said Danny. "Trying to get me, trying to get my own crew. That's it. No fuckin' [way]."

Danny described the way he turned McKay's plot against him by consulting with other members of the Indian Posse council. They all decided to back Danny. They entered McKay's cell together, Danny said, and murdered him right then and there. "Shook his hand, then boom, boom, boom . . . Next day drink coffee, play cards like nothing happened."

Perron listened, murmuring occasionally. Danny kept going.

"All of a sudden [McKay's] being called for a visit. Guard goes right to his cell, comes walking out. Running off the range, just closed the door. Lock down, lock up. We were locked down for two months after that . . . And [the authorities] didn't fucking really care, man . . . [Their attitude was] let [them] kill themselves."

"Yeah," said Perron.

"That was fucking wicked, man. [People were talking] about that," said Danny. "Killing their own now."

"Local or everywhere?" said Perron.

"All over the fucking place bros were talking, 'What the fuck's going on? Bros taking out other bros there, man.'"

That snippet of conversation provided the RCMP with a first-hand explanation for McKay's murder. The RCMP hadn't been able to solve it, even though the killing happened on a closed prison range, which necessarily limited its scope to a handful of suspects, because up to that point the inmates had successfully stonewalled the detectives. Danny's slip would eventually help police solve the case and charge half a dozen of the gang's leadership with Sheldon McKay's murder. But that was not the key piece of information that Perron was seeking. He had to keep Danny talking.

"I gotta get married right away, man," said Danny, still pondering the life sentence that he felt sure awaited him. "I want fucking trailer [visits] at least."

Then he returned to mulling over his interrogation. He remarked that LeRat was clearly a specialist in talking to suspects. He was very good at his job. "I'm surprised that I didn't even break down and [cry] you know," said Danny. He said LeRat's theory was that Granbois and James had gone with him to the house on Pasqua Avenue to "get their shit right," to earn their place in the gang or pay a debt. "The kid didn't say nothing," said Danny, pleasantly surprised by this. "And then he [LeRat] kept telling me 'You're done.' I'm laughing. I said 'I know.' Like three times, eh. We'd be in the middle of conversation, he'd say, 'You know you're done, eh?' Yeah, I'm fucking done, man . . . I says 'Either way, my rival gang, my own bros, somebody will step up and [kill me].'"

"Fucking right," said Perron.

"Give them the fucking glory."

Danny mentioned that he wanted to do something to help his little brother Preston, who was facing a murder charge. Since Danny saw no future for himself, maybe he could take the fall for his brother. Others were pinning it on Preston, he said, people who were probably already in the witness protection program. If he could find a way to save him, he'd feel better about himself, Danny said.

Danny and Perron started murmuring and the conversation was too quiet to be captured by the RCMP listening devices. It might have been at this point that Danny suggested that he and Perron should try to overpower the guards, which Perron later said Danny tried to convince him to do.

After a pause, Danny began describing what happened that September night at the bar in Fort Qu'Appelle. He recalled Pudge Pascal mouthing off, and how he grabbed pool balls from the pool table and twisted them up in his socks. He talked about how Pudge and his group left the bar and how he followed them. "I'm walking right outside and I'm looking at them, and they're sitting there in their truck fucking looking at me and I'm like 'What's up, man, what's up?' waiting for them. They took off."

"Fucked up," said Perron. "They didn't know who they were fucking with."

Danny said his mother was scared that he might take his own life. "She thinks I might go out [and] string up," said Danny. "I thought about it but I was like, fuck. Maybe," said Danny.

He described how, early on in the interrogation, he whipped around the desk and saw what was on LeRat's computer. He spotted a file called Granbois, he said, but before he could get back in his own seat the interrogator walked back in and spotted him. Then LeRat showed him the video.

"As soon as I seen that my heart went back to normal. That was it," Danny said. "He showed me right from my house on the reserve.

What I did, how I picked up the route. Took 'em right from the fucking house, took the route that I took, all the way down . . . Tells 'em what I did, tells them what he did, what he heard, boom, boom, boom."

Just then a guard came in to check for garbage. Danny and Perron had no idea what time it was but they knew it was late. They complained about the lights, asking if they could be turned off, but were told the lights were kept on at all times for safety reasons.

"I can't believe this fucking guy," said Danny, talking about Granbois again. "I'm never, ever gonna fucking forget it. I hope he knows it."

"I'm sure you'll remind him," said Perron.

"I'll kill him with my bare fucking hands," said Danny.

The conversation moved into a long discussion about the power of First Nations ceremonies such as the sun dance and the sweat lodge. Perron asked Danny how they worked. Danny provided an enthusiastic explanation.

"It's wild, man. It's like a vision. You either have visions or the *Mooshum* will work through the old guy and he'll get the answers."

"So [when the] buffalo is hitting you on the back, who's the buffalo?" said Perron, referring to the vision Danny had described earlier.

"He's the *Mooshum*," said Danny. "The guy who runs it, [the elder], all the spirits go through him."

"So he's like the interpreter?" Perron asked.

"Yeah, he'll translate for us from the spirit. I haven't seen [a spirit]. I only felt, like, in my heart . . . I can tell when there's a ghost around or something. I can tell when there's something wrong with me. I don't know if you can, but I can. I can sit in one spot and all of a sudden I can feel them. And I know. I don't get scared . . . My mom taught me not to be scared. She was telling me to pray."

"Your culture is very spiritual, eh," said Perron. "Can the same person do good or bad, or is that different people?"

"In the [gang] business there's always [something]. If I wanted someone to get hurt, I could do it but [the spirit will] tell me, 'If I do this with you and shit goes wrong, it'll fall back on you or your kid,'" said Danny. "So like right now, my situation. My mother told me . . . 'If you don't stop drinking and you don't stop doing this shit, it's going back onto your kids.'"

"Fuck, that's pretty powerful," said Perron.

"I was trying to lie to myself and I was trying to lie to the spirits. You know, I pray and pray and pray every day. It's good, but I was praying for the wrong reasons," Danny said. "So now I fucked up and this is what I did. This is it."

"So basically the spirit is saying . . ." Perron's voice trailed off.

"You fucked up," Danny said, completing the thought. "I believe in my heart that's what happened, and that's what I mean. Because I tried lying. I tried lying to my mom, eh. I told her I'll straighten out but I can't say I was . . . She told me, 'If I do this for you, you got to do it right, because if you don't do it right, you're gonna hurt me and you're gonna hurt yourself and you're gonna hurt your kids. You gotta stay cool.'"

"Now [it] went sideways, that's what you're saying. That's where you fucked up," said Perron.

"That was it, that was the sign. All last week I couldn't sleep, I couldn't eat, I couldn't think. I tried talking to my girlfriends. Every time I told them, 'I'm getting out, don't worry, baby, I'm doing well,' the knot just knotted up."

"Do they know now?" Perron asked.

"They know now. They're having a feast for me tomorrow," said Danny. "A feast is like a giving thanks, spiritual . . . make sure my daughter and my girlfriend [Shenoa] is there. I told her I'm charged with murder."

Danny's feelings of responsibility quickly returned to anger and regret. He focused his thoughts on Granbois. How could he have been so foolish? Danny wondered aloud whether he would feel better if he strangled Granbois with his bare hands.

"Choke the fucking life right out of him. I know I can do that shit [but] it wouldn't make me happier. No, it wouldn't. Beat it out of him? Tell him 'You fucking stupid,' boom, boom, boom, punch the shit out of him and then just leave him?" said Danny.

"Think about it," said Perron, egging him on.

"Think about it, fuck, for how much time you're going to get. Two first-degree and three attempts?" said Danny, assuming that Granbois would have to get some prison time for his role, even if he cooperated with police.

"Well, if he thinks he's walking?" said Perron, raising the possibility that the Crown would drop the charges completely in exchange for Granbois's testimony.

"I put it in his fucking head right after we were done. 'Shut the fuck up. Keep your fucking mouth shut.' Weak, weak."

"What do you think your buddy's thinking about right now?" Perron said.

Danny got so upset he could barely utter a coherent sentence. "You know what he said, he goes, 'If you go to the Correctional,' he told me to come to his range. That's what he told me," Danny said. He was incredulous. Could Granbois really be that naive? Did he not realize that Danny would have him killed?

"We kill. We don't give a fuck, man," said Danny. "Nothing's sweeter than fucking revenge."

It was getting late. Danny was yawning. Danny said his lawyer had advised him before today's interrogation that under no circumstances was he to say anything to police. It was fine to listen, to figure out what the police knew, but he shouldn't say a word.

He said that despite his mother's fear that he might commit suicide he couldn't abandon his little brother Preston. Preston had two little kids, Danny said, and a shot at a better life, if he could beat this murder charge. He told Perron that he had told Preston, "They got all this on me, man. But you, you got a second chance. You got a second chance to get out of here . . ."

"When he gets out I'll be fucking happy," Danny told Perron.

Danny said he would be a failure for as long as it took to get Preston out of jail. If Danny was ever able to get out again, he said, he wanted to have more children. "I want to watch my kids grow up . . . I did that to my first son and that ain't the way, man. You know what? I didn't even get a chance to see my son this time when I was out. Nine years old, man. He's back out in Winnipeg. It's been killing him what happened. He knows about me and about IP."

The two men fell silent for a while. The night was dragging on. Danny said he probably had another full day of interrogation to look forward to. The "special guy," as Danny called him, had said "See you tomorrow" when they parted.

"Fucking special guy. The fuck you going to take me for?" said Danny. "Almost made me cry on my mother."

"Yeah," said Perron, ignoring the emotional element of what Danny had just said. Perron just carried on probing Danny about Granbois. He needed to seal the deal before they both fell asleep.

"Wonder if he gave everything up, like?" said Perron.

"Yeah. He rolled," said Danny.

"Oh, you're [sure]?"

"He showed me the video and everything. Gave up the young guy and me. Gave us up," said Danny.

"Jesus Christ," Perron muttered.

"They had fucking nothing, man. No prints, no gun. Got rid of that. Nothing. No hair. No spit," said Danny. "Fucking nothing, man. They had nothing."

Except Granbois gave them everything, Perron prodded again.

"And that's what sewered you. Well, you said, too, they had the little things," said Perron.

"Yeah, but that still doesn't put me at the fucking scene," said Danny. "They couldn't prove that I was there . . . But they got me. They originally charged me with possession of a firearm, discharging a firearm on my reserve, off my back deck, shooting into the trees," said Danny. "They linked the three different spots [with] the same fucking hammer on the back [of the shell casings]. Couple in the van, twenty-one casings found at my house in the back yard, they found twenty-two casings at the scene."

"With the same hammer," said Perron. "But they don't have [the gun]."

"They don't need it," said Danny.

"That takes some of the weight off though, don't it?"

"Oh, fuck no. No, no. [Granbois] tells them that that [gun] is [mine]," said Danny.

"You never know," said Perron. "Don't think a guy's going to be that dumb, right? Jesus Christ."

Danny would just have to resign himself to his fate, he decided. It would be life in the penitentiary, for as long as he could take it anyway. "But the fucking pens today, man. Fucking wild. There's no old-school rules anymore," Danny complained. "It's not inmates for inmates, you know. It's like informants and rats. Penitentiaries have changed, man. And the fucking guys who testify on the stand are running around, guys who are known pedophiles are running around. Can't do nothing to them without being ratted out. And shipped out," Danny said.

"Really?" Perron maintained his curiousity.

"Pedophiles, rats, they let you know straight up, like if they owe you money, they fucking tell on you, man. You know, 'Just try it, I'll tell on you.'"

"Fuck," said Perron.

"You got a handful of guys who are solid, keep their mouth shut, that's it, man. That's why they don't like IP."

"Who don't?"

"Correctional Service of Canada," said Danny. "Because we're old school inside the pen. Not one of our guys yet charged with first-degree inside. There's a couple guys who were charged with murder inside but they beat it."

It was cold in the cell that night. Both Danny and Perron complained about a draft of cold air blowing from the vent, but eventually they settled down for a few hours of sleep. At about 6:00 a.m. they were served frozen waffles for breakfast. Perron was supposedly told he'd be getting on a plane to be shipped back east. Danny's resolve had hardened somewhat with the sleep. He said he'd refuse to leave the cell if Sergeant LeRat wanted to interrogate him again that day. Officers finally came to extract Perron at about 9:00 a.m.

Staff Sergeant Wilkie had been up all night monitoring the audio and video coming in from the cell. A team was in the special investigations monitoring room with her, typing up a transcript in real time. She conferred briefly with Perron and then let him head home for some rest. She then sent a text message to the entire homicide investigation team: *We got a confession*, it said in essence.

There was no celebration, Staff Sergeant Wilkie said, just a sense of an important job done. But there was one apparently insignificant piece of conversation in the cell that night that would soon loom large for RCMP across the country. Danny had mentioned to Perron that the range where he was locked up at the Regina Correctional Centre was loaded with serious criminals. They had eight people charged with murder, including himself and his brother.

"No way?" said Perron. "Won the lottery."

"My time is coming, man," said Danny. "What to do now?"

21

THE GREAT ESCAPE
JANUARY–AUGUST 2008

It was roughly a month after that night in the cells with the RCMP undercover officer when Danny met with defence lawyer Estes Fonkalsrud to discuss his case. By that time Fonkalsrud had told him that the RCMP had placed an undercover cop in his cell. Danny knew he had said too much. By now he was certain his fate was sealed.

"He was quiet, calm," Fonkalsrud said. "He always stayed quiet. Daniel was not very talkative. You never got any emotional response from him on anything . . . There's no doubt he was intelligent, but he wouldn't get upset and he wouldn't get happy."

There was some question about whether the undercover evidence would be admissible at trial. Fonkalsrud would at least try to argue that Danny's attempts to remain silent were violated by police. He had been questioned for more than ten hours by Sergeant LeRat and then immediately after was subjected to an undercover officer trying to extract information. That could be interpreted as a violation of his rights. But Fonkalsrud had his doubts about whether the argument would succeed. The undercover officer's evidence was going to make a big difference to Danny's prospects at trial, and they both knew it.

"Without that undercover operation the Crown would have been [looking at] a second-degree murder charge and looking to make a deal," Fonkalsrud said. They would have had a cooperating witness in Gerrard Granbois, but he was also present at the scene of the killings. Danny's defence strategy would have been to simply point the finger back at Granbois, who had escaped any criminal charge in exchange for his testimony. Doing so would have created enough doubt to make a conviction on first-degree murder unlikely.

"The undercover evidence, that just completely sunk him," Fonkalsrud said.

With his trial more than a year away, Danny was returned to the Regina Correctional Centre in January 2008. Not much had changed: he was placed on Unit 3A, the Indian Posse range, with his brother Preston and several members of the NSK, the Native Syndicate Killers, a Regina gang that was allied with the Indian Posse.

As the prospect of a lifetime in the federal penitentiary loomed ever larger, Danny started to dream of escape. Accused murderers don't normally have an easy time in jail, and Danny's unit, where nearly all fifteen people were accused of either murder or manslaughter, was deemed a high-security section with a fairly high level of monitoring. Escape should have been inconceivable, but Danny was a believer, and he proved both lucky and capable in its pursuit.

In May, a contractor booking off work on a Friday afternoon, forgot to lock the door to a maintenance tunnel on Unit 3A, which was a serious oversight. Danny walked past the following day and noticed that the door, normally locked tight, was slightly ajar. He quickly ducked inside, closing the door behind. Inside, he saw narrow stairs leading to the upper floors of the prison and surmised that they might take him all the way to the roof. He looked through a vent and could see right into the other unit, 3B, through a small opening. He observed the activity on the other range for a minute but was afraid he might reveal himself if he watched for too long. He climbed further up the stairs and found a door that was locked with a heavy chain and lock. He wondered if it would be possible to get through. This was an opportunity, he realized. Danny went back down the stairs to get help from his comrades.

He returned to Unit 3A with wide-eyed excitement, Preston recalled, gesturing for everyone to come over and see what he had found. He opened the door with dramatic flair and then let his jaw drop wide open. "Check it out," Danny said.

About six others went into the maintenance tunnel and climbed the stairs with Danny. Together they decided they might be able to snap the chain by brute force. They went back downstairs to their unit and got a metal rod from the shower, which they could unscrew using a piece of metal broken off from one of the beds as a makeshift screwdriver. They slipped the bar into the chain and twisted it tighter and tighter until the old, rusty links gave way. Danny let the chain fall to the ground and proceeded through the door, which led to another set of stairs that took them even higher, until they reached a maintenance room on the prison roof. This was where air vented to the outside. They could see the outdoors and the surface of the roof just beyond the walls. From there it would be quite feasible to get down to the ground and climb over the remaining fences, Danny reasoned, if they picked their spots. But the door leading outside was also locked, and this time the chain was in better shape, so the trick with the shower rod didn't work.

Danny led the group back downstairs to mull how they might seize this tantalizing chance. They spent the next day, Sunday, brainstorming methods to get through the final door, but nothing worked, and for various reasons they didn't get another opportunity to sneak away into the tunnel that day. The next morning the maintenance man was back at work and realized his mistake. Danny was frustrated to have missed his chance but was more convinced than ever that escape was possible.

The unit they lived in was in the old, dilapidated main building at the Regina Correctional Centre, built in 1915 and expanded in 1960. The cells, twelve in all, were arranged in a row along one side of a depressing corridor of peeling pink and green paint. The wall across from the cells had narrow windows at the top and three-foot-high heating grilles at regular intervals on the bottom. At one end of the corridor was a common room, and at the other was the guards' station, where one or sometimes two guards sat and occasionally poked their heads out for a visual check. The surveillance camera, which was mounted on the ceiling at the common room end and looked back down the hall toward the guard station, was located about ten feet in from the end of the corridor. That left a large blind spot underneath, giving Danny all the freedom he needed to work unobserved.

Around March 2008, a few months before the maintenance tunnel was left open, Danny had discovered he could remove the grille covering on a radiator located in the camera's blind spot. He had been playing with his nail clippers and found that one edge could be used like an Allen key to unscrew the grille cover. At first he stored his metal and plastic shanks in the heater space. But then, while he was in the maintenance tunnel months later, Danny found a number of tools and pieces of metal, including a drill bit, which he had kept. As he stored them away one evening, Danny realized that the hiding spot was also a route to a vulnerable outer wall. With the right tools and enough time, he was certain that he'd be able to dig his way out.

Blocking his path was the pipe setup of the radiator's heating mechanism, and then a sheet of thick metal, which covered a layer of cinder blocks. He was able to figure out how to make the heating mechanism swivel out of his way, so he could get a clearer path to the wall. Preston told him he didn't think it would work, that they would get caught. But Danny, with his energy and charisma, persuaded the others to hope.

He'd puzzle over his project in the evening after dinner, while the other inmates milled around in the corridor. Danny would arrange for a few guys to play cards in the area where he was working so that the guards, from their station at the end of the hallway, couldn't see what he was doing. He crouched at floor level, safely in the camera's blind spot, relying mainly on Preston to assist him. Preston was responsible for holding the grille cover while Danny worked, prepared to replace it in less than three seconds if one of the lookouts whistled a warning. Preston used to practise the motion over and over to be sure he could do it perfectly, without stumbling.

The biggest challenge was getting through the metal sheet, which proved frustratingly difficult to penetrate. At first Danny could only scratch the surface; then, with a great deal of effort, he could make small punctures with the drill bit he found in the maintenance tunnel. But it was a long way from tiny punctures to a human-sized hole. The work proceeded for a few months. Trying to get through the metal produced a lot of suspicious noise, so they would turn the showers on or turn up the radio to mask it, Preston said. At the end of the night they swept up the debris and flushed it down the toilet.

After a while Danny began to make progress. The key moment was when he figured out how to build a tool that could defeat the sheet metal. Someone on the range already had a small saw blade that they had smuggled in from somewhere, a very tiny blade of the kind that might be on a Swiss Army knife, but with no handle, which meant getting a sufficient grip on it to saw through the metal was difficult. Danny kept cutting his hand. Then one of the other inmates had the idea of making a handle from an old broomstick by cutting a groove just wide enough for the saw blade in the wood. They wrapped fabric around it, and then had something that they could use to poke, penetrate, and then pry the metal apart – like an old-style can opener, Preston said. Next Danny devised something like a crowbar from a utensil holder that was attached to a cell desk, where a knife and spoon were supposed to rest. That tool was used to punch into an existing hole to rip it wider. They worked at it every night for a month, and were often left sweating and bleeding. Progress was slow.

They worked most evenings, Danny and Preston, mainly, taking turns, but others participated as well. As lights-out approached they wrapped up their half-dozen homemade tools, hid them in the radiator, and replaced the grille. They even hung a piece of canvas torn from a prisoner's winter coat behind the grille so that if a guard peered inside he would see only a flat, dark background. But they weren't much troubled by the guards, Preston said. Normally just one person staffed the guard station, assisted by a colleague who moved between Units 3A and 3B. The inmates could go hours without seeing any prison authorities.

"The guards didn't come down because there were guys standing in the middle of the range, talking, working out. It seemed like they didn't want to come. They would look out [of their station] but they'd just see a bunch of people standing around," Preston said.

On June 21, when they were getting tantalizingly close to breaching the outer wall, a guard on a routine check noticed blood seeping from a cut on the back of Danny's left hand and asked how he'd hurt himself. Danny shrugged it off, saying he caught his hand on something sharp on his bed. The guard suspected the gang leader was lying but did not order a full search of the unit. A few days later, Regina police got a tip saying that the inmates on Unit 3A were planning an escape. The source of that tip has not been revealed, but subsequent investigations make it clear it was either a prisoner acting as an informant or someone on the outside who was speaking to a prisoner and then brought the information to police. Soon after that, on June 26, a corrections worker at the Regina jail got an email that said the word on the street was that some gang members would be coming out soon and would be "doing it like the movies." The worker forwarded it to a supervisor, who didn't even reply.

A week later, on July 3, Regina police phoned the prison and warned that they had heard the Indian Posse and Native Syndicate Killers were planning an escape for that very night. The prison responded by ordering a lockdown. All cell doors were checked and an additional guard was assigned to watch the Indian Posse and Unit 3A. On July 9, guards searched the cells and found hidden shanks and pepper bombs and a balaclava made from sweat pants. But they did not find the hole.

The heightened level of institutional alarm exacerbated tensions on the range. Fights broke out between inmates. Danny and Preston suspected an informant was leaking information to authorities, but they didn't know who was to blame. Guards patrolled more carefully, and took note of the inmates' sudden interest in the work schedule of the rookie employees. One guard later claimed, although it couldn't be verified, that after he grew suspicious he asked that all radiator covers be removed and searched, but he said he was turned down because maintenance staff weren't available. In any case, Unit 3A was placed on lockdown for most of July and early August, which kept inmates confined to their cells twenty-three hours a day. Danny had to wait.

"They knew something was up," Preston said. "Somebody said something on that range."

While the prison was on lockdown the authorities forced the men on Unit 3A to wear bright yellow clothing, hardly an ideal colour for a breakout. In August they were permitted to go to 50 per cent status, which meant half the inmates were allowed out of their cells together for a few hours at a time, a major improvement on being locked up twenty-three hours a day. Inmates in cells two to seven would be allowed out for the morning, for example, while those in cells eight to fourteen would get the afternoon.

Preston shared cell two with Cody Keenatch, a nineteen-year-old IP member from Saskatoon; Danny shared cell six with James Pewean, a twenty-five-year-old charged with second-degree murder for allegedly beating a man to death. Everyone on the range knew about Danny's digging and Danny had said all were welcome to escape with him, but that he and his brother and their cellmates would go first. He was hoping larger numbers would improve his odds of evading arrest.

Danny told everyone they had to exercise to prepare for the physical demands of the breakout. When they were locked down they did push-ups and sit-ups in their cells and ran in place for long periods. Once they were allowed outside again, they ran in the exercise yard and worked on their arm and shoulder strength in anticipation of a difficult climb over prison walls. "We were in good shape," Preston said.

Danny was now focused on chipping and scraping his way through the cinder block and brick. He knew he was close, but he also knew that he had to move quickly. A new, high-security building at the prison was nearing completion and the inmates on Unit 3A were set to be transferred there. They watched as inmates from other units marched across the grounds carrying their stuff, headed for the new building. Danny's time was running out.

By the middle of August, Danny could sense that fresh air was just a few inches away. He and Preston closed the grille and paused before going any further. They didn't want to ruin the scheme by accidentally opening a hole in the wall before they were ready to go. Danny spent a week planning the last step, trying to gauge when the prison would be at its quietest. The discussions were frustrating, Preston recalled, because he and Danny and their cellmates talked in circles about what-ifs and couldn't settle on where to go or what to do if they succeeded. Ultimately they gave up looking for consensus and Danny, the unquestioned leader, kept the decisions to himself.

He waited until Sunday, August 24, to make his move. He originally wanted to wait until the range was taken off 50 per cent status, so more people could join the escape, but he feared that if he waited any longer he would miss his opportunity. That evening he kept himself glued to the phone. If the escape was botched, if the hole proved too small to fit through, Danny's plan was to start a siege and set the prison alight.

The guard had completed the evening count and retreated to his station. It was just after 8:30 p.m. when Danny walked up to Preston, who was playing cards, and tapped him on the shoulder. "Let's go," he said. "Get the stuff you need."

The breakout was on. Preston felt a surge of adrenaline as he hurried to his cell and grabbed blankets and a small, red address book, thinking he'd need his contacts if they made it out safely. Then he walked quickly to the end of the corridor. Danny told the other half-dozen inmates to block the view from the guard post.

Preston bent down and unscrewed the heating grille with the nail clippers and placed the cover on the floor. Then he swivelled the heating unit out of the way to expose the hole they had dug. Danny, who had grabbed the shower rod, started smashing away at the remaining layer of brick, destroying the remnants of eight or ten bricks as he heaved and grunted. Finally they broke through. It was a titanic moment, Preston said.

"Anyone who wants to go can go," Danny said before slipping through the small hole and out into the night. Preston came after him, followed by Keenatch, James Pewean, Ryan Agecoutay, and Ken Iron.

At first, it was strangely quiet. No one seemed to have noticed that they had gone. Roughly fifteen minutes after the six slipped through the hole, word reached the Regina police service that the inmates had escaped, presumably from an informant on the unit or from someone in contact with an inmate on the unit. The police had that information at 8:50 p.m., according to a subsequent investigation, but there was a delay of more than forty minutes in getting that crucial information to the prison. Finally an officer with the Regina police called the central police station to get a number for the jail. At 9:40 p.m., police called the jail, more than an hour after the inmates had scaled the fence. The first question the officer asked was, "Have you had an escape tonight?"

The person who took that call, whose name has been redacted from the investigation documents, immediately called the guard on Unit 3A and ordered a head count. Then he rushed out of his office to go look for himself. He ran to the nearest window and saw something hanging from the razor wire outside Unit 3. He grabbed his radio and ordered an emergency lockdown across the prison. Another guard rushed to the compound outside Unit 3 and saw a gaping hole in the wall above him and ropes that extended from the hole to the razor wire. The two guards started searching the fence areas for clues that might indicate which direction the escapees were headed. They found none.

At 10:08 p.m., roughly thirty minutes after Regina police called to tell them about the escape, the jail called them back to confirm that some prisoners, they didn't yet know how many, had broken free. Police were now on high alert, but they were about ninety minutes behind Danny and company. Jail guards jumped into their own vehicles to search the surrounding farm fields. It was dark by this time and visibility was poor. The guards also personally knocked on doors to warn residents to beware and to stay indoors.

Back inside the jail, guards tried to enter Unit 3A to find out who was missing. Since they were on half-day lockdown, six of the seventeen men on the unit were locked up in their cells and six were gone.

The five who could have joined the escape but didn't (probably because they thought it was doomed), in an act of solidarity with Danny and the other escapees, smashed windows, threw toilet paper over security cameras, and generally created a mini-riot when the guards arrived, which slowed them down even further. The guards had to stop and get into riot gear before going in, then had to fire pepper spray to get the inmates under control. The inmates were told to lie face-down on the floor so they could be handcuffed. But to make things difficult for the guards, the inmates wouldn't look at their captors and wouldn't reveal their names. It took about twenty minutes to figure out who was who. Eventually photos were printed out and matched up to the remaining faces. By 10:40 p.m., two hours after the escape, the prison was finally able to provide police with the names of those who were missing. It was possibly even later before photos were distributed.

By 11:15 p.m., the search had reached the Trans-Canada Highway. A guard stopped at a hockey rink, where even in late summer a game was on. He wanted to speak with the manager, but as he walked down the corridor he noticed a young man headed in his direction. The man was walking with his head down, trying not to look suspicious. As they passed in the hall the guard recognized him as an escapee and swivelled round and grabbed the young man in an arm lock. As they struggled he threw him against the wall, wrestled him to the ground, and put him in handcuffs. Meanwhile, he asked the astonished hockey fans, who had turned away from the game to watch the scuffle, to call the RCMP. They had one of the escaped inmates back in custody: Ken Iron.

Danny Wolfe was well on his way to freedom. He waded through the long grass in the fields and kept looking back for Preston, who struggled to keep up with his older brother. Eventually Danny jogged back to Preston to encourage him to keep moving. They would run hard for a while, taking a faster pace than they could realistically maintain, and then walk until they caught their breath. They paused on a prairie back road, gravel crunching under their feet. There were no vehicles in sight and the only sound was the hum of insects in the night air. They walked a little further and eventually met up with Cody Keenatch, Preston's cellmate and a fellow Indian Posse member, by the railway tracks (Pewean and Agecoutay had already peeled off on their own).

"I can't believe it, we made it," Danny said.

They had just pulled off one of the most spectacular prison breaks in Canadian history. It was a product of incredible determination and cunning, and now five of them were on the loose.

Months later an independent investigation would catalogue the long list of errors and inadequacies of training or infrastructure at the prison that contributed to the escape. Among them: the security camera that couldn't see the end of the Unit 3A corridor; the failure to mount an effective search of Unit 3A, despite credible rumours of a planned escape; the obvious inattention to human intelligence gathering. Not a single guard tried to obtain information from inmates on Unit 3A about whether an escape was being planned, even though someone was clearly willing to reveal information about Danny's plans. One guard was even quoted as saying, "It's not my job to talk to inmates." Another guard later told investigators, "We look but we don't see." As many as eighty-seven different corrections workers had contact with the inmates on Unit 3A and yet not one had detected anything amiss.

One of the biggest questions arising from the escape is whether Danny and the Indian Posse paid their jailers to turn a blind eye. They certainly had the financial clout to do so: Danny was a successful prison smuggler who made thousands selling contraband in jail and had been bribing guards elsewhere. In 2012 a former guard at the Regina Correctional Centre was convicted of smuggling narcotics and tobacco into the jail at the request of prisoners. Another guard was convicted of the same offence a year earlier. Clearly, some guards made deals with prisoners in the period before Danny broke out, but several inmates who were there say Danny didn't make any deals and didn't need any help.

As darkness gathered that night, Danny, Preston, and Cody followed the railway tracks into Regina. It took about an hour to get to the city and then they crept through the industrial area at Regina's eastern edge. They were cold and exhausted. They had no phone. Their clothes were bloodied and torn. They did not have a ride arranged or even a place to stay, so they went to the home of someone Danny knew and trusted. He was not thrilled to see them, given the risks of harbouring fugitives, and told them to wait in the alley outside. They drank thirstily from a garden hose and waited until he brought out a cordless phone to let them make some calls. Danny reached his cousin, Kelly Goforth, who walked to the alley where they were hiding, carrying a coat for each of them and some food to eat. By 3:00 a.m. they had not yet found anyone with a vehicle willing to help them, nor did they have a place to spend the night. With no better options available, Preston suggested he steal a car, and Danny agreed. They got a screwdriver and walked down a nearby street, looking for an easy target, preferably an older North American brand. Preston, who was the most skilled car thief, spotted an old, four-door GM sedan, smashed the window, and all three hopped inside. He slammed the screwdriver into the steering column and they took off.

They headed out of town on the main roads, prepared for the possibility that police might have set up checkpoints, but found none. They scanned the radio dial, wondering if there would be news of their escape, but they heard nothing. Was it possible they had gone out unnoticed? Around White City, Preston got off the highway and took side roads all the way back home, to the Okanese First Nation, about an hour and a half outside Regina. They knew it was a crazy decision, that it was the obvious and foolish thing to do, but there were people there who would help them, and at that moment they needed it.

Danny told Preston to drive to Tatiana's place. He hadn't been there since he was arrested nearly eleven months earlier, but they were in and out quickly, stopping only to grab sleeping bags. Then they drove out into the middle of the bush, the area that locals call the Big Bush, a forest of trees and brush populated by deer and other woodland animals. It felt great to be outside again, but they were on the run and feeling paranoid, alert to every sound of a vehicle travelling on distant roads. They bunked down for the night, scared of what the next day might bring.

22

ON THE RUN
AUGUST–SEPTEMBER 2008

That Monday morning, RCMP Sergeant Brent Ross was returning to work after being on vacation. He had not yet heard about the breakout because the news hadn't been made public. The first he learned of it was when he arrived at RCMP headquarters in Regina.

Ross was a veteran officer with more than 30 years' experience. He'd seen nearly everything in his time, but this prison break was about as big as it gets. He knew both Danny and Preston well: he had been involved in the investigations that led to their arrests, and he considered them both very dangerous.

Ross had also investigated the murder of Sheldon McKay at Stony Mountain. Danny was a person of interest in the case, although no one had yet been charged. And of course everyone knew about the murders in Fort Qu'Appelle nearly a year before. In the words of Danny's lawyer, it was probably the highest-profile killing in the province since a government minister, Colin Thatcher, was convicted of murdering his wife.

Sergeant Ross was quickly put in charge of a task force of four officers and some administrative staff. He was beside himself – the escapees could be anywhere at this point. The RCMP was roughly twelve hours behind. Ross couldn't understand why they had waited this long to get the task force up and running, but there was no point complaining. He immediately started making phone calls to RCMP and local police forces in Alberta and Manitoba, as well as to those in Regina and Saskatoon. He asked them to contact their informants and pump them about the whereabouts of Danny and the others.

"We were convinced, knowing Preston Buffalocalf, knowing Danny Wolfe, that they would have no qualms killing. This became a divisional priority because of the danger," Ross said.

Finding and capturing Danny was now the RCMP's prime focus.

The task force began their probe by questioning Ken Iron, the one escapee who had been arrested. He didn't give them anything, Ross said, except to say it was possible they were all travelling alone. That would have been the most difficult scenario for the RCMP to handle. In fact, Danny, Preston, and Cody were together, while Ryan Agecoutay and James Pewean travelled alone.

Ross knew that they would have to go to the media to get tips rolling in from the public. But for the provincial government – the government responsible for overseeing the Regina Correctional Centre – everything about this situation was bad. Just one prisoner escaping is bad news; six is ridiculous. To make matters worse, most were accused murderers and high-ranking gang members with the resources to stay on the run for a while. There was a significant chance that this escape would lead to more killings. Danny, for one, had vowed to kill Granbois, and since nearly all of the escapees were facing life terms, there was a chance they would refuse to be captured, taking police and bystanders with them in a hail of gunfire.

Tips started coming in to Sergeant Ross's task force once news of the escape broke in the media on Monday afternoon. By then Danny and company had been gone for nearly sixteen hours. Sergeant

Ross thought the odds were about even that they'd stay in Saskatchewan or head for Manitoba or Alberta, but they could have been anywhere in Western Canada at that point. Sergeant Ross coordinated and farmed out any leads to local agencies for follow-up. On day one, not a single tip checked out. It was the same on day two and day three. The division's highest-ranking officers were in his office every day to check up on the search. Everyone was edgy.

"They weren't putting pressure on, but they were tense, we all were; if any of these men were cornered, they would kill, no doubt," said Sergeant Ross.

Police had wiretaps monitoring phones connected to Indian Posse members in various cities, trying to track Danny's movements. Susan said they were definitely listening to her calls, but Danny never phoned directly; he always used intermediaries to let her know they were okay, she said. The RCMP admits wiretaps were very useful in their investigation, but information was slow to develop.

Danny, meanwhile, awoke on Monday morning in the Big Bush near Okanese, ravenous, and unsure of his next move. Would he hunt down Granbois and the other witnesses who might testify in his case? He had to decide.

A witness to the Fort Qu'Appelle murders who survived the Pasqua Avenue shooting gallery told the media following the escape that she was afraid Danny might come after her and others who had spoken to police. That whipped up a sense of fear in the community, and the witnesses in both Danny's and Preston's homicide cases were all living not far from the spot where the men spent that first night on the run.

"They were terrified," said an RCMP officer who worked the case.

Danny eventually decided not to pursue the witnesses, because it was too risky. For several months before the escape he had said his plan was to rough it in the wild for a year or more, hunting and fishing and living off the land. It was almost a point of pride; he wanted to prove he was capable of living as his ancestors had for generations before. But he and Preston had no supplies. That first day they sent Cody out to the highway to try to get them some food and clothing, thinking that since he wasn't from the area he'd be less likely to be recognized. Cody walked a straight line out of the bush to the road and dropped his coat near the shoulder, so he could remember roughly where his friends were hiding. He walked for a while until he got back to Okanese and followed the directions that Danny had made him commit to memory. He found the help they were seeking. A few hours later, a friend dropped Cody off at the spot where he'd left his coat, and he made his way back into the woods with some sandwiches and other provisions. The three of them spent that night in the woods again, anxiously watching for signs of movement coming from the road. They saw several RCMP vehicles roll past, but none stopped. Danny hoped to arrange a ride that would get them out of Saskatchewan, but it took longer than he expected. His friends were afraid to help him.

Their legs and feet ached from the exertion of the escape. Preston had never run that far in his life, and Danny had done it in cheap, prison-made runners that left his feet covered in blisters. The break-out was also mentally exhausting. Beforehand, they'd had nothing but questions. Would they be flexible or skinny enough to squeeze through the tiny hole they'd made in the brick? Would they make it over the various walls or slip and injure themselves? If Preston was hurt, would Danny go on without him? Would they die trying? But now, ever since they burst through that wall, Preston had been looking over his shoulder, and it was wearing him down.

Their ride finally materialized on Wednesday when a friend came through for them. They piled in to the back seat and lay down as they drove off down the highway. No one will say who drove the car. They stopped in Brandon at a house and spent the night sleeping in a garage that belonged to someone connected to the Indian Posse.

Danny asked for some weed to help them relax, although it had the effect of also enhancing their paranoia. Every bump in the night conjured an image of a police SWAT team assembling, Preston said. The three of them got a few hours of uncomfortable sleep on the hard garage floor.

Years later, Danny's lawyer Estes Fonkalsrud said he wondered, when he heard of the escape that night, whether Danny had the wherewithal to disappear. "Would he go, get across the border, never pick up the phone, never refer to himself as Daniel Wolfe again?" He had a well-funded gang at his disposal and the open road ahead of him. But Danny went back to what he knew.

Hundreds of miles away in an Ontario prison, Danny's brother Richard watched the story unfold. He was older now, almost thirty-four, and had left the gang behind him years ago to focus on doing his time quietly, with as little drama as possible. He was still in regular contact with Danny and some others from the Indian Posse. He was living in a lower-security cabin setting with a few other prisoners who had spent many years in the system. Some were members of what the police call "Traditional Organized Crime," more commonly known as the Italian Mafia, who had status and respect in the institution. Richard was honoured that they'd chosen him to live among them. They told him they had done some research on him and were very impressed with how he'd built the Indian Posse. They'd taught Richard how to cook some of their favourite meals, and one of his occasional roles was to be the chef for the group.

Richard was nearing the final stretch of his sentence, having served thirteen years of his nineteen-year term (release is mandatory at the two-thirds point, but Richard had two years added for the stabbing he'd committed inside a decade earlier). He had asked to be transferred back to Saskatchewan to be closer to his family and was still awaiting word when the escape happened. It was the following afternoon when a guard approached, smiling.

"I have some news," he said. "Your brother broke out."

Richard's heart jumped. Escaping was great, but he worried police would simply shoot Danny on sight. "Did he get caught yet?" asked Richard.

"He had a good head start," the guard said.

"Good," said Richard.

Richard didn't know that Preston was with Danny, because at the time the media hadn't been told that Danny and Preston were brothers. As he considered the situation, Richard concluded that Danny would probably be killed. He was an accused killer on the run, presumed to be armed and dangerous – why would a police officer take a chance? Danny would probably prefer to go down in a shootout anyway, Richard thought.

As the days passed and Danny remained at large, Richard fretted about his brother non-stop. The stress took its toll. He was standing at the stove cooking one evening when he felt a powerful pain in his chest and collapsed. The next thing he knew, he was in hospital being treated for a serious heart attack.

After a night in Brandon, Danny, Preston, and Cody headed for Winnipeg. Their faces were plastered all over the news. Even though they knew they had to lie low, they wanted to be where they had a network. Danny had ex-girlfriends in the city and the Indian Posse still had hundreds of members in Winnipeg with money and resources to help them hide. The trouble was that the city police, as well as the RCMP, were going flat-out to find them, tapping every network and informant they could, offering thousands of dollars for tips on Danny. But the information police got usually left them a day or more behind. They needed to land a decisive bit of intelligence that would get them to Danny at the right moment.

"We knew they were constantly on the move," said Sergeant Ross. "No one wanted them. They were bringing way too much heat. [Friends] harboured them, but they couldn't stay [for long]. They had to keep moving."

Danny was returning to Winnipeg as both a feared gangster and a folk hero, seen by some as an aspiring revolutionary who had successfully thumbed his nose at the authorities. But not everyone in the Indian Posse was happy to see him. There was conflict within the leadership, as there had been more or less since McKay's killing. Danny was identified with an old-school leadership group, and some gang members emerging on the street weren't necessarily keen to see someone who could challenge their authority or bring unwanted police attention their way. Sergeant Ross said police intelligence indicated that some Indian Posse factions were unhappy with Danny's presence in Winnipeg. He wouldn't be able to issue orders and get them carried out as easily as he would like. If he needed to move, he couldn't snap his fingers and get a car and driver at his disposal. It was the same issue that Sergeant LeRat had alluded to in his interview with Danny: people weren't doing what he asked.

Danny did not have huge financial resources to call on either. One of the puzzling aspects of the Indian Posse is that although they always made money, they were never able to consistently amass and retain wealth, whether in the form of cars, or property or savings, as other organized crime groups have done. There are exceptions, and some members have done well personally for long periods, but for the most part police have never identified signs that the Indian Posse was putting away cash as part of a larger plan. The money they had was usually spent and shared widely in the group. Danny's philosophy was to ensure that everyone had enough to live well and enjoy themselves today, but he tended to plan for the weeks ahead, not years. Now that he was out he had to find a way to get some money to fund his time on the run.

He left Preston and Cody to lie low for a day in an apartment in the West Broadway area while they recuperated from the physical demands of the escape. Neither had ever run so much in their lives and they were still so sore they could barely move. Danny came back with a fistful of cash, roughly $3,000, for food, clothes, and partying, according to Preston – money he either borrowed, or made from selling drugs or doing an armed robbery. Danny also had some new green contact lenses for himself, a pair of dark sunglasses, and a baseball cap to disguise his appearance. He had a silver hoop earring in each ear.

"Your new name is Warren," Danny told Preston. "Now memorize your birthday." He handed Preston and Cody new identities that they could use if they got stopped by police. "Warren" was the name of a real person with a clean record and no legal entanglements. Preston committed the details to memory so he could rattle off his new name and age with ease.

That night, with fresh identities, new clothes, and pockets full of money, they went to a house party in the city's West End. There were other Indian Posse members there and a lot of girls. At first no one really noticed the three new faces, Preston said.

"People were like, 'Who are these guys? Oh, just some Indians.'"

But gradually word started to get around that these were Canada's most wanted criminals. They were infamous and in demand.

"What did we do?" said Cody. "Live the life, obviously."

The photos from that night show Danny surrounded by four or five girls in their late teens or early twenties. His face is tanned and lean, his arms chiselled, and he wears a confidence he seldom showed in earlier pictures. In one he's shirtless, showing off his back tattoos for the camera. In others his eyes look bleary and unfocused and he's wearing a happy half-smile. He was constantly raising a bottle to the camera, flashing an IP sign, or throwing his arms around the laughing girls, unafraid that these photos might lead to his downfall.

"The best part?" said Preston. "The girls, man, the girls. There were lots, coming and going. They took advantage of us," Preston said with a laugh.

Danny was the most heavily pursued, according to Preston. He was like a rock star. Women were charmed by his aura, hanging on his every word and attaching themselves to him. Danny was constantly in danger but he woke every day hungry to live as much as he could every hour, every day. In some of the photos he's surrounded by old friends, looking comfortable and happy, a bottle of Bud in his hand.

He even enjoyed the cat-and-mouse with the police, taunting them with online messages. A few days after the breakout, he, or someone acting on his behalf, updated his status on a social networking account with a simple "What's up? I'm out." And later, "Don't catch you slippin! 187 on that ass!" That might have been a threat for the witnesses in his case, as 187 is the radio code for homicide used by American police and popularized in gangster rap music. The RCMP, keeping an eye on his online profiles for any clues, carefully printed out each one and followed any leads.

The search for Danny was top of the news in Winnipeg for days, as it continued for more than a week. The city police were receiving lots of tips, but so were police in other parts of the country. The RCMP had a reliable source telling them that Danny was in Edmonton, so they devoted a lot of energy and resources to looking in the Alberta capital. But it turned out to be a false tip, deliberate misinformation engineered by Danny to throw the Mounties off the trail. There were reports of Danny in Onion Lake, Saskatchewan, and in other places in Alberta. The search stretched on and on, and by day ten there was still, improbably, no end in sight. James Pewean was caught by chance in Regina, after police responded to a call about a disturbance and were told that Pewean was hanging around the area. That left four of Canada's most sought-after criminals still on the loose.

Sergeant Ross is not the type to praise criminals. In fact, he's wary of speaking publicly about the case, for fear it might glorify Danny's actions. But he had to admit that what Danny had pulled off was impressive, in its own way. "Yes, I was impressed by the plan," said Sergeant Ross. "It wasn't a quick thing. It took months. Was it ingenious? Yeah. They got away with it," he said.

Officers delved into Danny's prison and police files, tracking down his known associates, friends, relatives, girlfriends, and children, trying to develop investigative leads. To Sergeant Ross, the Indian Posse leader was merely an above-average criminal who used his abilities to manipulate people for his own enrichment, and that infuriated him.

"This guy had no conscience. He might have been well-spoken but he didn't give a rat's ass about anybody," Sergeant Ross said.

On September 10, police finally got a tip that Preston was in Winnipeg, hanging around an address in the West Broadway neighbourhood. The Winnipeg police started surveillance on Balmoral Street near the Assiniboine River.

Preston was having the time of his life, but he knew it couldn't go on forever. As the heat from the police intensified, fewer people were willing to help the escapees. They had cousins in Winnipeg, Cody had an ex-girlfriend, and Danny knew lots of people, but Preston was younger and had spent the better part of ten years living in Saskatchewan. Where could he turn?

"We didn't know anybody," he said. He and Danny were thinking that their next move would be to head back to Saskatchewan, where they thought they could live in the bush for a while, build a shelter, and hunt for food. It was a romantic idea, following in the footsteps of their grandfather Bill Creeley. Susan says she thinks they would have been able to survive, as she had taught Danny and Preston the traditional skills they would have needed. But Preston couldn't get out before the police caught up with him.

Preston and Cody were together that evening while Danny was off on his own somewhere. The two of them had just bedded down in a new apartment, a place that belonged to a friend of a friend, where they could stay awhile. Around 10:00 p.m. Cody walked to the corner to use the pay phone and Preston went downstairs to smoke. He was sitting on the steps outside when he saw two patrol cars roll up. He kept his head down to hide his face, trying to look casual. The police cars stopped and Preston immediately sensed trouble. He turned, dropped his cigarette, and headed back into the building, breaking into a run as he climbed the stairs to the floor where he had been staying. He assumed, correctly, that the police had probably nabbed Cody, since they were coming from the direction of the pay phone. Preston re-entered the apartment and immediately tuned in the lobby camera on the TV. He could see two plainclothes police officers come into view and he knew they were looking for him. The girl he was with took him back out into the hall and they raced up another floor, where they were let into another apartment. Preston introduced himself using his false name and thanked his host for letting him stay for a minute. He struggled to keep his cool. He called Danny on a cell phone, panicked and out of breath. "They're coming for me," Preston said. "I don't know what to do."

Danny tried to calm his little brother by telling him he was going to make it, that the police couldn't just burst into the apartment and arrest him.

"He told me not to open the door," Preston recalled. "He said [the cops] can't do it themselves without a warrant. He told me to just hide. I was freaking out. They had dogs."

The SWAT team had been brought in, along with police from the organized crime unit and the criminal investigation bureau, and the mass of officers blocked traffic as they prepared for a stand-off. The police started going door to door in the building, clipboard in hand, inviting residents to leave their units so they could be cleared and declared safe. This was a process of elimination, and it went on for hours.

"I sat and watched and smoked and smoked," Preston said. "I knew what was going on."

He paced inside the small apartment, trying to avoid the windows in case he was spotted. For weeks people had been telling him the cops would shoot him if they ever found him. Now it seemed like that's how it would end. The apartment's owner watched him and knew something was seriously wrong, but he sat frozen to the couch. He had a small child sleeping in another room. Preston was muttering that he knew who had ratted them out.

Danny made his way to the scene. He tried to get as close as possible without drawing attention to himself, but the area was crawling with cops. When he was about a block away he described what he saw to Preston over his cell phone. It didn't look good.

"They're opening every fucking door," Preston told Danny. "They're going to open the fucking door."

Danny finally realized this was the end of the road for his little brother. They said goodbye and good luck. Preston didn't know if he'd ever see Danny alive again.

"I told him I loved him. I told him to hide, to get out of town," Preston said.

The moment he hung up with Preston, Danny removed the SIM card from his phone and smashed it under his foot. Then he threw away the phone, turned his back, and walked north, away from the flashing red lights of police cars.

The police finally knocked at the apartment door. The man who lived there stood up, grabbed his sleeping child, and ran out. Several minutes passed while Preston stayed rooted to his chair. Then the door popped open again and a small robot, maybe a foot tall, scooted inside. Its head pivoted to one side and then the other, scanning the room. Preston tried to lean over to avoid its gaze but didn't want to make a sudden move, in case police interpreted it as threatening. He was 90 per cent convinced he was going to be shot. After a minute or so the robot retreated the way it came. Preston could hear the rip of Velcro as police strapped on their body armour, then the click of metal as they racked their weapons. The police stormed in with their guns pointed at him and he surrendered. At first he protested they had the wrong guy, but they scanned his tattoos and checked them against the list they had.

"It's him," one cop said.

It was another six days before police had any information on Danny. On Sunday afternoon the RCMP's Emergency Response Unit was dispatched by plane from Winnipeg to the area of The Pas, Manitoba, about eight hundred kilometres northwest of the capital. The tip said Danny was in a housing complex on the Opaskwayak Cree Nation, just across the river from the town. Police were still operating on their mistaken belief that Danny was from The Pas and that he might think it a likely place to hide out. RCMP officers said Danny was partying openly in the community and living a "Don Juan of The Pas" lifestyle while on the run. They surrounded the complex in full SWAT gear, guns at the ready, and apparently trying to open negotiations. The standoff lasted several hours but turned up nothing. The pictures of heavily armed police crouching outside an apartment building kept the story going in the national media. CTV News, one of the leading national broadcasters, said Danny and the Indian Posse cast themselves as Robin Hood types, stealing from the rich to give to the poor. The idea was seductive. It fuelled a perception that many people were rooting for Danny to elude capture.

The next day, organizers of the Treaty Four pow-wow in Saskatchewan, a massive gathering held annually in Fort Qu'Appelle and scheduled for that week, decided that the threat of violence was too great to go ahead. They announced they would cancel the event, presumably because of the fear that Danny might target people in attendance. In the end, elders prevailed upon them to put on a smaller program with a heavy police presence.

It had been nearly three weeks on the run for Danny. He was at times comfortable enough to walk around Winnipeg, much as he had done as a twelve-year-old, roaming far and wide and exploring new places. But after Preston's arrest he grew more cautious, relying on friends to keep him hidden.

On a hot September day with a clear blue sky, he was strolling up Vaughan Street downtown, close to the Hudson Bay Company department store. He was wearing shiny new clothes, he had his hair back in a slick ponytail, and he wore black, designer sunglasses. His uncle was walking down the street in the opposite direction and didn't recognize Danny at first. Danny reached out to stop him.

"Uncle, it's Danny," he said. "How are you?"

His uncle, who had worked for years as a nurse in Winnipeg, hadn't seen Danny in ages. He knew his nephew had been in trouble with the law, but he didn't know that at this moment Danny was the object of an intense cross-country manhunt. They chatted for a while. Danny looked terrific, his uncle said, with a bright, happy smile and his typically sharp, teasing sense of humour. After a while Danny said he had to get going. He had things to do.

"Oh, should I call your mother, let her know I saw you and that you're okay?" his uncle asked.

"No, no, don't do that," Danny said. "She knows I'm fine."

"Little did I know," his uncle recalled in an interview years later. "I hadn't heard the news."

Danny went on his way, but not long after he made a mistake. It was really the first and only time police had come close to him. Information gathered by RCMP in Saskatchewan turned up a hint of Danny's movements.

He needed a ride. He called someone to arrange it, but one of the phones involved was being monitored. Police swooped down on the address in Winnipeg's North End where they thought he would be, only to find it empty. Then they searched the surrounding area and spotted a car speeding away.

The police tore after the vehicle and forced it to stop at a nearby gas station at Flora and Salter, a crossroad at the mouth of the North End. It was an area that for years had been claimed by the Indian Posse. The police approached cautiously and spotted Danny stretched out on the floor of the back seat, a blanket only half covering him. They ordered him out of the car and Danny gave himself up without a fight. Police said they'd been told that he'd never willingly go back to prison, that he'd rather go down in a hail of bullets than give himself up. To get Danny without firing a shot was a triumph.

Police also arrested a twenty-five-year-old girl who was allegedly driving the getaway car. The CBC, the national public broadcaster, identified her as Daniella Bevacqua. She said she would do anything for Danny Wolfe. He was like a brother to her, she said.

"I stick for them. These are my bros," she told CBC. "They've always protected me and I protect them." She said she was surprised to have been caught with Danny. He'd been getting away with it for so long, after all. She was charged with aiding and abetting his escape.

"That's just the life. I chose to help them," she said.

23.

ON TRIAL
OCTOBER 2008–NOVEMBER 2009

A few days after his arrest in Winnipeg, the Mounties drove Danny back across the provincial border and returned him to the prison from which he had just escaped, the Regina Provincial Correctional Centre.

The guards weren't happy with him, Danny said, but his life wasn't any worse than usual. He didn't get beaten or suffer any undue retribution, just the regular crap. He still had a lot of good friends behind bars and access to all that he needed in the prison world.

About ten months earlier, while lodged in a cell with Sergeant Perron, the undercover officer, Danny had mentioned two important goals: one was ensuring that Preston beat his murder charge; the second was getting to see his son again. His son was nearly ten years old then, and although he kept in close contact with the boy and his mother through letters and phone calls, it seemed to hurt Danny deeply that he hadn't been able to see him face to face.

It's not clear whether Danny saw his son in Winnipeg in the three weeks he spent on the run. Lisa, his mother, says they never saw Danny. Of course, the police were probably monitoring her, since they knew of her connection to him. It's also possible Danny tried to watch the boy from afar without disturbing him. It's hard to believe that in those weeks, when he was bracing himself for a potentially violent showdown with police, that Danny made no attempt to see the son he talked about so much in his letters. He wanted badly to be a better father to his children than his father had been to him.

Danny had been looking for his own father, Richard Sr., in the prison system for years. He hadn't seen him since that brief encounter on the street when Danny had the crushing realization that his own father wanted nothing to do with him. More recently he had been following news of his father in the newspapers. Richard Sr., who was on the lam at the time, had been charged in Regina with stabbing a man to death with a screwdriver after the pair had spent the day drinking hairspray. It was the kind of awful killing that occasionally hits the pages of local newspapers, and it left readers wondering how someone could end their days in such squalid and depressing circumstances. When he was finally caught, Richard Sr. pleaded guilty to manslaughter, his fifty-fifth criminal conviction.

Danny's wish that Preston avoid going to jail for murder came true just a few months after they were returned to prison. Like his older brother, Preston was eventually moved north to the federal Saskatchewan Penitentiary in Prince Albert, and for a time they were on the same range. The case against Preston collapsed when the lone witness called in his defence, the girlfriend of the man who was killed, said she saw someone else fire the gun. The courtroom exploded in a mixture of disbelief and celebration when the jury announced its verdict, the local paper reported. Members of the victim's family were incredulous and Preston was spared a twenty-five-year sentence.

Over the next year Danny bided his time without incident. Preston, who was eventually convicted for the jailbreak and sentenced to another two years, was with him for a lot of it. Danny talked of wanting to make a documentary that would tell the real story of the Indian Posse, and in a letter to a journalist he said he wanted to make sure the gang's history was told in a way that didn't distort the truth. He had been very unhappy with a feature film called *Stryker*, directed by Winnipeg filmmaker Noam Gonick, which Danny felt had misrepresented the gang and embarrassed him. He had said back in 2006, "[As] for that bunk movie about the family, it sucks. Most of it ain't the real deal so I'm going to do my own project on that."

On October 20, 2009, Danny arrived for the opening of his trial at the Court of Queen's Bench in Regina under heavy security. Police snipers surveyed the scene from the rooftops of nearby buildings and heavily armoured officers carrying assault rifles stood watch on the ground, there to guard against any Indian Posse attempt to free Danny before trial or a rival gang's attempt to kill him. Danny was led out of a van with his hands and feet shackled. He was wearing wire-rimmed glasses and a prison parka over a white shirt. He looked as though he had aged a great deal in just a year. The energy and vitality he had while on the run were gone.

As the trial began, Danny had one move remaining. His lawyer, Estes Fonkalsrud, rose in front of Judge Eugene Scheibel and said he would have to withdraw as counsel because he could no longer work with his client. The judge was not happy about this development. The trial had already been delayed, in part due to Danny's escape. Danny would now require a new lawyer, who would have to become familiar with more than ten thousand pages of disclosure. It could mean a delay of six months or longer. The judge asked Danny what was happening.

"It's not a question of I'm not prepared. It's other reasons," Danny said quietly.

"You can't fire your lawyer fifteen minutes before the trial is supposed to begin," the judge replied.

Mr. Fonkalsrud said his request to withdraw was the result of an instruction he had received from his client at 9:00 p.m. the previous night. He would not say anything more specific. Years later he still did not want to say what had happened, for fear of breaching solicitor-client confidence. Whatever the reason, Danny might have been simply trying to maximize the amount of time he spent in pretrial custody, to reduce the length of his sentence.

The judge ruled that the trial would go ahead and that Mr. Fonkalsrud had to stay on to act in Danny's interest. They accepted the ruling without a fight.

On the first day, the court heard from the RCMP officer, Constable Jan Lussier, who had been first to arrive at the scene. He described the blood and carnage he saw on the night of September 20, 2008, at 302 Pasqua Avenue in Fort Qu'Appelle. A forensics officer described the matching shell casings that were discovered at the scene and at Danny's cousin's house on the Okanese reserve. Danny's cousin Tiffany Buffalocalf gave a testimony of mostly "I can't recall" answers that weren't particularly incriminating. Then she was asked who was carrying the gun that night. She took a breath, as if facing up to a difficult truth. After a short pause she said, "my cousin," meaning Danny.

The day's last witness was Christina "Granny" Cook, the sixty-three-year-old grandmother who had survived the shooting. Ms. Cook told the story of her husband Marvin Arnault's heroic death. She described for the court how he had jumped on top of her to protect her from the gunfire. The shooter said one thing before leaving, she testified: "That'll teach them to mess with IP."

"Did IP mean anything to you?" the prosecutor asked.

"Yes, I'm from Winnipeg," Ms. Cook replied, her tone suggesting that anyone from Winnipeg would know precisely what those initials represent. "It means Indian Posse."

Over the next several days, seven people who were in the Pasqua Avenue house that night took the stand to testify. They explained the sense of terror they felt: one moment they were happily talking and drinking; the next, the door broke open and two masked gunmen opened fire. It was pure horror. The walls were covered in blood. People ran around not knowing whether they'd been shot. There was screaming, shock, confusion, and fear. And not one person was able to identify Danny as the shooter.

The evidence to this point was circumstantial: the shell casings at the crime scene matched those found near the deck of the home where Danny was staying on the reserve. But in order to tie Danny to the casings found on the reserve, the Crown needed the testimony of Ernest Tuckanow, who had looked out his window to see Danny standing on the deck firing the gun. That was important evidence. For some reason, possibly out of fear of the Indian Posse, Mr. Tuckanow did not show up in court to give that testimony. The judge issued a warrant to force him to testify, but he never did.

Percy "Pudge" Pascal was similarly reluctant to appear in court. He was the original target of the attack and had been shot nine times at close range. He spent months in hospital and there were still shells lodged in his body that surgeons had been unable to remove. His childhood friend Michael "Mikey" Itittakoose was dead, and if anyone had reason to testify against Danny, it was Pudge. But when court officials asked that he be brought up from the cells, he refused to move. Was he afraid of the Indian Posse? Or was he just following the gangster's code? Pudge said later it was the code. He couldn't testify and maintain any credibility in the Native Syndicate, he said, and besides, he blacked out and couldn't remember anything. His evidence from the preliminary hearing was read into the record, but even then, given the chance to identify the killer, Pudge declined to point the finger at Danny.

The case was going about as well as Danny could hope. A reasonable person couldn't convict him based on what they'd heard to this point. Still, the major issues lay ahead. Danny watched the proceedings with a calm detachment, never betraying much emotion, his lawyer said. Susan said it was odd seeing him up close like this, day after day. He didn't quite look like himself; she prayed for him, but she also sat alongside the families of the victims. She could see that they were in pain and felt terribly for them.

On the trial's third day, Gerrard Granbois stepped into the witness box. He hadn't been seen around Fort Qu'Appelle in a while, not since he decided to turn on Danny. He had been placed in the witness protection program and he and his family had been given financial support to move to another province. He was still in the witness protection program when Danny broke out of prison in August 2008. All charges against Granbois stemming from the killings in Fort Qu'Appelle had been dropped in exchange for his testimony.

A defence lawyer faced with these facts is in a more favourable situation than it might seem. A witness like Granbois is expected to point the finger at the accused, and his obvious interest in keeping himself out of jail can be used to discredit his statements. Granbois also admitted he was present during the events in question. It wouldn't take much to catch him in a few contradictory statements, which would tarnish whatever he might say.

Granbois told the court everything he had told the officers in his videotaped statement a year earlier. He described the phone call he received from Danny at the bar, the route they took from the reserve back to Fort Qu'Appelle, the search for the blue truck, and then the shooting. It was damning but not decisive. After all, when the RCMP reached this point in their investigation, their detectives had felt that they still didn't have enough to secure a conviction. That's why Sergeant LeRat had spent more than ten hours trying to elicit a confession, and why they had put an undercover officer in Danny's cell.

But there remained the question of whether the RCMP's tactics were fair, and whether the conversation from the jail cell could be legitimately presented as evidence. These issues would have to be decided by the judge. One complicating factor was that the quality of the audio recorded in the cell was terrible. The police had typed up a transcript of the conversation between Perron and Danny that night, but it was filled with blank spots. The word "inaudible" appeared hundreds of times in the eighty-page document. The RCMP said they didn't know why the audio was so bad, but it was the worst they'd heard in fourteen years.

The judge decided the transcripts could not be relied upon as evidence because they were incomplete. Instead, the court would hear the testimony of Perron, who would be allowed to consult his notes. Perron's notes, though, were not written immediately after leaving the cell. That morning he had gone home, showered and slept, and only later that afternoon had he put together his thoughts about what had transpired in the cell. Fonkalsrud pointed out that not only had a whole day passed before he wrote his notes, but he had only documented evidence that pointed to Danny's guilt. Other statements, including moments when Danny called Granbois a liar, were left out of the officer's written version of events.

When he appeared before the court, Perron described his role in the cell as that of a "truth seeker." He said the first thing Danny asked him was whether he was a biker, and that he did so by making a revving gesture with his hand rather than say the word out loud. Danny told him that he had seen the guns, the AK-47 and the Uzi, in the police car. And then he told Perron he was there for two first-degree murders and three attempted, "the big one," he said, out in Fort

Qu'Appelle. Perron spoke with a gruff voice and provided sharp, concise answers to the lawyers:

> [Mr. Wolfe] stated that he was fucked, pardon the language, and that he would get life. Said that this is the life of a gangster.
>
> Mr. Wolfe stated that he should have shot – and then he made a gesture with his hand – both [his accomplices] and that he knew that he had, pardon the expression once again, fucked up.
>
> Mr. Wolfe states that the police had nothing and no other evidence. No hair – and he grabbed his hair – and no spit and no – again making a gun gesture – no gun. He goes on to state that he had used a .22 calibre with a twenty-five-round clip and that it was gone.
>
> Mr. Wolfe again states that he wants to kill Mr. Granbois and that he doesn't care how long it takes that he will get him. He goes on to say that he told both Mr. Granbois and the 15-year-old that the 15-year-old might get 10 years but that he and Mr. Granbois would be gone for life.
>
> He says that the police have everything on him, that the officer told him that he was done and that he actually agreed with the officer. Mr. Wolfe says that he knew it was coming and that when he saw Mr. Granbois's reenactment his heart was pounding. But that after his heart rate had returned to normal and he had accepted the fact he was done.

The undercover officer's evidence was devastating for Danny. Fonkalsrud tried to poke holes in the testimony, pointing out that early in the conversation Danny had said that Granbois was a liar. He was suggesting that Danny had said he was finished only because he expected a liar would convict him with lies. But these apparently frank statements, even if they were the product of nearly twenty-four hours of relentless interrogation, all pointed to Danny's guilt.

Danny fidgeted during Perron's testimony, staring up at the hypnotic white squares of light that covered the courtroom ceiling. Danny occasionally took notes, betraying no outward emotions, but he fumed about the direction of the case. When he had a moment to consult with Fonkalsrud privately, he lashed out.

"What the fuck are you doing up there? I should be the one wearing that cape," Danny said, referring to the long, dark gowns lawyers must wear in Canadian courtrooms. Danny was angry, perhaps as much at himself for falling for the RCMP's jailhouse ruse, but he insisted he should testify to contradict Perron. Fonkalsrud cautioned Danny against taking the stand. "Why won't you let me talk?" Danny demanded.

For a defendant, taking the stand is an inherently risky choice with many potential pitfalls. But Danny's options were dwindling and he needed to refute Perron's testimony.

When the case resumed, Danny strode across the courtroom and sat in the grey chair in the witness box to the judge's left. A Canadian flag stood in the courtroom's opposite corner and a bronzed Great Seal of Saskatchewan, including a beaver with the Crown on its back, was affixed to the dark wood that covered the wall behind him. Mr. Fonkalsrud asked Danny for his version of the conversation with Perron.

"I told him I was in for two first and three attempted – and he said, 'Oh, the big one,'" Danny said.

"I sat back down on the mattress and I was going to read and he said, 'What did they ask you?' I said they showed video of people making statements, video of me at the bar, warrants, and that they had searched my house.

"I said it was a bunch of fucking bullshit lies," Danny said.

Danny had made his point. His testimony was relatively short.

On October 28, Danny was brought into court for the last day of his trial.

His mother again noted how different he looked, how his colour was gone and he looked weary. As she sat in the courtroom watching her son and praying, she thought she could see signs that his soul was leaving his body. It was preparing for its next journey, she said. Danny as she had known him was no longer there.

"I was looking at the judge and all of a sudden I saw smoke leaving his body," Susan said. "It didn't look like him. The body was there but his spirit was gone."

Addressing the judge for the last time, Fonkalsrud raised several important points. He suggested that Ernest Tuckanow's evidence, which was read into the record, should be treated carefully because he hadn't seen the gun in Danny's hands, and because, if the judge were to accept that Danny was firing a gun a few days before the killings, it could prejudice his view of Danny. He said photos of Danny's tattoos, including those that said *Indian Posse* or *Red til Dead*, would also have a prejudicial effect, since the victims said the shooters mentioned the Indian Posse. And then there was Granbois's testimony.

"The court," Fonkalsurd said, "needs to pay close attention to any self-interest that Mr. Granbois would have, his motive for giving testimony – not only the fact that he was provided financial compensation, but also that he was charged with the offence [and in exchange for his cooperation had his charges dropped].

"Only after his arrest did he become a cooperative witness. . . . I'd certainly suggest he has motives of his own in this regard to testify before the Court."

The undercover officer's evidence should also be treated skeptically, the lawyer said, because his ten hours of conversation in the cell with Danny were reduced to an eleven-page summary written from memory.

"Only the comments that the officer in his testimony felt were relevant were taken down . . . When we're looking at a confession, generally the Court wants to see the entire statement. Well, that's not possible here. Some weight has to be taken away, I would suggest, due to the fact that certain parts of the conversation to benefit Mr. Wolfe aren't recorded."

Crown attorney Alistair Johnston rose to make his closing statement immediately after the defence had finished.

"Mr. Wolfe is charged with two counts of first-degree murder which we allege we have proved beyond a reasonable doubt as being planned and deliberate murders. He is additionally charged with three attempted murders. We respectfully submit we have proved beyond a reasonable doubt that he shot and injured those men and that he intended to kill them," Johnston said.

He described the shooting as the product of a seemingly inconsequential encounter between Daniel Wolfe and Pudge Pascal, one with Indian Posse tattoos, the other with Native Syndicate tattoos, at Trapper's Bar in Fort Qu'Appelle. There was video of the testy exchange in the bar, video of Danny removing his socks and turning them into weapons with billiard balls. There was the evidence of bartender Joseph Crowe, who said he overheard Danny on the phone saying, "They don't know what's coming for them." There was the fact that Pudge, who sparked the confrontation in the bar, was shot nine times. There was Ernest Tuckanow's evidence that connected Danny to the firing of the gun on the back deck and thus to the matching shell casings found near the deck, at the crime scene, and in the van. And then there was eyewitness evidence from Mr. Granbois, as well as the evidence of a confession to the undercover officer, Mr. Johnston said. Motive, witnesses, confession, he said in summary. "It is our submission that all of that evidence proves beyond a reasonable doubt that Mr. Wolfe is guilty of two counts of planned and deliberate murder."

The Crown attorney took his seat again and the court process came to an end. Justice Scheibel retired to consider his verdict and Danny returned to the jail with his fate uncertain. Three weeks later, on November 18, 2009, the judge delivered his verdict.

He canvassed all the major points of evidence, from the autopsy to the forensic firearm evidence to witness testimony. He concluded that Danny's statements to Perron in the cell constituted a complete confession and that Granbois was telling the truth. Danny had thought carefully about what he was going to do that night, the judge said. He trekked back to the reserve to collect the gun, searched methodically for the blue pickup truck, and donned a mask before approaching the house. When he opened the door there was no argument or provocation, just gunfire. This was not done on the spur of the moment, he said.

"The Crown has proved to my satisfaction, beyond a reasonable doubt, that the murders were both planned and deliberate. Therefore the Crown has proven that Wolfe is guilty of first-degree murder in respect of the deaths of both Itittakoose and Arnault.

"Wolfe has proved the case against himself out of his own mouth by his lengthy, voluntary confession," Judge Scheibel said. "This case is evidence of Wolfe's callous disregard for human life. There are no mitigating circumstances in this vicious, gang-related home invasion. But for some luck, many more people would have been killed. It ranks as one of the worst of its type in the history of this province . . . Given the nature of this horrific crime, Wolfe should be sentenced to the maximum term permitted under the law."

He handed down five consecutive life sentences. Danny showed no emotion as the sentence was read. At one point he stifled a yawn, the local paper reported. The judge asked if he had anything to say. He did not, his lawyer said: "He realizes nothing can take back that terrible night."

The statements submitted by the family of his victims made clear their pain. Michael Itittakoose left behind a wife and a young son, a sister, and a nephew. In an eloquent letter, his mother explained the waves of anguish and suffering that continued to roll through their lives.

"My son, Michael Royce Itittakoose, *Hoto Wakiya Hokshila*, Rattling Thunder Boy, was taken violently before his time," Joyce Poitras wrote. "My son was a good young man, a good father and brother. After that fateful day, September 20th, I have felt very angry and hurt that my son's life was taken by a hardcore gang member with no compassion for life or the human race.

"As a mother I know the depth of pain which will forever scar my heart and soul . . . My life can never return to normal; what it once was is now buried with my son."

The depression and sense of loss touched many others in her family, she wrote. She described herself as a traditional person, and that long ago, in the customs of her people, those that broke the laws of the people were sent away, ostracized, and this is what must happen now, she said.

"As Daniel Wolfe took innocent lives he must be held accountable and locked up. I have seen no remorse in the eyes of this person," she wrote. She asked that Danny be forced to do his time in a place where there were no aboriginal gang members, so he could not seek shelter in the gang.

"I want Daniel Wolfe to remember, every time he hears the thunder, that he has to pay for the lives he took. Not only in this world with man's law, but in the next world with the Creator's law."

Outside the courthouse that day Susan spoke to the pack of reporters, trying to be as honest and accountable as she could. She said Danny turned to the gang because she had failed to provide him with a home. She had set a poor example by drinking and using drugs, she said. Danny had made bad choices, choices she wished he hadn't made, but she accepted responsibility for her own role in his criminality. It was a remarkably open statement to make to the press.

Susan went home to a community that still sometimes regarded her with suspicion. In some stores in Fort Qu'Appelle she was met with hard stares from relatives of those who had died or been injured. But she held her head up, she said, and told them if they had a problem with her she would address it. Danny was her child and she loved him as any parent would.

Danny left court that day with the words of the victims' families still in his ears. He was packed into a van and transported back to prison to begin his sentence, contrary to the wishes of the Itittakoose family, at the maximum-security wing of the federal penitentiary at Prince Albert, where the Indian Posse was waiting.

24

LIFE
2009–2010

Danny was placed in the maximum-security section of the federal Saskatchewan Penitentiary at Prince Albert, or the House of Misery, as he called it. Guards here patrolled with rifles, keeping an eye on some of the most dangerous criminals in the country via openings in the Plexiglas through which they could shoot if necessary. His range was semi-segregated, dedicated to Indian Posse inmates and gangs considered their allies, particularly the Native Syndicate Killers.

The atmosphere was tense. He had residual bad feelings about Sask Pen, dating back to his time there from 2002 to 2004. He had narrowly avoided being killed after the warden sent him out on an emergency transfer. Now, the conflict stemmed from how illicit drugs were being distributed. Someone had been stabbed over a drug deal just before Danny arrived, and the ripple effects of revenge and retaliation were still playing out.

Danny was a lifer now. He couldn't even apply for parole for another twenty-five years, so he had to adjust. In some ways his situation was not that different from the one that his brother Richard had once confronted. Richard had eventually found a way to do his time quietly, after walking away from the gang, and Danny wondered whether he had to start thinking that way, too. He had thoughts of getting married to his girlfriend, Shenoa, the mother of his young daughter. She lived about four hours away in southern Saskatchewan and her visits would give him something to look forward to. He couldn't bear the thought of going twenty-five years without sex. But he needed to show prison officials a year of an established relationship and good behaviour within the institution before he could be eligible for trailer visits.

The possibility of a quieter life existed, but Danny only ever flirted with the idea of leaving the gang. It meant too much to him, and leaving would be too hard, too dangerous. Even if he did leave, he would have been a high-profile target for a rival group, especially after all the media coverage he'd received during his escape and trial. There would always be someone gunning for him, maybe for the rest of his life. What's more, he liked the status and power the gang offered. He needed to hold on.

One person who was a prisoner at the Prince Albert penitentiary at the time said the trouble began with divisions in the Indian Posse that Danny was unable to bridge. "It was a power struggle," said Darren, a former inmate who asked not to be named as he feared his life was in danger.

Darren felt a great deal of loyalty to Danny because Danny had rescued him back when he was a young striker trying to climb the ranks in the Indian Posse. Darren had attacked a rival gang member and tried to go into hiding. He was a world removed from Danny, had only heard of him vaguely, but someone sounded the alarm and Danny came riding in like the cavalry, driving a black Cadillac SUV all the way across the Prairies from Alberta. He scooped up the young striker and hid him in Winnipeg, in the care of his own network. Darren was able to lie low for a while, and although he was eventually caught and sent to prison, Danny had earned his undying loyalty.

The divisions on the range emerged even before Danny arrived in the penitentiary, Darren said. What sparked them is unclear. Those who might know have said that they won't discuss it for fear of breaking the prisoner's code of silence. Darren, who was in the prison but not on the same range, said that the stabbing over drugs a few weeks earlier had left some of the NSK-affiliated inmates looking for revenge. Some also complained that drug shipments were not shared equally.

The rifts were a fairly typical aspect of gang life, according to Darren. The Indian Posse was often splintered and incoherent. "It's not an organized crew at all," he said. The ranks were fluid. Jealousy and rivalry were rampant. The leadership had insufficient control of the members. "No one has the brains to pull it off. D-Boy couldn't," said the inmate, using Danny's nickname. "He was smart, but not that smart."

Danny celebrated another New Year in jail on December 31, 2009. He was thirty-three years old. Two days later he phoned his mother and wished her Happy New Year. When she asked how he was holding up, he told her "everything is going crazy." Inmates were arguing and Danny didn't have a handle on it. In years past he had been able to bring people together and solve disputes. Not this time.

Susan remembers speaking to Danny on the telephone on January 3. She could hear the worry in his voice as he mentioned the deteriorating situation in the penitentiary. Someone was stabbed that day but hadn't gone for treatment, an investigation later revealed, so authorities didn't suspect that tensions were rising on Danny's unit. Susan told him to be careful. It was evening, so she told him to pray and to smudge with sweetgrass before he went to sleep.

The next day, January 4, 2010, Danny was in the common room with roughly ten other inmates. It was midday. He was at the back of the room and the others milled about. Some went to the phones; some stood and chatted.

Keith Coutu was standing several feet away from Danny. Danny had known Coutu, a long-time Indian Posse member, since they were teenagers. He even carried photos of him in his small duffel bag of keepsakes, which featured hundreds of photos of friends, family, and fellow gang members. In 2004, Coutu and his brother Jason had been kicked out of a house party in the North End. They went to the car, grabbed a sawed-off shotgun from the trunk, and stormed back into the house, seeking revenge. They shot dead the first man they encountered and chased a second man to a bedroom. The man tried to hide behind a closed door but Coutu and his brother smashed it down and shot the man three times. Coutu was sentenced to life in prison.

KC, as he was known, was in hot water with some of the other inmates. His closest ally on the range, other than Danny, was Cheyenne Nelson. Nelson was also from Manitoba and was serving time for a second-degree murder conviction. Nelson had just been charged in connection with a stabbing that occurred in the penitentiary on November 15. His co-accused in that case, Nolan Turcotte and Michael Slippery, were among the half-dozen members of the Native Syndicate Killers housed on Danny's range. Turcotte was infamous in Saskatchewan for murdering a good Samaritan who tried to intervene in a convenience store robbery on December 26, 2006, which earned him the nickname the Boxing Day Killer.

That day, Turcotte, Slippery, and their allies were planning to attack Coutu and Nelson to seek vengeance for earlier stabbings. They had each concealed a homemade knife somewhere in their clothing or had it close to hand. Danny was unarmed. He walked in looking relaxed, laughing, and chatting with some of the others.

Turcotte struck the first blow. He walked up behind Coutu carrying a homemade knife and unleashed a flurry of violent blows. He stuck the blade into Coutu's back, then whipped it out again, repeating the action over and over. Then a hulking man named Francis Yukon joined in, attacking Coutu with a knife and puncturing his back and abdomen. Yukon had murdered Danny's friend Ron Taylor in the same prison four years earlier.

Nelson, who was talking on the phone not far from Danny, was then attacked by Ryan Agecoutay. Agecoutay, who had escaped the Regina jail with Danny, walked up and punched Nelson in the face, catching him off guard. As the blows rained down, Nelson fell to the ground. Jacob Worm joined in the attack on Nelson, stabbing him in the back and head.

According to the Crown lawyer who later prosecuted the case, the video shows that Danny is clearly not the target. As the swarming began, Danny looked surprised and confused, the Crown said. In the first moments, Michael Slippery physically blocked Danny from coming to Nelson's aid. Slippery then turned away from Danny and joined in the attack on Nelson. Danny tried again to jump in to help his friend, but he was spotted by Jacob Worm, who had been stabbing Coutu. Worm lunged at Danny and his blade hit Danny in the chest, twice. The Crown described the blows as "get the hell out of here" stabs. The first was a glancing blow. The second punched through the skin, and Danny staggered back.

Coutu and Nelson were screaming for help and bleeding all over the floor. The stabbing went on for about thirty seconds. Each had been stabbed more than twenty times. A prison guard watching from the gallery above rushed over and saw the victims covered in blood. He fired a warning shot to disperse the attackers, who backed off, only to pick up a microwave and heave it at the victims as they lay on the floor. A guard down below fired another warning shot and deployed a canister of pepper spray to force the attackers away from the victims. The NSK group moved to the back of the room. Danny stayed with his two fellow IP members. Somehow, Coutu and Nelson had survived the attack.

Danny calmly sat down. He picked up a cup of coffee and took a sip. He picked up his slippers, which had come off in the commotion, and put them back on. He didn't look distressed. He sat there for a few moments. And then he slumped to the floor.

The second blow from the knife had pierced Danny's chest on the right side, about halfway up. It sliced his right coronary artery. Externally, the wound looked tiny, but the internal bleeding started immediately. Blood seeped into Danny's chest and accumulated in his chest cavity and in the pericardial sac, gradually putting more and more pressure on his heart. He might have felt the pressure building moments before the end; he might have been in shock; he might have already known that there was little hope. Five minutes after the stabbing began, corrections officers entered the common room to attend to the inmates. They immediately saw that Danny was the most seriously injured and hurried him out on a stretcher to the prison's main entrance to await an ambulance. Nurses arrived and saw that guards were already performing CPR. It looked grim. When he arrived at hospital, he was pronounced dead.

Danny had survived a harrowing childhood. He'd been pulled from the burning home he set on fire. He had driven on a highway at age seven; hopped trains as a nine-year-old; robbed homes; stolen cars; robbed drug dealers; survived car chases, gun battles, and prison brawls. He'd killed and seen others killed, but this was the end. He drew his last breath in the maximum-security unit of a federal penitentiary, his life taken by his fellow gang members. It was just as he predicted.

Susan was driving through the Saskatchewan countryside to a nearby reserve called Carry the Kettle First Nation that morning. She was looking outside at the snow-covered fields when she noticed an owl by the side of the road. As she passed, the owl turned its head and followed the car with its eyes, Susan said. She stopped immediately and made an offering of tobacco.

"In our spirituality owls give messages," she said. "I thought, 'This is not good.' I knew it was someone close to me because it was such a beautiful owl. Just white, so white."

Susan was back at work at the Wellness Centre on her home reserve that afternoon when she received a call from a prison chaplain.

"I have some bad news to tell you," the chaplain said.

With three sons in prison it could have been any of them, Susan said. But she knew right away that it was Danny.

She walked over to the band office and told the chief what had happened. The chief smudged with Susan and she cried. Then she fell into a trance, she said. She can't remember very much from that afternoon.

Richard was still in prison in Ontario, nine months remaining on his sentence. He was watching television when he saw the words in the news feed crawling across the bottom of the screen: *Saskatchewan inmate found dead.* He wondered who it might be. A few hours later, he was back on the range when a guard told him he needed to go see the elder.

"I knew something was wrong," Richard said. "He sat me down and said, 'Your mum phoned. You've got to call her immediately.' I remember clearly she said, 'They killed Danny.'"

Richard just held onto the phone silently. His mother called out "Richard, Richard" a few times but he couldn't answer. He couldn't believe it. Richard hadn't seen Danny since the day he was sent west to Edmonton from Stony Mountain nearly fourteen years earlier. He was devastated.

Richard asked to be released on a short-term pass to attend Danny's funeral. His request was denied. Too high a security risk, he was told. Preston was told the same. Neither would be allowed to say goodbye.

The news of Danny's death spread quickly. The first bulletin to hit the newswires said simply that an inmate had been killed at Prince Albert. But it was only a matter of hours before reporters were quoting unnamed sources confirming that it was Danny. After leading the breakout from the Regina prison, Danny had gained a rare level of notoriety among Canadian criminals. His slaying was a top story across the country.

In Winnipeg, Danny's ex-girlfriend Lisa got a phone call from Danny's uncle. She had been in some ways expecting and dreading this call for years. Her son was still at school. She would have to tell him, but she didn't know how she would put it into words. He was only ten years old.

"I sat there all day because my son was at school, contemplating how to tell him. Should I let him watch the news? This is a mother's worst fear, to have to tell her son his dad is gone," Lisa said.

She phoned the school and the after-school program he attended and asked them to make sure that he wouldn't watch any television. She didn't want him to know that his father had been murdered. Maybe she could put it in different words to soften the blow. Unfortunately, her plan failed, and he saw a news update with his father's photo: *killed in prison brawl.* When she finally saw him, their son burst into tears.

"It was really hard," Lisa said. "I said, 'I'm really sorry but that's the lifestyle your dad chose.'"

Her son was heartbroken. He didn't know his father well but he longed to see him.

"He wanted to ask his dad why he lived the life that he did, why he had made those choices," Lisa said.

The boy was going through a hard time before Danny died. His grandfather had recently died, and now his father was dead. He was living a few blocks from where Danny grew up, an area where gangs held significant sway on the streets. The dark forces that terrorize so many in the neighbourhood were pulling at him.

"He was setting fires, doing everything Danny was doing when he was that age. It was my worst nightmare. I thought, 'My God, I've got Danny all over again. What am I going to do?'" Lisa would do everything she could to keep him safe.

Three days after Danny's death Susan drove into Regina to collect his body. The investigators and coroner had finished their examinations and the funeral home had prepared him for burial. She asked that he be dressed in jeans and brought the ones his lawyer had bought for him to wear to his trial a few months earlier. She also brought a red ribbon shirt for him, a formal, ceremonial shirt with ribbon attached across the chest. As much as red stood for the Indian Posse, it was the colour he always wore.

Susan spent a long time with him that morning. She noticed his hair was sticking out at the back, tangled. She spoke to him quietly, saying, "We don't want you to go with messy hair." Braids would look nice, she thought.

"I was just talking to him in my own mind," she said. "I must have spent an hour doing that. I just smoothed his hair and said, 'You start your journey home.'"

His body was placed on a blanket and laid in a casket made of birch.

More than one hundred people came from across the West to see Danny buried on the Okanese First Nation. Some pages of the guest book read like a who's who of the early days of the Indian Posse. In adulthood many had graduated to serious crime and served long sentences, but to Susan they were still the little kids she knew from the neighbourhood. The mention of their names brings a smile to her face.

Some of the gang called beforehand to let Susan know they wanted to come. She said they were welcome as long as they didn't wear their colours.

To the RCMP the funeral was a potentially volatile situation. There were about two dozen police officers there, Susan said. They checked on vehicles and sat among the mourners in plainclothes. They asked people what gang they represented, but they weren't too intrusive, Susan said.

Danny's father, Richard Sr., spoke to Susan in the days after Danny's death and she told him the date and time of the service. Richard Sr. had been released from prison following his conviction for manslaughter but was hard up for cash. He was living on a reserve a short distance away and asked Susan for gas money. Susan said she'd pay but he never showed up at the funeral.

Susan remembers the service with a mixture of happiness and sadness. She says the grandfathers, the *Mooshums*, were present that day to help usher Danny into the next world.

The hearse brought Danny's body right to the door of the reserve school. There were traditional dancers, drumming and singing. Susan walked to the front of the school carrying her son's picture and a special starblanket, which she draped over the casket. Then there were prayers and smudging. After the chief and an elder spoke, the assembled crowd walked past the open casket.

"After the viewing we went to the gravesite. It was wintertime but I didn't feel the cold. I stayed right 'til the end to put flowers there," Susan said.

Danny Wolfe was buried in a clearing sheltered by a stand of trees, near his grandfather, Bill Creeley, a private in the Canadian Infantry Corps. His great-grandfather Leonard Creeley was buried there too, the site marked only by a wooden cross.

Danny's grave was marked by a small piece of plastic, his name inscribed in the blocky white-on-black type of a label maker, intended to be a placeholder until a proper headstone could be made.

Susan stayed until the backhoe covered the casket with earth.

TODAY
2016

Danny Wolfe belongs to the first generation of indigenous children raised after the closing of Canada's residential schools. The impact of those schools on his family was catastrophic. His mother, who suffered years of abuse and, in the aftermath, struggled with addictions, regrets that she raised her sons in an environment marred by alcohol and violence. Her own childhood, however, was shaped by similar forces: her father and mother, with whom she lived only sporadically, both attended residential schools and their lives were also beset by addiction and violence. They, in turn, were influenced by their parents' experiences; Danny's great-grandfather, Leonard Creeley, was removed from his family and placed at the File Hills residential school, where he was forced to reject his own language, culture, and the way of life of his ancestors. When he returned from war, his injuries made it impossible to keep up the farm, and he soon lost everything.

That is just one family's experience of the legacy of colonialism in Canada, and it is a history shared by thousands of other indigenous people. Only a tiny minority have been involved in gangs, but in

Danny's lifetime gangs became a significant influence, particularly among young men from troubled backgrounds. In 2014, indigenous men were seven times more likely, and indigenous women six times more likely, to be victims of homicide than their non-indigenous counterparts. Gang violence was part of that equation, as were the still-considerable gaps in wealth, education, and opportunity that continue to cleave the population. When Danny received his first adult conviction, the unemployment rate for indigenous people his age was 33 per cent, more than three times the national average. Thirty years ago, 10 per cent of federal inmates were aboriginal; today, it's more than 25 per cent, a rate more than five times greater than their share of the population.

Danny was often identified as a young man with potential, yet he dedicated his energy to crime, drug trafficking, and the exploitation of others. Different, legitimate paths in life existed, and sometimes he even aspired to them, but he never followed through. As one close friend put it, Danny was too caught up in the gang life to get out. He was the consummate "suit," wearing his gangster identity at all times, unable to separate himself and his purpose from the gang's.

A year after Danny was killed, I sat outside a halfway house in Regina with his brother Richard. He was still angry about his younger brother's death. His mother had told him to forgive, to let go, but he couldn't. "I wish [Danny] wasn't so deep in it, so he could see that he [had] a lot of people on the rez that loved him. I tried to get him to open his eyes, but he was so proud of what he made he couldn't turn his back on the family."

They always told each other, "Be proud of who you are." It was how they signed off their letters, it was the phrase Richard wrote above the framed photo he kept of Danny, and it was the last thing they said to one another fifteen years earlier at Stony Mountain, just as Danny was beginning his adult criminal career.

"We did feel pride, me and Danny," Richard said. "No matter what, when we pass away, fifty years down the road, when they bring up the Indian Posse, they're going to remember our names."

Danny's life was in some ways defined by that search for pride. The gang was the vehicle they created to survive. He dreamed that it could become something bigger; a movement that stretched from coast to coast and would lift others out of poverty. It eventually enslaved and damaged young people by the hundreds, even the thousands, and its promises proved mostly empty.

Not long after Danny died, police put a significant dent in the Indian Posse. Several people in the gang turned on the leadership and testified against them. The murder of Sheldon McKay led to charges and convictions against a half-dozen top leaders. Other gang leaders on the outside were swept up in a Winnipeg police operation.

As I rummaged through the beaten up canvas bag of personal effects taken from Danny's cell after he died I came across seven poems he had written in black ink, now all folded together. The poems suggest he knew his own death was approaching. They are at times maudlin and self-pitying, and at times defiant. Mostly, Danny sounds as though he's sad and alone and in pain.

The waves of grief Danny left behind were immense. First, there were the victims of his crimes, whose families struggled to carry on without their loved ones. A few weeks after he was killed, his girl-friend Shenoa took her own life, leaving his daughter to be raised by relatives. There was his son in Winnipeg, who struggled to understand his father but, while growing up in his dad's old stomping grounds, has managed to avoid following in his footsteps.

Danny's father was released from prison in 2011, but he drank so heavily that within six months he fell into a coma and died in hospital. Richard spoke at anti-gang sessions around Saskatchewan, telling young people to stay away from the gang life, or get out if they still could. He moved in with a woman and became a father, but when his partner's son died tragically his life and relationship ran off the rails. His statutory release was revoked, and at the time of writing, he was imprisoned and awaiting trial on serious charges. Danny's brother Preston returned for a brief stint in jail, but was doing his best to start a new life.

Susan regularly attends cultural ceremonies in her community and continues to work at the reserve's wellness centre. She says some days are better than others.

ACKNOWLEDGEMENTS

This book owes a great debt to all those who took the time to share their experience and knowledge with me. In particular, Richard Wolfe and Susan Creeley were very patient to always answer my phone calls and correspondence. Current and former gang members were often wary of speaking to a journalist, but some did, and I'm grateful to them. Several told me they did so because they wanted others to understand Danny Wolfe and the world in which he grew up.

I'm grateful also to the RCMP and Winnipeg Police Service, who made their officers available for interviews. The officers I spoke with were all very generous with their time. The staff at the provincial court house in Winnipeg and the Court of Queen's Bench in Regina, as well as those of the National Parole Board, were always professional, capable, and eager to help me find the materials I needed.

It would have been impossible to write this book without the help, support, and understanding of my wife. Somehow, between her own career and the arrival of our two children, she made this book feasible. Thank you. Thank you also to my children, who put up with their dad's reporting trips, and to Mimi for looking after them during these trips. I'd also like to thank my parents and my brother for their wisdom, and I thank Julie for her enthusiasm and advice.

My colleagues at the *Globe and Mail* encouraged me to pursue this subject. There are too many to name, but thank you to Gabe Gonda, who commissioned the first story and gave it its title. Thank you also to Sinclair Stewart, Dennis Choquette, Christine Brousseau, and Chris Wilson-Smith, the editors who gave me the time to do it; and David Walmsley and John Stackhouse, who were in charge of it all. I'd like to also thank my friends and fellow reporters: Greg McArthur, Patrick White, Colin Freeze, Tu Thanh Ha, Robyn Doolittle, Renata D'Aliesio, Kathryn Blaze Baum, Karen Howlett, Liz Church, James Bradshaw, Graeme Smith, Sandra Martin, Kirk Makin, Ian Brown, Peter Cheney, John Allemang, Ann Hui, Oliver Moore, Ivan Semeniuk, Simona Chiose, Caroline Alphonso, Tim Appleby, Kate Hammer, Grant Robertson, Kelly Grant, Jill Mahoney, and so many others, who listened to my stories and helped me with their insights. My former colleague Kim Mackrael very helpfully gathered some materials for me in the National Archives of Canada.

Thank you to Doug Pepper of McClelland & Stewart and Penguin Random House Canada for his vision and encouragement, and to my colleague Craig Offman for introducing us. A special thank you to Bhavna Chauhan for the skillful editing that brought this book to life.

A NOTE ON THE SOURCES

The descriptions of events in this book are drawn from many sources, primarily personal interviews, but also voluminous documentary records and personal correspondence. Thanks to the help of Danny's family and friends, I had access to more than 30,000 words of Danny's letters and more than 1,200 pages of his prison records and psychological reports.

The passages that deal with the commission of crimes or the criminal court system are bolstered by the evidence presented in those cases, including videos of Danny's interrogation, photos, transcripts, and the testimony of witnesses.

Passages on incidents that occurred in prison benefited from documents obtained under access to information laws, as well as publicly commissioned reports and inquiries. Information on Danny's ancestors was drawn from documents found in the National Archives of Canada and historical census records.

Local newspapers and broadcasters, particularly the *Winnipeg Free Press*, *Regina Leader-Post*, CTV and CBC, produced hundreds of items on the Indian Posse and other gangs that I relied on for a picture of the gang's development and its historical context. There are too many to produce a comprehensive list here, but they were all valuable to the research. Also, a number of academic studies were useful for context, as well as publicly available reports from Criminal Intelligence Service of Canada and Saskatchewan. The following is a selected list of works referred to in the text or that were crucial to informing my understanding. A full list will be available on my website.

Carter, Sarah. "An Infamous Proposal: Prairie Indian Reserve Land and Soldier Settlement after World War I," *Manitoba History* 37 (Spring/Summer 1999).

Comack, Elizabeth, Lawrence Deane, Jim Silver, and Larry Morrissette. "Indians Wear Red": Colonialism, Resistance, and Aboriginal Street Gangs (Winnipeg: Fernwood, 2013).

Fort Qu'Appelle and District History Book Committee, Fort Qu'Appelle and Area: A History (1996).

Giles, Christopher, "The History of Street Gangs in Winnipeg from 1945 to 1997: A Qualitative Newspaper Analysis of Street Gang Activity" (MA thesis, Simon Fraser University, 2000).

Hagedorn, John. A World of Gangs: Armed Young Men and Gangsta Culture. (Minneapolis: U of Minnesota, 2008).

Hughes, The Hon. E.N. (Ted), *Report of the Independent Review of the circumstances surrounding the April 25-26, 1996, Riot at the Headingley Correctional Institution* (Winnipeg, 1996).

Marlyn, John. Under the Ribs of Death. (Toronto: McClelland & Stewart, 1964).

Peet, William, Bob Vogelsang and Dan Wiks, Regina Provincial Correctional Centre Escape, August 24, 2008 (Report produced for Government of Saskatchewan, 2008).

Shakur, Sanyika. Monster: The Autobiography of an L.A. Gang Member (New York: Atlantic Monthly, 1993).

Sinclair, C.M, Hamilton, A.C., Report of the Aboriginal Justice Inquiry of Manitoba (1991).

Sinclair, Gordon. Cowboys and Indians: The Shooting of J.J. Harper (Toronto: McClelland & Stewart, 1999).

Skarbek, David. The Social Order of the Underworld: How Prison Gangs Govern the American Penal System (Oxford University Press, 2014).

Stevens, Critchley et al., the Balcarres Book Committee, Furrows in Time: A History of Balcarres and District (Focus Publishing, 1987).

Truth and Reconciliation Commission of Canada, Honouring the Truth, Reconciling for the Future: Summary of the Final Report of the Truth and Reconciliation Commission of Canada (2015).

Winegard, Timothy C. For King and Kanata: Canadian Indians and the First World War (Winnipeg: University of Manitoba Press, 2012).

INDEX

The Ballad of Danny Wolfe is set in Adobe Caslon, a digitized typeface based on the original 1734 designs of William Caslon. Caslon is generally regarded as the first British typefounder of consequence and his fonts are considered, then as now, to be among the world's most "user-friendly" text faces.